ANALYZING FUGUE

A Schenkerian Approach

For Islay-May

ANALYZING FUGUE

A Schenkerian Approach

by William Renwick

HARMONOLOGIA SERIES No. 8
General Editor: Joel Lester

PENDRAGON PRESS
STUYVESANT, NY

Other Titles in the Series HARMONOLOGIA: STUDIES IN THE HISTORY OF HARMONY

No. 1 *Heinrich Schenker: Index to Analyses* by Larry Laskowski (1978) ISBN 0-918728-06-1

No. 2 *F.W. Marpurg's* Thoroughbass and Composition Handbook: *A Narrative Translation and Critical Study* by David A. Sheldon (1989) ISBN 0-918728-55-X

No. 3 *Between Modes and Keys: German Theory 1592–1802* by Joel Lester (1990) ISBN 0-918728-77-0

No. 4 *Music Theory from Zarlino to Schenker: A Bibliography and Guide* by David Damschroder and David Russell Williams (1991) ISBN 0-918728-99-1

No. 5 *Musical Time: The Sense of Order* by Barbara Barry (1990) ISBN 0-945193-01-7

No. 6 *Formalized Music: Thought and Mathematics in Composition* (revised edition) by Iannis Xenakis (1992) ISBN 0-945193-24-6

No. 7 *Esquisse de l'histoire de l'harmonie: An English-Language Translation of the François-Joseph Fétis History of Harmony* by Mary I. Arlin (1994) ISBN 0-945193-51-3

No. 9 *Bach's Modal Chorales* by Lori Burns (in press) ISBN 0-945193-74-2

Library of Congress Cataloging-in-Publication Data
Renwick, William. 1958–
    Analyzing Fugue : a Schenkerian Approach / by William Renwick.
        p. cm. — (Harmonologia series : no. 8)
    Includes bibliographical references and index.
    ISBN 0-945193-52-1
    1. Fugue. 2. Schenkerian Analysis. I. Title. II. Series.
MT59.R27 1995
784.18'72—dc20   94-47622
                                                                CIP
                                                                 MN

Copyright Pendragon Press 1995

Contents

Preface		vii
Chapter	1. Approaches to Fugal Analysis	1
	Thoroughbass: Foundation of Baroque Composition	2
	Patterns of Structure	11
	Improvisation and Composition	17
	2. Subject and Answer	19
	Tonality in Subject and Answer	21
	Subject Categories and Paradigms	24
	Subject and Answer Paradigms for Category 1	26
	Subject and Answer Paradigms for Category 2	55
	Subject and Answer Paradigms for Category 3	63
	Paradigms in Perspective	73
	3. Invertible Counterpoint	79
	The Voice-leading Matrix	81
	The Voice-leading Complex	83
	Invertible Counterpoint for Category 1 Subjects	86
	Invertible Counterpoint for Category 2 Subjects	100
	Invertible Counterpoint for Category 3 Subjects	101
	Invertible Counterpoint at the Tenth and Twelfth	102
	4. Exposition	109
	Tonal Structure in Fugal Exposition	109
	Exposition Schemes	111
	Exposition Patterns for Category 1 Subjects	113
	Exposition Patterns for Category 2 Subjects	128
	Exposition Patterns for Category 3 Subjects	132
	Subject Paradigms and Exposition Patterns	134

5.	Sequence and Episode	139
	The Voice-leading Structure of Sequences	140
	Sequence Pattern 1: Descent by Step	143
	Sequence Pattern 2: Descent by Third	150
	Sequence Pattern 3: Descent by Fifth	152
	Sequence Pattern 4: Ascent by Step	155
	Sequence Pattern 5: Ascent by Third	160
	Sequence Pattern 6: Ascent by Fifth	162
6.	Stretto and Other Devices	165
	Prolonged Harmony	165
	Linear Progression	172
	Tetrachordal Stretto	182
	Voice-leading Complex	185
	Sequential Stretto	187
7.	Complete Fugue	189
	Bach, Fugue 1 in C Major (*WTC II*)	191
	Bach, Fugue 13 in F-sharp Major (*WTC I*)	195
	Bach, Fugue 22 in B-flat Minor (*WTC II*)	199
	Form and Tonal Structure	202
	The Fundamental Line	205
	Epilogue	209
Appendix:	Bach, Fugue 1 in C Major (*WTC II*)	211
	Bach, Fugue 13 in F-sharp Major (*WTC I*)	212
	Bach, Fugue 22 in B-flat Minor (*WTC II*)	213
Bibliography		219
Index of Compositions		225

Preface

Since Heinrich Schenker's death in 1935, the analytical techniques which he developed have increasingly become dominant in the analysis of tonal music, and have provided a rich and powerful means of understanding the complexities of great masterworks of the western tradition. Schenker's method is based on two cardinal concepts: a hierarchy of tones grouped into structural levels, and a recognition of the importance of strict voice-leading at all structural levels. This study utilizes Schenkerian techniques in exploring the relationship between imitative counterpoint and voice-leading in fugue. Schenker himself touched upon issues of fugal structure from time to time and published a complete analysis of Bach's Fugue in C minor (*Well-Tempered Clavier I*), but he did not explore the genre systematically or comprehensively.[1] Several important but isolated studies of fugue from a Schenkerian perspective, particularly Carl Schachter's analysis of Bach's Fugue in B-flat major (*WTC I*), have highlighted analytical problems and pointed to the complexity of the challenges which the genre poses.[2]

The greatest difficulties encountered in structural analysis of fugue arise from its principal design factor: three or more contrapuntal parts, each carrying a proportionate and similar motivic content. Schenker's ideal of tonal structure distinguishes melody, bass and inner voices as having different content and function. But in fugue, where the upper part has by and large the same content as the bass and the inner parts, does the upper part carry the fundamental line? Indeed, is a fundamental line generally discernible in fugue, and if so, how is it realized? In what ways does the structure of a fugue subject determine and control the tonal structure of the exposition and the fugue as a whole? What effect does invertible counterpoint have on deep structure? How does the bass express Schenker's concept of scale steps, despite being constructed largely of subject and countersubject statements and other imitative materials? In what ways do fugues, each of which develops its own unique form, reflect Schenker's conceptions of formal structure in the large? In addressing these issues, this study may provide more analytical problems than solutions, but this is after all the nature of healthy intellectual inquiry.

---

[1] Heinrich Schenker, "Das Organische der Fuge," *Das Meisterwerk in der Musik*, 2:55–95. This essay is translated by Sylvan Kalib in "Thirteen Essays from the Three Yearbooks *Das Meisterwerk in der Musik* by Heinrich Schenker: An Annotated Translation" (Ph.D. diss., Northwestern University, 1973), 2:245–320.

[2] Carl Schachter, "Bach's Fugue in B-flat Major, Well-Tempered Clavier, Book I, No. XXI," *The Music Forum* III (1973): 239–67.

The detailed consideration of tonal structure as it relates to imitative counterpoint and the attempt to formalize general principles of their interrelation have led inevitably to the consideration of normative patterns in fugue and have motivated a central focus on the work of J. S. Bach above all others. Apart from the deepest background levels, Schenker concerned himself in his own analytical work with characteristics of individuation rather than features of similarity, and in this regard the present study represents a divergence of emphasis. Instead, the normative patterns identified here bear a loose philosophical kinship to the type of patterning developed by Leonard Meyer and illustrated in detail in Robert Gjerdingen's *A Classic Turn of Phrase*.[3] The essential differences are to be found in the structural basis of the patterns shown here in tonal voice-leading, and the omission in this study of consideration of patterning in relationship to stylistic change and development. Such considerations may well be the fruit of further study.

As powerful and revealing as theories of music can be, if they bear no relation to the ways that composers themselves conceptualize music their relevance and importance is critically diminished. In this book, relating theoretical issues to documents that illuminate the Baroque conception of fugue as it was understood by theorists of the time curtails this danger as far as possible and in fact helps to show that Schenker's theories accord in multifarious ways with conceptions of musical structure current in the Baroque era.

In the text, pitches in the octave from middle C to the B above are identified by lower case letters with a superscript "1"; the octave above uses "2" and so on; the octave below has no superscript, and the lower octave uses upper case. Scale-steps are notated with carets according to Schenker's practice: e.g., $\hat{5}$ is the fifth note of the scale.

The notions developed in this book could not have emerged without the inspiration of several dedicated theorists and musicians to whom I extend my deepest gratitude: William Benjamin, Charles Burkhart, Joel Lester, Carl Schachter, and George Stauffer. I am also grateful to several colleagues who have assisted me in points of musicological or historical importance: Arnim Eisenach, Staatsbibliothek Preussischer Kulturbesitz, Musikabteilung, Professor Yoshitake Kobayashi, Johann Sebastian-Bach-Institut, Göttingen, Robert Kosovsky, New York Public Library, Music Division, and Alan Walker, McMaster University. Special thanks to Kimberly Banfield for assisting in the preparation of the examples.

William Renwick
Hamilton, 1994

---

[3] Leonard B. Meyer, *Explaining Music: Essays and Explorations* (Chicago: University of Chicago Press, 1973); Robert O. Gjerdingen, *A Classic Turn of Phrase: Music and the Psychology of Convention* (Philadelphia, University of Pennsylvania Press, 1988).

CHAPTER 1

Approaches to Fugal Analysis

Example 1-1 shows three fugue subjects, strikingly different in range, rhythm, length, and type of motion. Two are by J. S. Bach; one is by Handel. The first, for unaccompanied violin, is brief, occupies a narrow range, and uses primarily conjunct motion. The second, for organ, is lengthy, covers a wide range through an ascent followed by a descent, and makes extensive use of arpeggiation. The third, in a major key and for clavier, contains descending and ascending conjunct lines broken by a wide leap at the midpoint. Observations such as these characterize the elements that distinguish these subjects from each other. The common features are not so obvious, for it is not their stylistic attributes but their structural aspects that are similar.

Example 1-1. a, J. S. Bach, Sonata 1 in G minor for solo violin BWV 1001, *Fuga*; b, Bach, Prelude and Fugue in A minor BWV 543; c, G. F. Handel, Suite 2 in F, *Fuga*

The analytical graphs of example 1-1 illustrate the tonal and voice-leading structures of each subject.[1] All three subjects project a clear sense of key by beginning and ending with one or more notes of the tonic chord.

[1] The analysis of Handel's subject follows that in Heinrich Schenker, *Free Composition*, trans. and ed. by Ernst Oster (New York: Longman, 1979), Fig. 92-1.

All three express a sense of motion and resolution by passing through one or more intermediate notes of the dominant chord which resolve to the final tonic chord in an authentic cadence. Finally, and most specifically, each subject projects a descending third progression $\hat{5}$ - $\hat{4}$ - $\hat{3}$ as its underlying melodic basis (shown by the beamed notes). In the G minor subject the $\hat{5}$ - $\hat{4}$ - $\hat{3}$ progression can be found in the pitches that occur on the beats. In the A minor subject the descent is drawn out by several means: the initial tonic chord is expanded by arpeggiation and a rising third progression, and the broad $\hat{5}$ - $\hat{4}$ - $\hat{3}$ progression is prolonged by a sequential arpeggiation and an upper neighbor, giving $\hat{5}$ - $\hat{4}$ - $\hat{3}$ as the melodic contour. The $\hat{5}$ - $\hat{4}$ - $\hat{3}$ pattern arises in Handel's subject by associating the music in the higher register at the beginning and the end, while the other notes form subsidiary linear progressions that reinforce the basic harmony.

What is to be made of the observation that the three subjects exhibit contrasting styles but similar structure—distinctive content within analogous form? First, the compositional process of baroque imitative counterpoint involves far more than a question of intervallic consonance and dissonance or of thoroughbass at surface levels. Rather, it involves voice-leading and harmony at deeper levels of structure—levels which can only be systematically understood by analysis. Second, repetitive patterning beneath the contrasting surface of different compositions may play a significant role in the genre of fugue. This role may be secondary to other structures, or it may indeed be central in the structures of fugue. Chapter 1 explores in detail two concepts that underlie these thoughts: first, a chain of practice in Baroque compositional and pedagogical methods that provides a step-by-step link from the most elementary thoroughbass right through to fugue, and second, a pattern-based approach to imitative counterpoint.

Thoroughbass: Foundation of Baroque Composition

The remarkably swift and universal development of thoroughbass in western music in the decades following 1600 represented a complete and irreversible shift in the focus of musical thought from consonance and dissonance treatment to harmonic progression and tonality.[2] In learning to use the new harmonic system, composers developed powerful new means of expression: tonicization, modulation, and chromaticism, the full exploitation of which was left to the later generations of the eighteenth and nineteenth centuries. For contrapuntists the challenge was to develop a contrapuntal art within the new parameters of what came to be known as common-practice tonality. Fugue was established as an independent genre and reached its full development entirely within the thoroughbass period. The masterfugues which resulted, especially those of Bach and Handel, demonstrate

---

[2]This topic receives detailed treatment in Joel Lester, *Between Modes and Keys: German Theory 1592–1802* (Stuyvesant, New York: Pendragon Press, 1989), and *Compositional Theory in the Eighteenth Century* (Cambridge, Massachusetts: Harvard University Press, 1992).

the perfect reconciliation and union of the old art of counterpoint, the legacy of Palestrina, with the new art of triadic harmony.

In the search for new means of expressing counterpoint in tonal music, patterns of voice-leading were established by which individual melodic lines could work together to express harmonic motion and direction. Contrapuntal composition by the layering of melodies or counterpoints on a given *cantus firmus* was replaced by a new harmonic and voice-leading approach:

> Since he [Bach] himself had composed the most instructive pieces for the clavier, he brought up his pupils on them.... he started his pupils right with what was practical, and omitted all the *dry species* of counterpoint that are given in Fux and others. His pupils had to begin their studies by learning pure four-part thorough bass.[3]

This testimony forms the basis of various discussions of Bach's teaching methods, from Forkel's biography—for which it supplied the direct source—down to the present day. Here is an important example by Bach's pupil, Johann Philipp Kirnberger:

> His [Bach's] method is the best, for he proceeds steadily, step by step, from the easiest to the most difficult, and as a result even the step to the fugue has only the difficulty of passing from one step to the next. On this ground I hold the method of Johann Sebastian Bach to be the best and only one. It is to be regretted that this great man never wrote anything theoretical about music, and that his teachings have reached posterity only through his pupils. I have sought to reduce the method of the late Joh. Seb. Bach to principles, and to lay his teaching before the world to the best of my powers, in my *Art of Strict Music Composition (Kunst des reinen Satzes)*.[4]

These quotations summarize the basic methodology by which Bach and his contemporaries developed their contrapuntal art, a method quite distinct from the older contrapuntal tradition codified by Fux. As outlined by Kirnberger in *The Art of Strict Musical Composition*, harmony is considered before counterpoint; first in four parts, then in three, then in two, and finally in one part.[5] Music in fewer than four parts is understood to be based on the principles of four part thoroughbass, but with certain less important notes or voices omitted.[6] Even fugue is considered simply one more stage of complexity from the simple beginnings of thoroughbass. Existing documents from the period illustrate this method in all its steps from simple harmony to complex fugue.

---

[3] C.P.E. Bach's letter to Forkel, January 13, 1775, trans. in Hans David and Arthur Mendel, *The Bach Reader* (New York: Norton, 1966), 278.

[4] Johann Philipp Kirnberger, *Gedanken uber die verschiedenen Lehrarten in der Komposition als Vorbereitung zur Fugenkenntniss* (1782), 4–5, trans. in David and Mendel, *The Bach Reader*, 262. Other examples are in Johann Nicholaus Forkel, *On Johann Sebastian Bach's Life, Genius, and Works* (Leipzig, 1802), trans. by A. F. C. Kollmann in David and Mendel, *The Bach Reader*, 329; Philipp Spitta, *Johann Sebastian Bach*, 3 vols., trans. by Clara Bell and J. A. Fuller-Maitland (London: Novello, 1883–85), 3:120; and David and Mendel, *The Bach Reader*, 39.

[5] Johann Philipp Kirnberger, *The Art of Strict Musical Composition*, 4 vols. (1771–79), trans. (Vol. 1 and part 1 of Vol. 2 only) by David Beach and Jurgen Tym (New Haven: Yale University Press, 1982).

[6] Spitta, *J. S. Bach*, 3:120.

Among the innumerable thoroughbass treatises of the time, no work better shows the connection of thoroughbass to composition than *The Musical Guide* of Friderich Erhard Niedt (1674–1708).[7] It typifies the kind of practical guide to accompaniment, improvisation, and composition in general use, and its only defect is a limited display of musical imagination. That Niedt was a pupil of Johann Nicolaus Bach (1669–1753) and that parts of *The Musical Guide* were dictated by J.S. Bach to his students at the *Thomas Schule* confirms that Niedt's method is in close accord with Bach's. Following an amusing allegory known as the "Narrative of Tacitus," *The Musical Guide* introduces the reader directly to the principles of thoroughbass and four-part harmony. Part 2 deals almost entirely with the art of diminution, first in the bass, then in the treble, and then in combination, but in all cases within the context of thoroughbass.[8] Example 1-2 illustrates Niedt's systematic method for transforming a simple implied homophony (a) into a three-part polyphony of fluid and active contrapuntal lines, first by adding diminutions in the bass (b), and then by adding diminutions in the upper parts (c).

Example 1-2. Niedt, *The Musical Guide*, pp. 41–42

Diminution of the type espoused by Niedt was constantly practiced. Airs, chorales, passacaglias, chaconnes, and suites all held unlimited potential for variation. Two more sophisticated examples illustrate: Example 1-3 compares Bach's *stylus simplex* chorale harmonization of *O Mensch, bewein' dein' Sünde gross* with the highly ornamented version found in *Das Orgel-Büchlein*. In mm. 1, 5 and 6, the voice leading of the ornamented version is so similar to the simple chorale that one may speculate that Bach consciously utilized the choral arrangement as the

---

[7]Friderich Erhart Niedt, *The Musical Guide (Musicalische Handleitung)* 3 parts, (Hamburg, 1700, 1706, and 1717), trans. Pamela L. Poulin and Irmgard C. Taylor (Oxford: Oxford University Press, 1989).

[8]Diminution, in this context, is a technique of variation in which longer note values are replaced by groups of shorter notes which enliven the texture and add complexity. This should not be confused with the more familiar meaning in which a series of notes is restated in shorter note values.

basis of the ornamented chorale or improvised the ornamentation while reading the simple choral arrangement. Example 1-4 illustrates a similar approach but a different result. Again, the *Orgel-Büchlein* version exhibits similar voice-leading to the choral version, especially in mm. 1–2, but here the accompanying voices are subjected to diminutions which begin to exhibit imitative development. Indeed, the impulse to imitate the descending motive and establish a repetition in the pedals in m. 3 clearly accounts for the altered harmony at this point. It is in passages such as this that we can see imitation beginning to assume a role as a shaping force in voice-leading that leads far beyond any technique illustrated in Niedt's treatise.

Example 1-3. Bach, *O Mensch, bewein' dein' Sünde gross*, mm. 1–2, 5–6; a, four-part chorale BWV 402; b, *Orgel-Büchlein* BWV 622

Example 1-4. Bach, *Christ lag in Todesbanden*, mm. 1–4; a, four-part chorale BWV 278; b, *Orgel-Büchlein* BWV 625

Further and more specific evidence that the methods of thoroughbass instruction and improvisation have a demonstrable relationship with the composition of fugue is provided by *partimento* fugue, a little discussed but fascinating genre of the period. A partimento fugue is a fugue notated as a figured bass. Thus for the most part only the lowest sounding part is given in notes. Figures represent the harmony and voice-leading of the upper parts, and in some instances indications of subject statements are included as well. When only two parts are to be heard, both are fully notated on a single staff. The realization of the details is left to the ingenuity of the performer. Although partimento fugue is a rare genre, examples occur in treatises and manuals by Handel, Heinichen, Keller, and Niedt.

That Bach himself advocated partimento fugue can be adduced from the examples in the Brussels manuscript, *Elementary Instruction in Figured Bass*, a work attributed to Bach and stemming from his circle.[9] This manuscript contains five brief partimento fugues ranging from 14 to 21 measures in length. Example 1-5 shows the first. The figures have been realized on the upper staff, probably by a student of Bach's.[10] Imitation is rudimentary here, and the subject occurs only in the lowest sounding voice, yet we can discern an attempt to realize a figured bass in a fugal style.

Example 1-5. *Elementary Instruction in Figured Bass*, Example 12

[9] The full title is *The Precepts and Principles for Playing the Thorough-bass or Accompanying in Four Parts by the Royal Court Composer and Capellmeister as well as Director of Music and Cantor of the Thomas Schule, Mr. Johann Sebastian Bach, at Leipzig for his Students in Music, 1738* (Der Königlichen Hoff-Compositeurs und Capellmeisters ingleichen Directoris Musices wie auch Cantoris der Thomas-Schule Herrn Johann Sebastian Bach zu Leipzig Vorschriften und Grundätze zum 333 vierstimmigen Spielen des General-Bass oder Accompagnement für seine Scholaren in der Music, 1738). Brussels, Bibliotheque du Conservatoire Royal de Musique, MS AA 27.224. It is printed in Spitta, *J.S. Bach*, 3:315–47 (Appendix 12), and translated in David and Mendel, *The Bach Reader*, 392–98. Parts of the work are taken from Niedt's *Musical Guide* (see pp. xi–xiii). Carl August Thieme, one of the hands that has been identified, was a student at the Thomas-Schule from 1735–45. See Hans-Joachim Schulze, "'Das Stücke im Goldpapier' Ermittlungen zu einigen Bach-Abschriften des frühen 18. Jahrhunderts," *Bach Jahrbuch* LXIV (1978): 19–42.

[10] All of the partimento fugues are printed in Spitta, *J. S. Bach*, 3:336–39. The realizations display a rudimentary style and glaring errors noted by Spitta and also by Franck Thomas Arnold in *The Art of Accompaniment from a Thorough-Bass*, 2 vols. (London: Oxford University Press, 1931), 1:215.

APPROACHES TO FUGAL ANALYSIS

In the course of Niedt's "Narrative of Tacitus" it is suggested that the thoroughbass method allows students quite easily to "make a fugue and the like *ex tempore.*"[11] Perhaps in order to support this claim, Niedt included an example of partimento fugue near the end his treatise. Example 1-6 is much longer than any in the *Vorschriften*, and it includes several subject statements in each part. In this particular type of partimento fugue, all entries of the subject are notated. (Incidentally, the subject of this partimento fugue is almost identical to Bach's G minor subject shown in example 1-1.)

Example 1-6. Niedt, *The Musical Guide*, pp. 48–49

Handel composed several partimento fugues in the course of his instructions for Princess Anne, eldest daughter of George II.[12] Somewhat more sophisticated, Handel's examples indicate in letter notation the starting pitch of each entry of the subject, thereby allowing entries in the upper parts above the bass. Example 1-7 shows a fairly elaborate composition on a more lengthy subject. Handel also composed partimento double fugues, with indications for the entrance of the subject and countersubject. In his commentary on Handel's sketches and thoroughbass exercises, Alfred

---

[11] Arnold, *The Art of Accompaniment from a Thorough-Bass*, 1:222.
[12] George Frederick Handel, *"Aufzeichnungen zur Kompositionslehre"* ("Composition Lessons"), published as *Hallische Händel-Ausgabe, Supplement, Band I*, ed. Alfred Mann. (Kassel: Bärenreiter, 1978). See especially pp. 44–52. See also David Ledbetter, *Continuo Playing According to Handel* (Oxford: Oxford University Press, 1990).

Mann concludes that "in Handel's instruction the study of fugue evolved from thoroughbass technique."[13]

Example 1-7. Handel, *Lessons for Princess Anne*, Fugue 4

The largest extant collection of partimento fugues is attributed to Bach, but is again of doubtful authorship. Known as the "Langloz" manuscript after its owner and scribe, A. W. Langloz, and titled *Praeludia et Fugen del Signor Johann Sebastian Bach*, it contains two sets of pieces. The first set contains 38 partimento fugues arranged in an ascending series of 15 major and minor keys. The second set contains 17 works: 14 preludes and fugues, one prelude, and two fugues, arranged in an ascending sequence of nine keys.[14] Example 1-8 shows one of the more fully developed composi-

---

[13]*Ibid.*, 45.

[14]Berlin, *Staatsbibliothek Preussischer Kulturbesitz, Musikabteilung, Mus. Mn. P 296*, listed in Wolfgang Schmieder, *Thematisch-systematisches Verzeichnis der musikalischen Werke von Johann Sebastian Bach* (Wiesbaden: Breitkopf & Härtel, 1990), item 22, pp. xxxi–xxxii. The owner's name is inscribed *possessor A. W. Langloz Anno 1763*. An *Aria*, included at the end in another hand, belongs to a later period.

APPROACHES TO FUGAL ANALYSIS

tions. The fact that Niedt's partimento fugue (example 1-6) appears as *Fuga 22* in the Langloz manuscript, with several variants in the figures, indicates at least that the whole of the Langloz manuscript cannot possibly be by Bach. Considering that Niedt mentions at the end of *The Musical Guide*, Part 1 (p. 49) that he intends to write a treatise on the performance of fugues *ex tempore*, it is more likely that the Langloz manuscript is the work of Niedt than Bach.

Example 1-8. *Langloz ms., Praeludium et fuga 52. Dis dur*

Partimento fugue adds imitative counterpoint to the framework of pure voice leading, and it is the essential link between a basic harmonic framework and an elaborative contrapuntal texture.[15] Partimento fugue reflects a method of conceptualizing fugal composition and improvisation as an extension and refinement of thoroughbass, rather than as an extension of counterpoint. These pieces, whether composed by Bach or someone else, nevertheless illustrate a harmonic rather than contrapuntal conception of fugue, and attest to the attempt on the part of composers and improvisors to conceive of fugue in terms of thoroughbass during the Baroque era.[16]

The step from partimento fugue to fully-composed fugue marks the final phase of a gradual process which is documented at each step as a pedagogical tradition. Example 1-9, from an organ prelude by Buxtehude, shows how little additional detail is in fact required beyond the partimento to realize a simple yet genuine fugue. The descending order of entries here allows complete freedom of motion in the upper parts, just as in a typical partimento fugue, and once the music reaches three parts in m. 48, the counterpoints revert to the simplest continuo harmony, throwing the quicker notes of the subject into relief.

Example 1-9. Buxtehude, Prelude in G minor BuxWV 163, mm. 44–52

[15]Partimento fugue was also used to train in the accompaniment of imitative vocal polyphony. Indeed, occasionally the continuo part of a concerted fugue taken by itself closely resembles a partimento fugue. The partimento fugue in Johann David Heinichen's *Der General-Bass in der Composition* (Dresden, 1728) is conceived in terms of an accompaniment to a concerted fugue. See George J. Buelow, *Thorough-Bass Accompaniment According to Johann David Heinichen*, revised edition (Ann Arbor: UMI Research Press, 1986), 208–10.

[16]Alfred Mann, "Bach and Handel as Teachers of Thoroughbass," in *Bach, Handel, Scarlatti Tercentenary Essays*, ed. Peter Williams (Cambridge: Cambridge University Press, 1985), 256, and Handel, *Aufzeichnungen zur Kompositionslehre*, 47.

Pachelbel's fugues in C major and A minor, and the first fugato of Bach's early Prelude and Fugue in A minor BWV 551, are conceived on equally simple lines.[17] These fugues may be the most accurate preserved examples of the nature of extemporized fugue as it was actually practiced throughout Europe around the beginning of the eighteenth century. Also among the works attributed to Bach, the Fantasy and Fughetta in B-flat major BWV 907 and the Fantasy and Fughetta in D major BWV 908 stand midway between partimento fugue and fully-composed fugue.[18] They are notated partly in staff notation and partly in figures. A lost art today, partimento fugue makes clear Kirnberger's point that even the fugue, as taught by Bach, is only one further step along a continuous path of ever growing complexity.

On two occasions Kirnberger published fundamental-bass analyses of complete fugues—his own Fugue in E minor and the concluding fugue in B minor of Bach's *Well-Tempered Clavier I* (*WTC I*).[19] In the context of this discussion, Kirnberger's analyses represent the reverse process, relating complete fugues back to the simplest voice-leading and harmony. For the complete baroque musician, performance, thoroughbass, improvisation, composition and theory formed an unbroken continuum as united aspects of a single art. Thoroughbass, representing the center of the system, provides a wonderful bridge that unites theory and composition, performance and improvisation, in a manner that we may well envy in our present age of specialization and diversity.

Patterns of Structure

Perhaps the most remarkable observation concerning the three subjects of example 1-1 is that they exhibit similar patterns of voice-leading structure. What kinds of implications might such patterning have for the structure of imitative counterpoint in general and of fugue in particular? How pervasive is repetitive and stereotyped patterning in Baroque music? The unity of language and of style which mark the Baroque period (and indeed the Classical period which followed it), reflect prerevolutionary attitudes of positivism and universality which were to be shattered by the romantic rebellion. For music this meant the rise of individualism and the elevation of the musician from artisan to artist, involving a rejection of traditional patterns in favor of original and novel means of expression, thereby

---

[17]Johann Pachelbel, *Orgelwerke*, ed. Traugott Fedtke (New York: C. F. Peters, 1973), 4:20–23 and 101–104.

[18]Both are attributed to Bach, but are possibly the work of G. Kirchoff. See *The New Grove Bach Family*, ed. Christoph Wolff (New York: Norton, 1983), 210. See also Russel Stimson, *The Manuscripts of Johann Peter Kellner and his Circle* (Durham and London: Duke University Press, 1989), 127–29.

[19]Johann Philipp Kirnberger, *The True Principles for the Practice of Harmony* (1773), trans. by David Beach and Jurgen Thym in *Journal of Music Theory* XXIII/2 (Fall, 1979): 210–22, and *The Art of Strict Musical Composition*, 270–75. The first treatise is possibly the work of Kirnberger's student J. A. P. Schulz (see Lester, *Compositional Theory*, 240).

establishing in the artist a unique and inimitable personal style. The following series of examples illustrates the potency of repetitive patterning in the Baroque style by tracing a continuum of practice in the use of the scale from simple exercises to complex and fully worked-out contrapuntal structures.

The art of playing from a figured bass in itself represents a challenge to the performer. So much more so for unfigured bass, where the choice of notes, as well as their arrangement, depends on the skill and knowledge of the player. One method for developing this art was to base chordal realizations on harmonization of a scale. This was known as the *regola del l'ottova* (rule of the octave). Examples can be found in treatises by Francesco Gasparini, Heinichen, Rameau, Niedt, and Kirnberger, among others.[20] Mattheson's figured scales are typical (see example 1-10).[21]

Example 1-10. Mattheson, *Kleine General-Bass Schule*, pp. 250, 252.

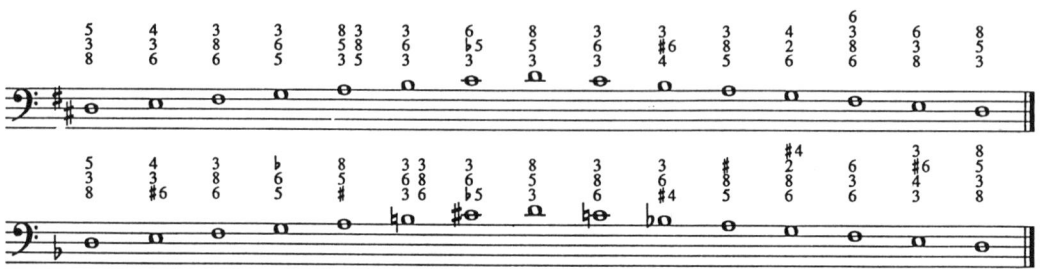

The fact that the figures are different in the ascending and descending portions of the scale indicates that context is important here—in other words, voice-leading is a component of the theory of figured bass. Thus each note of the scale, ascending and descending, is associated with a single, most appropriate harmonization. Further, Mattheson's complete figuring indicates not only the chords but also the basic voice-leading patterns. A musician who had memorized the rule of the octave in a variety of keys was capable of quickly inventing a convincing harmony for any simple thoroughbass by rearranging these familiar patterns. Gasparini's scale (example 1-11) rises only to $\hat{6}$ and descends all the way to $\hat{5}$, perhaps suggesting a *prima prattica* origin of the *regola del l'ottava* in the hexachord, *ut re mi fa sol la*, yet it essentially serves the same function.[22]

---

[20]This practice has been well documented in Arnold, *The Art of Accompaniment from a Thoroughbass*, Vol. 1, where examples by Heinichen (p. 265), Rameau (p. 266), and Gasparini (p. 280, fn. 20) are presented. See also Kirnberger, *The Art of Strict Musical Composition*, 70.
[21]Johann Mattheson, *Kleine General-Bass Schule* (Hamburg, 1735), 250, 252. Mattheson's figured bass scales are almost identical to, and nearly certainly based upon those of Rameau. See Jean-Philippe Rameau, *Treatise on Harmony*, trans. Philip Gosset (New York: Dover, 1971), 396–97.
[22]Francesco Gasparini, *L'armonico pratico al cimbalo* (Venice, 1708), 83–86.

Example 1-11. Gasparini, *L'armonico practico*, pp. 84–85

Bach himself evidently endorsed the rule of the octave, for the Bach/Thieme manuscript contains fourteen figured-bass exercises founded on descending scales and sequences in a section titled "Rules for Playing *en quatre*." Each exercise utilizes a different figure. The exercise shown in example 1-12 teaches the resolution of suspension chords in third inversion. Simple cadences, repetition in closely related keys, and a *da capo* develop a rudimentary ternary form in this elementary figured-bass exercise. Interestingly, several of the preludes in the "Langloz" manuscript follow a similar formal structure. In example 1-8 the opening passage is repeated in the dominant (m. 4), the supertonic (m. 7), and the relative minor (m. 9), after which it returns again in the tonic (m. 12).

Example 1-12. Rules for playing *en quatre*, No. 13.

One must look no further than the first page of *WTC I* to see the influence of this type of patterning on Bach's compositional process. The structural basis of the C major Prelude is no more than a descending scale followed by an elaborated cadence (example 1-13).[23] This is no isolated instance. The preludes in C minor, D major and E minor from the same book all follow this model, with increasing degrees of elaboration and extension. Example 1-14, showing the structure of the C minor prelude, provides a basis of comparison.[24]

Example 1-13. Middleground analysis, Bach, Prelude 1 in C major (*WTC I*)

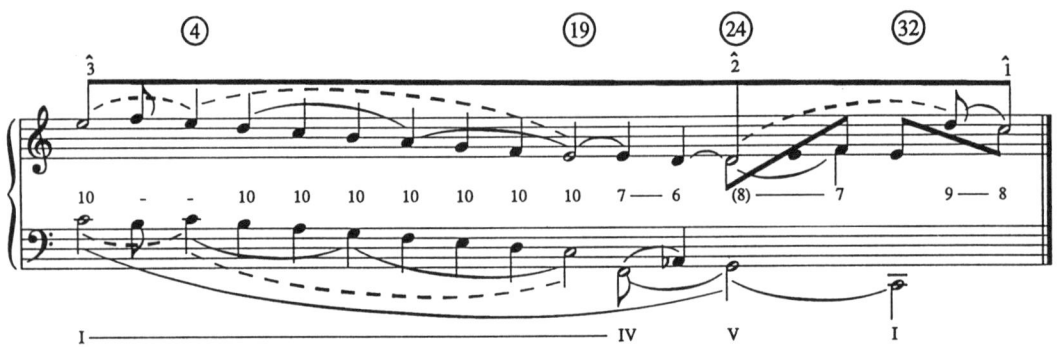

Example 1-14. Middleground analysis, Bach, Prelude 2 in C minor (*WTC I*)

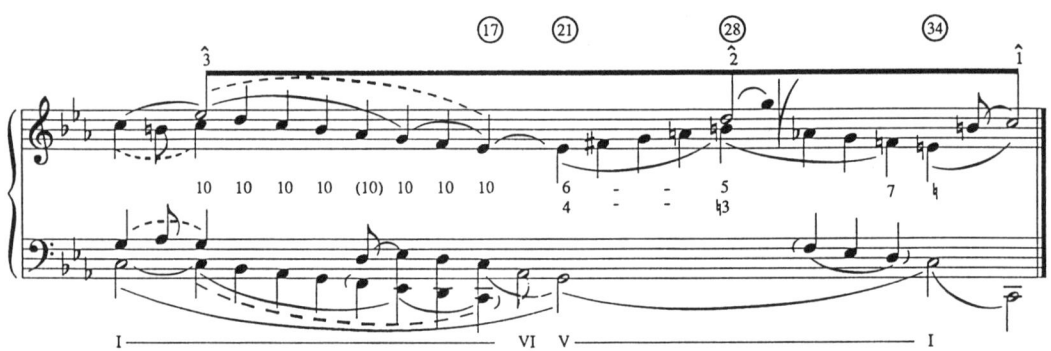

In earlier versions, these preludes were among the first pieces that Bach devised as lessons for his eldest son, Wilhelm Friedemann. The *Clavier-Buchlein vor Wilhelm Friedemann Bach* versions of these preludes consist only of the descending octave-progression followed by a final cadence.

---

[23] This analysis is based largely on Schenker's. See *Five Graphic Music Analyses* (New York: Dover, 1969), 36–37.

[24] Schenker's analysis of this prelude is given in *Das Meisterwerk in der Musik*, Vol. 2 (1926): 85. C. P. E. Bach uses a similar approach albeit based on a freely composed figured bass in his directions for improvising fantasies in *Essay on the True Art of Playing Keyboard Instruments* (1753), trans. by William Mitchell (New York: Cassel, 1949), 440–45.

APPROACHES TO FUGAL ANALYSIS

Much of the music in the C major prelude is notated simply as block chords.[25] There can be no stronger evidence of the centrality of such patterns in Bach's thought and in his teaching. Other compositions by Bach which exhibit a similar scalar basis include the Fantasy in G major for organ BWV 572 and the Invention in G major BWV 781.[26] These compositions demonstrate a technique based on the development and extrapolation of a simple underlying pattern into several distinct but related compositions.

It is not difficult to see the close relationship of thoroughbass scales to the arpeggiated harmonies of simple preludes in *WTC I*, but we must look deeper to see comparable patterning in more complex textures. The *Allemande* from Bach's French Suite in D minor BWV 812 illustrates the same pattern in the *stile brise* as the opening of a binary dance movement (see example 1-15). As the graph shows, the outer voices again form a series of descending tenths, albeit heavily overladen with diminutions.[27]

Example 1-15. Bach, French Suite 1 in D minor BWV 812, *Allemande*, mm. 1–5

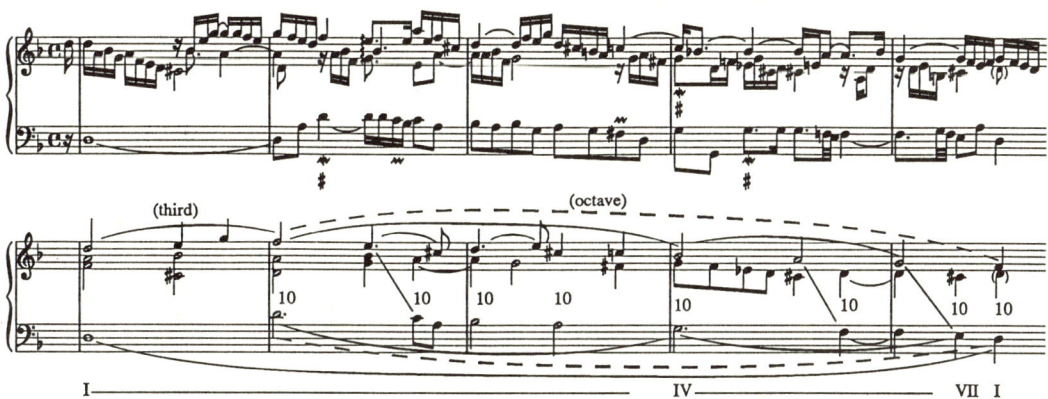

Fugal texture constitutes an even greater challenge. Example 1-16 illustrates the exposition and opening sequence of Bach's Fugue in C-sharp major (*WTC I*). The graph, which reduces the contrapuntal texture to an underlying homophony, illustrates that the entire exposition and subsequent episode are an imitative working out of a continuous scalar descent in the bass from g-sharp[1] to G-sharp, harmonized principally in chains of parallel sixths and tenths.

---

[25]Johann Sebastian Bach, *Clavier-Buchlein vor Wilhelm Friedemann Bach*, ed. in facsimile with a preface by Ralph Kirkpatrick (New Haven: Yale University Press, 1959).

[26]In the possibly spurious G major Fantasy BWV 571, the third movement is built entirely on the descending hexachords G–B and E–G deployed in a variety of registers. The final measures (30–33) include a full octave-descent, g–G.

[27]Robert L. Marshall, *The Compositional Process of J.S. Bach*, 2 Vols. (Princeton: Princeton University Press, 1972), 1:126–27, illustrates how a descending scale spans the melody of the ritornello of BWV 43-7.

Example 1-16. Bach, Fugue 3 in C-sharp major (*WTC I*), mm. 1–10

Similar examples are found in the C major and G minor fugues of *WTC II*. In each case a descending scale in the bass, supporting sixths and tenths in the upper voices, forms the structural framework, and a harmonic, vertical concept underlies a contrapuntal, linear texture.[28] Consider example 1-7 again. The subject of Handel's partimento fugue reduces to a simple scale-segment, continued through the introduction of succeeding entries in lower parts. Following the exposition, the sequence that follows is no different from the pattern of Bach's descending scale in example 1-12. Buxtehude's Prelude in G minor (example 1-9) also exhibits a fugal exposition based entirely on a descent by step. While in fugal exposition the texture is more highly detailed and intricate than in other genres, the underlying structure is the same.

---

[28]Compare Example 4-3.

Improvisation and Composition

The improvisation of a fugue has been considered by many as the definitive test of musical accomplishment. Bach and Handel both held high reputations as improvisors. Improvised fugue combines a full knowledge of harmony and counterpoint with complete command of a keyboard instrument, and above all an ability to create and develop a coherent musical form instantaneously and without prior preparation. The stylistic consistency which characterizes the Baroque (and indeed any well-defined musical period), and particularly the type of repetitive patterning shown here, provides the necessary basis for the high level of development attained by Bach and his contemporaries in improvisation. Creative freedom in improvisation comes from combining well-known and often repeated fragments into a whole. Only when many of the patterns and processes have become habitual through repetition can the improvisor focus on the refinement and creative arrangement of such patterns. Internalization of familiar patterns allows the performer to concentrate on the individualization of such patterns into specific and characteristic musical compositions.

> When Johann Sebastian Bach seated himself at the organ when there was no divine service, which he was often requested to do by strangers, he used to choose some subject and to execute it in all the various forms of organ composition so that the subject constantly remained his material, even if he had played without intermission, for two hours or more. First, he used this theme for a prelude and a fugue, with the full organ. Then he showed his art of using the stops for a trio, quartet, etc., always upon the same subject. Afterwards followed a chorale, the melody of which was playfully surrounded in the most diversified manner by the original subject, in three or four parts. Finally, the conclusion was made by a fugue, with the full organ, in which either another treatment only of the first subject predominated or one or, according to its nature, two others were mixed with it. This is the art which old Reinken, at Hamburg, considered as being already lost in his time, but which, as he later found, not only lived in Johann Sebastian Bach, but had attained through him the highest degree of perfection.[29]

One of J. S. Bach's last pupils, Johann Christian Kittel (1732–1809), who also claims to have grounded his method in the principles of Bach, provides further insight into this technique. In Book III of *Der angehende praktische Organist*, a series of thirteen examples illustrates how a wide variety of textures—melodic, contrapuntal, and fugal—can be developed from a simple subject.[30] The subject, the opening of the chorale *Warum soll ich mich denn grämen* is the familiar melodic fragment $\hat{5} - \hat{6} - \hat{5} - \hat{4} - \hat{3}$. Among the fugal openings, Kittel's first example is in three parts, and the second shows the same opening but with a more ornamented version of the subject. The third example shows a simpler form of the subject combined with a countersubject.[31] The thirteenth and final movement treats the subject as

---

[29] Forkel, *On J.S. Bach's Life, Genius, and Works*, trans. in David and Mendel, *The Bach Reader*, 315–16.
[30] Johann Christian Kittel, *Der angehende praktische Organist*, 3 vols. (Erfurt, 1801–1809), 3:5–9.
[31] This countersubject has the same structure as the second countersubject of the F-sharp major fugue of *WTC I*.

a simple chorale over an imitative texture. Although the music of these examples is merely competent, in its systematic development of a wide range of styles from a simple subject, Kittel's scheme echoes Forkel's description of Bach's improvisational art with remarkable precision.

According to Spitta, "thoroughbass is the beginning of composition," and "imprinting it on the memory is a great part of the whole art [of composition]."[32] For the Baroque composer and improvisor, memory of basic voice-leading patterns is fundamental to the development of a ready and fluent technique. One of the major thrusts of this book is the recognition of basic tonal structures that are repeated frequently enough to be recognized as standards. The three subjects discussed at the beginning of this chapter, three representatives of the simple underlying pattern $\hat{5}$ - $\hat{4}$ - $\hat{3}$, suggest voice-leading and structural levels as a promising avenue for fugal analysis, for it was Schenker's method of structural analysis that facilitated the comparisons made between the three subjects and which showed that radically different musical surfaces can share identical underlying patterns. Schenker's method also permitted the comparisons of scalar structure in the later examples of chapter 1. The following chapters investigate the roles of voice-leading and patterning in the various parts of fugue, beginning in chapter 2 with a detailed exploration of the patterns found in the corpus of Baroque fugue subjects.

---

[32]Spitta, *J.S. Bach*, 3:119–20.

CHAPTER 2

Subject and Answer

> The fugue subjects of J. S. Bach, with only few exceptions, convey self-substantiation within themselves as they reveal a strictly compact course of action.[1]

Schenker's typically concentrated locution implies that the fugue subject embodies the characteristics of unity and wholeness—the prime requisites which he also ascribed to deeper levels in his "organic" conception of musical structure. Schenker explains his meaning and supports these assertions through a detailed analysis of the subject from Bach's C minor fugue in *WTC I*. In example 2-1, Schenker illustrates how a structural unity remains the basis of a multi-layered structure that develops the unique motivic qualities of this familiar subject.[2] Level (a) proposes that the structural basis of the subject is a third-progression, $\hat{5}$ - $\hat{4}$ - $\hat{3}$, which arises through a passing motion from $\hat{5}$ to $\hat{3}$. (This subject also uses the $\hat{5}$ - $\hat{4}$ - $\hat{3}$ progression seen in example 1-1.) Schenker's comment "the falling third progression g^1–f^1–e-flat^1 determines the content of the subject"[3] suggests that this underlying linear progression embodies the tonal and motivic essence of this subject. Levels (a)1 and (a)2 show two different ways of establishing a contrapuntal bass for this third progression. Each fulfills the harmonic and voice-leading implications of the third-progression. At this deep level the structure already projects "self-substantiation" or unity in that it prolongs a given sonority, I, and it conveys a "strictly compact course of action" as it proceeds in a direct manner between two chord tones, g^1 and e-flat^1. Thus the simple $\hat{5}$ - $\hat{4}$ - $\hat{3}$ progression embodies the essence of structural unity and directed motion.

Example 2-1. Schenker, analysis of Bach, C minor fugue subject (*WTC I*)

[1]Schenker, "The Organic Aspect of the Fugue," trans. by Sylvan Kalib in "Thirteen Essays," 2:25.
[2]Schenker, "Das Organische der Fuge," *Das Meisterwerk in der Musik*, 2:60.
[3]*Ibid.*

It is the task of subsequent levels to embellish and prolong, without undermining the established structural coherence. At (b) an upper neighbor is introduced, accompanied by a pre-dominant (IV), and in this upper neighbor Schenker sees the contrapuntal origin not only of the main outline of the subject, but also of the sequential repetitions a-flat^1–g^1–f^1 and g^1–f^1–e-flat^1 shown by the brackets in level (c). In this manner, the original underlying third, which is purely structural, becomes embedded in the motivic surface of the subject. Level (d) introduces a third contrapuntal line, and (e) a fourth, all of which fill out the basic harmony and clarify the voice leading. The passing g^1 at the beginning of m. 2 is thus given consonant support by a contrapuntal I chord that links pre-dominant to dominant. At (f) the upper neighbor a-flat^1 is contrasted by a lower neighbor c^2–b^1–c^2, which completes the motivic development of the subject.

Schenker's discussion of the structural genesis of the *WTC I* C-minor subject beautifully illustrates his idea that structure and motive are organic and inseparable in masterworks of the tonal era. In this case the upper neighbor provides the basis for all other elaborations. Likewise the genesis of harmony and melody are one here. Schenker's conception here is that the harmonic development and its implications grow out of the original melodic segment $\hat{5}$ - $\hat{4}$ - $\hat{3}$ which itself stems from the *Klang* or tonic triad. The two chief elements in the structure of the subject are thus tonal coherence and linear direction. In this context, Schenker's "compact course of action" signifies the underlying linear-progression which gives direction and motion to a subject, while "self-substantiation" is the sense of unity that such an unfolding of the tonic chord provides.

The analysis described above is the most complete analysis of a fugue subject published by Schenker. However, each of his other analyses of baroque fugue subjects points to similar concerns of unity and directed motion, and as Figure 2-1 shows, in each case he uncovers an elementary structural basis in a fundamental linear-progression connecting notes of the tonic triad.[4]

Figure 2-1. Summary of Schenker's analyses of fugue subjects

Fugue subject	Linear progression
Bach	
Fugue 2 in C minor (WTC I)	$\hat{5}$ - $\hat{4}$ - $\hat{3}$
Fugue 3 in C-sharp major (WTC I)	$\hat{3}$ - $\hat{2}$ - $\hat{1}$
Fugue 4 in C-sharp minor (WTC I)	$\hat{3}$ - $\hat{2}$ - $\hat{1}$
Fugue 6 in D minor (WTC I)	$\hat{1}$ - $\hat{2}$ - $\hat{3}$ - $\hat{4}$ - $\hat{5}$
Fugue 8 in D-sharp minor (WTC I)	$\hat{5}$ - $\hat{4}$ - $\hat{3}$ - $\hat{2}$ - $\hat{1}$
Fugue 22 in B-flat minor (WTC I)	$\hat{5}$ - $\hat{4}$ - $\hat{3}$
Fugue 23 in B major (*WTC II*)	$\hat{5}$ - $\hat{6}$ - $\hat{7}$ - $\hat{8}$

[4] These analyses can be found in Schenker, *Das Meisterwerk in der Musik*, 1:97, 2:33, 60, and 63; *Free Composition*, Figs. 53-5, 92-1, 102-4, 103-3a, 109-e5, and 133-1; *J. S. Bach's Chromatic Fantasy and Fugue*, (1910) trans. and ed. Hedi Siegel (New York: Longman, 1984), 45.

Chromatic Fantasy and Fugue in D minor	$\hat{5}$-$\hat{4}$-$\hat{3}$-$\hat{2}$-$\hat{1}$
Invention No. 15 in B minor	$\hat{5}$-$\hat{4}$-$\hat{3}$
Handel	
Harpsichord Suite in F major, *Fuga*	$\hat{5}$-$\hat{4}$-$\hat{3}$
Concerto Grosso, Op. 6, No. 6, *Allegro ma non troppo*	$\hat{8}$-$\hat{7}$-$\hat{6}$-$\hat{5}$

These observations are the basis of a systematic approach to structural analysis of fugue subjects set forth below, an approach which considers both of Schenker's main ideas, tonal unity and directed motion, as a means of understanding the compositional procedures outlined in chapter 1.

Tonality in Subject and Answer

The two points of greatest structural importance in any fugue subject are the beginning and the ending. Together, they define the limits of its tonal expression and largely determine the tonal structure of the answer. It can be stated as a premise that the first important structural harmony expressed by any baroque fugue subject is the tonic chord.[5] Further, $\hat{1}$ and $\hat{5}$ are the notes of fundamental importance at the beginning of a subject. The mediant alone is inadequate as a representative of I here, since, in the absence of $\hat{1}$ or $\hat{5}$, $\hat{3}$ of a major key by itself implies the Phrygian mode, while $\hat{3}$ of a minor key implies the relative major. Any initial notes of a subject that are not part of tonic harmony act as melodic embellishments of chord members of I. Bach's Fugue in F-sharp major (*WTC II*) is a good example: the leading tone with which the subject begins is a lower neighbor and anacrusis to the following tonic.

The tonal implications of the end of the subject are even more important than those of the beginning, since they determine the main harmonic activity of the subject and the answer, hence of the exposition as a whole. With rare exceptions, usually framed along the lines of a "close fugue,"[6] any subject will end in one of three possible cadence forms: (1) an authentic cadence in I, (2) an authentic cadence in V, or (3) a half-cadence in I. Thus the underlying harmony of a subject as a whole takes one of three forms: (1) I–V–I, (2) I–V/V–V, or (3) I–V.[7] In structural terms, all else of a harmonic nature is subordinate and elaborative. These three tonal types determine the three broad categories of subject structure discussed below.

Despite the importance of cadence, a recurring difficulty in fugal analysis is the establishment of the *precise* ending point of a subject. The E-major subject of *WTC I* is one of the most intractable cases. Higgs, Norden, Von Bruyck

---

[5]Exceptions occur only in the case of fugatos within larger movements, particularly in those based on incipits of chorales or other *canti fermi*.
[6]Such unusual constructions must be analyzed in context, which is often a larger sequential passage.
[7]Iwan Knorr, *Lehrbuch der Fugen Komposition* (Leipzig: Breitkopf & Härtel, 1911) is one of the few theorists to define the end of a fugue subject by its cadence.

and Verrall suggest that the subject is ten notes in length. Prout and Iliffe, the latter probably following the view of the former, propose fourteen notes. Czackzes concurs. Keller, on the other hand, conjectures twenty-two notes and considers it a modulating subject. Tovey skirts the issue: "it is not worth settling where the subject ends and where the countersubject begins," and Knorr states categorically that "it is impossible to determine absolutely where the subject ends."[8] All of this disagreement and confusion results from failure to distinguish the various aspects which comprise a subject. Many texts focus on the melodic aspect and declare that the length of a subject is determined by the largest segment that is consistently repeated, regardless of cadential gesture or harmonic implication. This view guides those who maintain that the *WTC I* E-major subject ends at the fourteenth note, since the following d-sharp^1 is not strictly imitated by the corresponding a^1 in the second part. Keller's analysis, along the same lines of reasoning, disregards the exact intervallic imitation and thus extends the subject a further eight notes. Others, focusing on the rhythmic aspect, declare that the subject should end on the accented part of the beat, at the beginning of the answer or on the nearest accented beat before, hence in this instance on the second beat of m. 2, giving ten notes. Usually analysts also take into account cadential implications. But a further factor, perhaps the most important since it determines the basic tonal coherence, is generally overlooked: the completion of structural units of voice leading.

In problematic cases such as this the analyst needs greater precision. In stating that a given subject ends at a certain point, does the analyst mean that a cadence occurs, that a melodic segment ends, that a particular point in a metric plan has been reached, that a voice-leading motion has been completed, or some combination of factors? In the preponderance of instances where all or most of these factors coincide, an analytical decision is easy, but it is in the more complex and contradictory cases that difficulties arise. Consideration of the voice-leading structure or the E-major subject suggests that it extends only through the first ten notes, despite the fact that motivic imitation continues in a more or less rigorous fashion for twelve notes more.

The importance of the cadence of the subject rests in the fact that it is a hub of tonal activity, at once the conclusion of the subject and the beginning of the answer. In the usual course of a fugal exposition, the cadence of the subject marks the point of entry of the answer, and in many cases an overlap occurs, such that

---

[8]James Higgs, *Fugue* (London: Novello [1878]), 16; Hugo Norden, *Foundation Studies in Fugue* (New York: Crescendo Publishing, 1957), 3; Carl Von Bruyck, *Technische und äesthetische Analysen des Wohltemperierte Clavier*, 2nd. ed. (Leipzig: Breitkopf & Härtel, 1899), 180; John W. Verrall, *Fugue in Theory and Practice* (Palo Alto, California: Pacific Books, 1966), 66; Ebenezer Prout, *Fugue* (London: Augener, 1891), 19; Frederick Iliffe, *The Forty-Eight Preludes and Fugues of Johann Sebastian Bach Analyzed for the use of Students* (London: Novello [1897]), 33; L. Czackzes, *Analyse des WTC: Form und Aufbau der Fuge bei Bach*, 2 vols. (Wien und Müchen: Österreichischen Bundesverlag, 1965), 135; Hermann Keller, *The Well-Tempered Clavier by Johann Sebastian Bach*, trans. Leigh Gerdine (New York: Norton, 1976), 85; Donald Francis Tovey, *Forty-eight Preludes and Fugues by J. S. Bach*, 2 vols. (London: The Associated Board of the Royal Schools of Music, 1924), 1:15; Iwan Knorr, *Die Fugen des Wohltemperierte Clavier in bildischen Darstellung*, 2nd. ed. (Leipzig: Breitkopf & Härtel, 1926), 9.

the beginning of the answer occurs at the same time as the end of the subject. Whether the answer begins exactly at the point of cadence, immediately after, or immediately before is often more a matter of motivic and rhythmic detail than of structural significance. As a result of overlap, the opening of the answer must express whatever harmony the subject ends on, either I, or V—tonicized or not. For this reason the characteristic cadence of the subject conditions the form of the answer. And it is here that the problem of the tonal answer for the non-modulating subject is at issue.

> Tonal answer ... requires that the tonic-tone and the fifth-tone of the subject be replied to by the fifth-tone and the tonic-tone in the answer, respectively. Since this rule overlooks the core of the question—that is, the necessity of leading the tonic chord of the subject to the dominant chord of the answer—it was unable to progress beyond superficially descriptive words, and was forced to admit one exception after another.[9]

In most instances the subject begins with either $\hat{5}$ or $\hat{1}$ as a primary note. If the subject ends on I, $\hat{5}$ and $\hat{1}$ are answered by their complements, $\hat{1}$ and $\hat{5}$. If, however, the subject ends on V, $\hat{5}$ and $\hat{1}$ are answered by their transpositions, $\hat{5}$ and $\hat{1}$ of V, simply in order to harmonize with the end of the subject.

Schenker's discussion of the answer for the *WTC I*, C-minor subject clarifies this point (see example 2-2). "The answer, mm. 3–5, responds to the subject with the dominant chord or—in a foreground sense—in the dominant key."[10] After illustrating how in a simple transposition of the subject and its implied structure the answer would begin in and on G minor, he goes on to explain how the overlap which occurs at this point prevents the answer from beginning on G minor, and in fact necessitates the tonal alteration of the answer, such that the answer begins as a continuation of tonic harmony. It is thus the overlap which accounts fundamentally for the tonal answer. In this example the tonic of C minor acts as a pivot chord, becoming IV in G minor, as Schenker shows in example 2-2, and the fourth note of the answer is altered from d^2 to c^2, giving a tonal answer. The answer can therefore be thought of structurally as a transposition of the subject to the dominant level, but conjoined harmonically to the end of the subject.

Example 2-2. Schenker, analysis of Bach, C-minor fugue answer (*WTC I*)

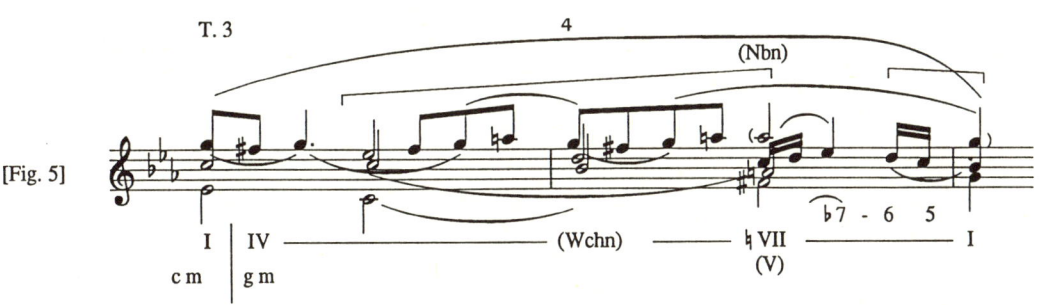

[9]Schenker, "The Organic Aspect of the Fugue," trans. by Kalib in "Thirteen Essays," 2:259. Charles Naldin has effectively proven Schenker's claim here regarding the necessity of exception after exception in *Fugal Answer* (London: Oxford University Press, 1969).
[10]Schenker, "Das Organische der Fuge," *Das Meisterwerk in der Musik*, 2:64.

The fugato from Mozart's *Musical Joke* (*Musikalischer Spass*) illustrates the weakness of having no overlap between subject and answer (see example 2-3). Omission of overlap avoids any necessity for tonal change in the answer or countersubjects, but the squareness of rhythm and awkward segmentation destroy any cumulative effect.[11]

Example 2-3. Mozart, *Musical Joke* K. 522, Presto, mm. 291–344

Since overlap is the normative procedure in fugal exposition, and since overlap is for the most part responsible for the problems of tonal and real answer, overlap at the end of the subject and beginning of the answer can be considered the rule. However, there are cases in which the answer enters at some distance after the subject has concluded, for reasons of rhythm, counterpoint, or tonality. Since no overlap takes place in these cases, the answer is not bound to begin on the harmony with which the subject ends. Indeed, a codetta, or link following the subject may induce a change of key. In Bach's Fugue in G minor BWV 578 (example 2-25), the codetta shifts the tonal focus to the dominant key, while in the E-flat major fugue (*WTC I*), (example 2-48) the codetta serves as a return to I following a modulating subject.

Subject Categories and Paradigms

Traditional classifications of subject types separate subject and answer forms into paired opposites: tonal versus real and modulating versus nonmodulating.[12] This meritorious division isolates surface melodic and harmonic aspects, yet it fails to capture the essence of the underlying structural qualities that above all determine the tonal characteristics of the exposition as a whole. Early in this century, Marc-André Souchay classified Bach's fugue subjects according to melodic characteristics using analytical graphs reminiscent of Schenker's.[13] Although several of his graphs reveal simple underlying linear progressions, the absence of a rigorous distinction between structural and ornamental notes prevents a true structural analysis. Ultimately, his work must be

---

[11] Johann Mattheson illustrates the necessity of overlap in *Der vollkommene Capellmeister* (Hamburg, 1739), trans. by Ernest C. Harriss under the same title, (Ann Arbor: UMI Research Press, 1981), Part 3, Chapter 23, paragraph 40, with reference to a fugue by Kuhnau. Mozart may well have read Mattheson's discussion and then exemplified it in his parody.

[12] See for example Arthur W. Marchant, *Five Hundred Fugue Subjects and Answers: Selected, Arranged and Edited*, 2nd. ed. (London: Novello, 1892).

[13] Marc-André Souchay, "Das Thema in der Fuge Bachs," *Bach Jahrbuch* XXIV (1927): 1–102 and XXVII (1930): 1–48.

considered stylistic analysis. The following division of subjects into three categories on the basis of the three cadence types described above represents a first level of classification of fugue-subject types.[14]

Category 1: subjects that end on I (I–V–I)

The initial I is expressed by $\hat{1}$ and/or $\hat{5}$, possibly linked by $\hat{3}$. The cadence leads through one or more notes of V^7 or VII^7 to a termination on $\hat{1}$ or $\hat{3}$, representing the concluding I. The answer, transposing to the fifth, ends correspondingly with $\hat{5}$ or $\hat{7}$, resolving as an authentic cadence in the dominant key. Category 1 includes by far the greatest number of baroque fugue subjects. It accounts for fully four-fifths of Bach's subjects and corresponding proportions in the works of other composers.

Category 2: modulating subjects that end on V (I–V7/V–V)

In this case the end of the subject is $\hat{5}$ or $\hat{7}$ of the original key, representing the dominant chord, preceded by its dominant, giving an authentic cadence in the dominant key. A real answer would therefore modulate to II. The more usual tonal answer replicates the authentic cadence in the tonic, ending with $\hat{1}$ or $\hat{3}$. Category 2 thus represents a reversal of cadence types as compared to category 1.

Category 3: non-modulating subjects that end on V (I–V)

The third category is distinguished by ending on V as a half cadence with no modulation. The final structural note of the subject can be $\hat{5}$, $\hat{7}$, or $\hat{2}$. The answer is usually real, replicating the half cadence by ending on $\hat{2}$, sharp-$\hat{4}$ or $\hat{6}$, representing V in the dominant key. More rarely a tonal answer effects the return to I through an authentic cadence. Category 3 is often neglected within traditional classifications, or if included is subsumed within category 2 despite its lack of modulation.

Beyond the basic tonal characteristics of subject and answer outlined by these three categories, a Schenkerian approach also considers voice-leading, in this case underlying linear progressions as suggested in chapter 1. Within each of the three categories outlined above, melodic patterns define a series of *subject paradigms* and corresponding *answer paradigms* which express the essential tonal content in a variety of ways. Thus, each subject paradigm suggests a single model for the structure of numerous actual fugue subjects; each answer paradigm refers to the underlying form that the corresponding answer displays. Analysis of a large number of fugue subjects, coupled with a Schenkerian conception of the linear implications of basic harmonic progressions, yields some five or six distinct subject paradigms for each subject category, some of which have additional sub-paradigms as well. As an example, all three subjects in example 1-1 are based on the identical underlying paradigm, $\hat{5}$ - $\hat{4}$ - $\hat{3}$, identified below as paradigm 1.

---

[14]My earlier work, focusing on subjects that end on I, presents only a partial categorization of subject paradigms. See "Voice-leading Patterns in the Fugal Expositions of J. S. Bach's *Well-Tempered Clavier*" (Ph.D. diss., City University of New York, 1987), and "Structural Patterns in Fugue Subjects and Fugal Expositions," *Music Theory Spectrum* XIII/1 (1991): 197–218. Subject paradigms are labelled differently in these works.

Subject and Answer Paradigms For Category 1

For category 1, the set of subject and answer paradigms is illustrated in example 2-4. Each subject paradigm is represented by a series of notes connected by a beam. The corresponding answer paradigm, which can be inferred from the harmonic and melodic implications of the subject paradigm, is shown by a second set of beamed notes with stems in the opposite direction, representing a second voice. Each paradigm projects a simple linear basis that expresses the main harmonies involved. For the abstract purposes of example 2-4 it is of no consequence whether the answer enters above or below the subject. However, in practice there is often a significant correlation between paradigm and order of entries in an exposition.[15]

Example 2-4. Subject and answer paradigms for category 1

---

[15]See chapter 4.

SUBJECT AND ANSWER

In example 2-4, the paradigm number denotes one of the five possible subject endings in category 1, while any letter that follows represents an alternative opening position leading to the same ending. Thus subject paradigm 1 is the descent from fifth to third, but paradigm 1a extends the descent so that it begins a fourth higher, on the tonic. Paradigm 2 is the stepwise descent from third to tonic; paradigm 2a extends the opening up to the dominant and paradigm 2b extends through the entire octave; paradigm 2c compresses paradigm 2b into a simple neighbor motion. The essence of paradigm 3 is the resolution of the leading tone to the tonic, and paradigms 3a and 3b again extend the figure to other notes of the initial I chord. Paradigm 4 is the basic root motion of the harmony I–V–I. Paradigm 4a utilizes the same resolution but begins on the dominant. Paradigm 5 represents an ascending motion $\hat{1}$ - $\hat{2}$ - $\hat{3}$, and paradigm 5a extends the beginning of the ascent to the dominant.

In all cases in category 1, the answer replicates the close of the subject at the dominant pitch-level, yielding I–V/V–V as the basic harmonic structure of the answer. Any tonal modifications which the answer may undergo result from the altered harmonic structure of the answer. It is noteworthy that even at this most basic level of subject structure some answers are real and others are tonal. The choice of real or tonal answer for category 1 subjects has to do with the type of linear motion involved rather than with the harmonic implications. More specifically, any subject paradigm in category 1 that begins on $\hat{5}$ will have a tonal answer (paradigms 1, 2a, 3a, 4a, and 5a).

Paradigm 1: subject $\hat{5}$ - $\hat{4}$ - $\hat{3}$; answer $\hat{8}$ - $\hat{8}$ - $\hat{7}$

Subject paradigm 1 is simply the descending third-progression $\hat{5}$ - $\hat{4}$ - $\hat{3}$ previously introduced as example 1-1 in chapter 1. The subject of *WTC I*, Fugue 2 in C Minor (example 2-1) is another instance, and as Schenker notes, the answer begins on the tonic, but transposes the authentic cadence to the dominant, generating IV–V⁷–I in V, if the tonic that ends the subject is considered a pivot chord to the dominant. Thus, the basic answer paradigm, $\hat{8}$ - $\hat{8}$ - $\hat{7}$, embodies a tonal alteration: the descending third becomes a descending second. The whole issue surrounding paradigm 1 therefore is located in the means by which this tonal alteration and consequent melodic defect in the answer is made good by the surface texture.

Example 2-5 is a very simple instance of paradigm 1. The parenthetical notes in the graphic analysis of example 2-5 may be inferred as logical continuations of voices that are only partially represented in the surface texture. Arpeggiation of I prolongs the initial $\hat{5}$ of the subject before the main melodic motion continues to $\hat{4}$ and $\hat{3}$. The first note of the answer, c², provides a consonant harmonization of the end of the subject, but the following music now takes advantage of the subject's arpeggiation of I to form an arpeggiation of V. The arpeggiating notes, b-flat^1, d^2 and g^1, intervene between and thus ameliorate the repeated $\hat{8}$s of the answer paradigm.

Example 2-5. Bach, Fugue 2 in C minor (*WTC II*), mm. 1–3

The most common means of separating the $\hat{5}$ - $\hat{4}$ motion of the subject, and thus accommodating the tonal alteration of the answer, is evident in the C minor subject of example 2-1 and in the A minor subject of example 1-1: an upper neighbor, $\hat{6}$, embellishes the subject, giving the progression $\hat{5}$ - $\hat{6}$ - $\hat{5}$ - $\hat{4}$ - $\hat{3}$. This becomes $\hat{1}$ - $\hat{3}$ - $\hat{2}$ - $\hat{1}$ - $\hat{7}$ in the answer. The initial step, $\hat{5}$ - $\hat{6}$, becomes an arpeggiation $\hat{1}$ - $\hat{3}$, affirming the tonic harmony at the point of overlap and simultaneously providing for the tonal mutation. While the role of such a neighbor is strictly ornamental in the subject, it assumes structural importance in the answer as the third of the tonic chord and the initiator of a new linear progression. The resulting answer form replicates the contour of the subject very effectively.

In its directness and simplicity, the subject of Bach's *Kyrie eleison* from the *Mass in F major* BWV 233-1 can be regarded as a *locus classicus* of the upper-neighbor pattern. Example 2-6 illustrates how the upper neighbor allows the answer to replicate the contour of the subject while at the same time tonicizing V.

Example 2-6. Bach, *Kyrie eleison, Mass in F major* BWV 233, mm. 1–5

SUBJECT AND ANSWER

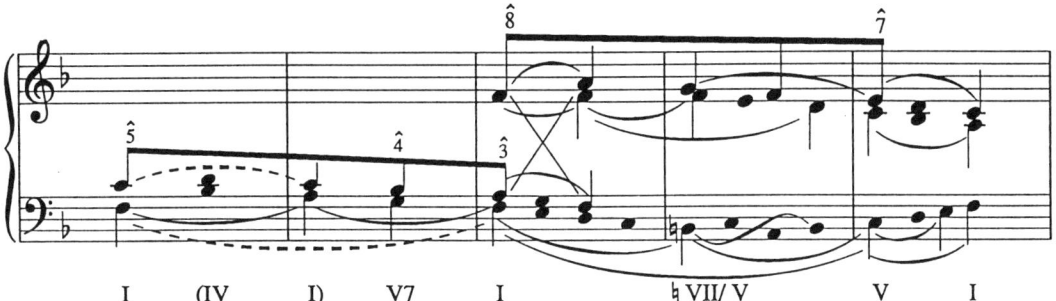

Although the main linear-progression of the subject is $\hat{5}$ - $\hat{4}$ - $\hat{3}$, the completion of the text *kyrie eleison* suggests that the subject in fact ends on f, not a. This is confirmed by repetition in the answer. A *final descent*[16] such as this, which follows after the main linear progression but is nevertheless part of the subject is a common feature of subjects that end on $\hat{3}$. The final descent provides for a root-position harmony when the subject appears in the bass and also serves to harmonize the mediant in the answer which arises from the upper neighbor of the subject. Thus the final descent forms a voice exchange with the arpeggiation $\hat{1}$ - $\hat{3}$ in the answer.

The compositional technique employed in François Roberday's twelve *Fugues et Caprices* of 1660 helps to clarify the role of paradigms in fugue.[17] In this collection the composer strives to provide motivic links between the fugues and the caprices in each mode, as well as to use varied forms of the same imitative motive within the sections of a given fugue or caprice. Example 2-7 shows an original subject (paradigm 1) and four transformations used in the later sections of *Fugue 9me* and in its companion *Caprice*.[18] While in each case the surface rhythm and ornamentation undergo alteration, including the introduction of new pitches in the later subject forms, the underlying structural pattern of paradigm 1 with the upper neighbor remains. What better example of Schenker's motto, *semper idem sed non eodem modo* (always the same, but not in the same way). In the consciousness of the composer, this structurally based approach must have been construed as a form of variation and diminution technique.

Example 2-7. Roberday, *Fugue 9me*, subjects; *Caprice*, subjects

[16]The term *final descent* is coined as a counterpart to Schenker's term *initial ascent*, discussed below.

[17]This is the only extant work of this little-known composer (1620–1690). The fact that three pieces in the collection are by Frescobaldi, Ebner, and Froberger places the origin of the entire collection in doubt. See Jean Ferrand, "Roberday," *The New Grove Dictionary of Music and Musicians*, ed. Stanley Sadie (London: Macmillan, 1980) 16:65.

[18]The term *varied fugue subjects* is used by Peter Williams. See *The Organ Music of J. S. Bach*, 2 vols. (Cambridge: Cambridge University Press, 1980), 1:225.

Example 2-8 shows a more fully developed instance of paradigm 1, again using the upper neighbor as the agent which transforms the answer in a convincing manner. The structural upper neighbor even becomes a motivic element, such that mm. 3–4 of the subject become a disguised sequential repetition of mm. 1–2. This underlying sequential structure is brought out later in the fugue, where three entries are given in a simplified form as shown in example 2-8 (b).[19] The answer again uses the upper neighbor to form a leap, c²-e², forming a voice-exchange with the continuation of the first part.

Example 2-8. Bach, Fugue 1 in C major (*WTC I*), a, mm. 1–9, b, mm. 76–80

Two of the subjects discussed thus far, *WTC I*, Fugue 2 in C minor and *WTC II*, Fugue 1 in C major, include an *initial tonic* at or near the beginning, even though the paradigm itself originates from $\hat{5}$. In the subject, this initial tonic assists in projecting the opening tonic sonority and can serve as a root when the subject is in the bass. An initial tonic need not be the very first note of a subject, as the term would seem to imply. Rather, it is a tonic note stated within the time-span of the initial tonic-chord. The answer replicates the initial tonic with $\hat{5}$, as part of its opening I chord. When an opening gesture boldly asserts the tonic and dominant in this manner, its implication for answer construction has traditionally been framed in one of the most familiar rules of tonal answer, that tonic responds to dominant and dominant to tonic, in an opposition of keys.[20] While it is true that $\hat{1}$ and $\hat{5}$ act in opposition, they combine to form a harmonic interval within the tonic chord rather than a melodic interval between I and V; their proper expression in the answer will thus be as an expression of the tonic harmony which ends the subject and simultaneously begins the answer: $\hat{1}$ - $\hat{5}$, signifying I, becomes $\hat{5}$ - $\hat{1}$, still signifying I. The traditional view of opposed tonic and dominant notes, which is so often linked incorrectly with the idea of opposing tonic and dominant keys in subject and answer, gives way to an associative view of tonic and dominant

---

[19]See chapter 7.

[20]For example, André Gedalge states that "the dominant of the main key is always considered as the first degree of the dominant key (root of the tonic triad of the dominant key) ... consequently every subject beginning with, or ending on the dominant is considered as modulating *a priori* to the dominant key." *Treatise on Fugue* (1901), trans. A. Levin, (Mattapan Mass.: Gamut Music Co., 1964.), 16.

SUBJECT AND ANSWER

notes as components of a single harmony. $\hat{1}$ and $\hat{5}$ act as opposing notes within a single harmony, not as roots of opposing tonic and dominant harmonies.

The brief subject of Bach's Fugue in C-sharp major (*WTC II*) (example 2-9), begins with an initial tonic, but rather than proceeding at once to $\hat{5}$, it fills out I by arpeggiating the full tonic chord. Like the initial tonic, this *initial arpeggiation* is frequently found in subject paradigms that begin on $\hat{5}$. While Schenker identified initial arpeggiation, particularly in the context of broader musical segments, as an ascending arpeggiation through notes of the tonic chord, culminating on a significant structural note, usually the *head tone (Kopfton)*,[21] the usage here is not confined to the ascending form. The *WTC II* C minor subject (example 2-5) represents a similar structural function, even though the arpeggiation follows the start of the linear progression and outlines I through a descent.[22]

Example 2-9. Bach, Fugue 3 in C-sharp minor (*WTC II*), mm. 1–3

Example 2-9 also illustrates what happens in the answer if there is no intervening music between $\hat{5}$ and $\hat{4}$ of the subject paradigm, thus between the repeated $\hat{8}$s of the answer paradigm. In most paradigm 1 subjects the motion from $\hat{5}$ to $\hat{4}$ is broken up, whether by an arpeggiation (example 2-5) or by an upper neighbor (examples 2-1, 2-6 and 2-8), allowing for the necessary melodic alteration. But if no upper neighbor, arpeggiation, or other motion intervenes at this point, the direct repetition $\hat{8}$-$\hat{8}$ of the answer paradigm gives a melodically deficient answer. Indeed, in cases which afford no opportunity of masking this repetition, composers give a plagal (subdominant) answer which respects the melodic condition but concedes the usual harmonic objective. The answer replicates the descending third, preserving the melodic contour, but moves to IV rather than V.[23]

In example 2-9 the answer could have taken advantage of the initial arpeggiation to provide a real answer. However, the harmonic requirements of the close imitation demand c-sharp² rather than d-sharp² to harmonize with the end of the subject. Other paradigm 1 subjects that possess the direct motion from $\hat{5}$ to $\hat{4}$ also give plagal answers. The fugue subject of Bach's Sonata 1 in G minor for solo violin BWV 1001-2 (example 1-1) has neither initial arpeggiation nor separation of $\hat{5}$ and $\hat{4}$, and consequently requires

---

[21]Schenker, *Free Composition*, 46–47; Fig. 40.

[22]This association becomes even more important when motivic inversion is considered. See chapter 6.

[23]See also example 1-6.

a plagal answer. In the Prelude and Fugue in C major BWV 531, one of Bach's earliest organ fugues, the direct sequential ornamentation of paradigm 1 again necessitates a plagal answer. Examples such as these clarify the vital relationships between structure and ornament that characterize the complex nature of fugal style and structure.

Example 2-10 takes the idea of initial arpeggiation one step further and fills in the gaps with a step-wise motion in a seamless *initial ascent*.[24] The space between $\hat{1}$ and $\hat{5}$ is completely filled by step-wise motion, yielding a subordinate rising fifth-progression. In example 2-10 the initial ascent occupies the first half of the subject. The structural paradigm itself occurs in m. 2, and the subject is completed by a final descent, d^1–b, which balances the initial ascent.[25]

Example 2-10. Bach, Prelude and Fugue in B minor BWV 544, fugue, mm. 1–4

Initial ascent serves an important new function for the answer: it delays the beginning of the main linear progression of the answer to such an extent that it is no longer obliged to reinforce the tonic harmony with which the subject ends. Indeed, the continuity of the step-wise ascent makes such a tonal mutation awkward. Thus, like initial arpeggiation, initial ascent allows paradigm 1 to give a real answer as a prolongation of V. The answer paradigm becomes $\hat{5}$ - $\hat{4}$ - $\hat{3}$ in V. Once again, structure and ornament can be seen working together in a systematic way.

It should also be noted that no overlap occurs in example 2-10. The subject ends on I in m. 2 and the answer begins a prolongation of V in m. 3. Had the answer begun in the middle of m. 2, a disturbing I six-four would

---

[24]Growing out of initial arpeggiation, initial ascent is also derived from Schenkerian terminology. See Schenker, *Free Composition*, 45.

[25]Although one may be unsatisfied with the analysis that the $\hat{5}$-$\hat{4}$-$\hat{3}$ descent is of greater significance than any other portion of this entirely conjunct subject, chapter 3 illustrates how $\hat{5}$ - $\hat{4}$ - $\hat{3}$ operates in a more significant manner in the context of the invertible counterpoint which develops later in the fugue.

have resulted, caused by the answer entering below the subject. The delayed answer allows for a change of harmony and the new entry coincides with the beginning of a prolongation of V.

All three phenomena, initial tonic, initial arpeggiation, and initial ascent, are variant means of expressing the opening I with increasing degrees of fullness and progressive ways of separating the linear progressions of paradigm 1 so that a real answer can be acheived.

The lengthy and complex subject in example 2-11 includes an initial ascent and a final descent which again complement each other, providing an arched contour. The initial ascent again permits a real answer (not shown). In example 2-11, the upper neighbor occurs twice, first as part of a lengthy descent to the leading tone, and second as part of the motion to $\hat{4}$ of the main linear progression in m. 5. The first and last notes of the subject (supplied by the initial ascent and final descent) plus the lowest note, d-sharp^1, project a second voice, $\hat{8}$ - $\hat{7}$ - $\hat{8}$ which acts as a contrapuntal basis for the main linear progression. At this stage of development the simple $\hat{5}$ - $\hat{4}$ - $\hat{3}$ paradigm has assumed all the qualities of a brief yet complete tonal utterance.

Example 2-11. Bach, Fugue 10 in E minor (*WTC II*), mm. 1–6

The *WTC II* B-flat minor subject also contains a lengthy initial ascent to $\hat{5}$, and again the apex is capped by the upper neighbor $\hat{6}$ which moves directly to $\hat{4}$ rather than returning to $\hat{5}$ (see example 2-12). The initial ascent again leads to a real answer. The two notes which follow the end of the subject, a and b-flat, complete an implied lower voice, b-flat-a-b-flat ($\hat{8}$ - $\hat{7}$ - $\hat{8}$).

Example 2-12. Bach, Fugue 22 in B-flat minor (*WTC II*), mm. 1–5

A remarkable feature of this subject is that its structural meaning remains essentially unchanged when the subject appears in inversion in the middle portion of the fugue. See example 2-13. This type of melodic inversion has the third note of the scale as its axis of inversion, and is especially suited to the minor key, where the lowered sixth becomes the raised seventh.

Example 2-13. Bach, Fugue 22 in B-flat minor (*WTC II*), mm. 42–46

The principal theme from the *Art of Fugue* is perhaps the most familiar example of thematic inversion, since the inverted subject forms the basis of complete fugues. The original theme and its inversion are shown in example 2-14 (a) and (b). The tonal structure of the inverted form is in fact a most compelling representation of paradigm 1, including the upper neighbor, whereas the prime form omits the $\hat{4}$ of paradigm 1. In the subject itself the final descent ($\hat{2}$ - $\hat{1}$) is also present, completing a lower voice. Examples 2-14 (c) and (d) illustrate the tonal structures of the corresponding answer forms, while (e), (f) and (g) show how, in connection with the final descent or its inversion, other forms yield new paradigms. It is just this malleability that allows this innocuous theme to unfold so many imitative possibilities throughout the *Art of Fugue*, and as Tovey points out, provides a simple means of incorporating transitory modulations to related keys within thematic statements.[26]

Example 2-14. Bach, *Art of Fugue*, a, *Contrapunctus 1*, mm. 1–5; b, *Contrapunctus 3*, mm. 5–9; c, *Contrapunctus 2*, mm. 38–42; d, *Contrapunctus 4*, mm. 39–43; e, *Contrapunctus 4*, mm. 73–77; f, *Contrapunctus 3*, mm. 1–5; g, *Contrapunctus 1*, mm. 5–9

[26] See Donald Francis Tovey, *A Companion to "The Art of Fugue"* (London: Oxford University Press, 1931), 3. In *Untersuchungen zur Struktur der "Kunst der Fuge" J. S. Bachs* (Regensburg: Gustav Bosse Verlag, 1941), Bernhard Martin analyses the first four fugues of the *Art of Fugue* in a quasi-Schenkerian manner. Despite his brave acknowledgement and open support of the theories of Schenker (labelled *Jude* in accordance with Nazi policy) and no doubt hampered by the intellectual and cultural prohibitions of the regime, his understanding of deeper levels is not sufficiently developed for the analyses to be of much significance today.

SUBJECT AND ANSWER

Paradigm 1 occurs more frequently than any other subject paradigm in the baroque era, in perhaps one quarter of all fugues. Common as it is in the fugues of such diverse composers as Corelli, Buxtehude, Fischer, Frescobaldi, and Handel, Bach seems to have been particularly consistent in his use of paradigm 1: it occurs in fully forty percent of all Bach's fugue subjects. We have already seen how paradigm 1 can effectively accommodate a wide range of styles and forms. The following chapters which deal with the contrapuntal applications of paradigms give additional explanations as to why paradigm 1 is so prevalent. The ornamental features illustrated for paradigm 1, initial tonic, initial arpeggiation, initial ascent, upper neighbor, and final descent, are also widely applicable to other paradigms, as the following examples show.

Paradigm 1a: subject $\hat{8}-\hat{7}-\hat{6}-\hat{5}-\hat{4}-\hat{3}$; answer $\hat{5}-\hat{4}-\hat{3}-\hat{2}-\hat{1}-\hat{7}$

By contrast with paradigm 1, paradigm 1a is extremely rare. It is natural to perceive lengthy linear progressions or paradigms that exceed the span of a fifth as shorter underlying progressions elaborated by chordal unfolding.[27] In paradigm 1a, the span from $\hat{8}$ to $\hat{5}$ is easily understood as an unfolding of the initial tonic. Thus, although paradigm 1a is structurally an expansion of paradigm 1, the fact that the two segments, $\hat{8}-\hat{7}-\hat{6}-\hat{5}$ and $\hat{5}-\hat{4}-\hat{3}$, form a continuous, unidirectional line, supports the idea that the two shorter progressions may in some cases be best perceived as a unified sixth-progression. While the descending fourth that begins paradigm 1a might be construed as an *initial descent* in analogy with initial ascent, the resultant unidirectional sixth progression has a greater degree of melodic continuity. In any case, the letter system with which these paradigms are identified makes explicit the relationship between the simple and expanded forms which these two paradigms represent.

Only a small number of the many imitative movements in baroque trio-sonatas are genuine fugues, yet the imitative procedures are often identical to those of fugues. In example 2-15 the descending sixth is clearly broken into a fourth and third, both rhythmically and harmonically. Although the answer is real in its basic outline and could have ended with an authentic cadence in V (f-sharp and d-sharp^2 would replace f and d^2 in m. 6), Purcell raises g^1 to g-sharp^1, maintaining the key of A minor and giving instead a Phrygian cadence which conveniently sets up the return to I for the bass entry of the subject in m. 8.

---

[27]Similarly, Schenker's octave-spanning fundamental line is extremely rare, and for similar reasons.

Example 2-15. Purcell, Trio Sonata V in A minor, iii, mm. 1–7

The lengthy subject in example 2-16 contains two important deviations from the basic form of paradigm 1a: (1) the first note of the linear progression occurs in the lower octave, giving an expansive ascending seventh in place of the descending second. (2) the second note of the main linear-progression is chromatically altered (g-natural^1 instead of g-sharp^1). This alteration, which converts the tonic of m. 30 into a secondary dominant, yields a sequential motivic repetition of the previous measure and also respects the melodic principle that an upper neighbor to $\hat{6}$ should be lowered.[28] The remainder of the subject is harmonized as a series of descending tenths. The answer (not shown) is a strict transposition of the subject.

Example 2-16. Bach, Cantata BWV 17-1, mm. 28–34

[28]*"Una nota sopra la semper est canendem fa"* (a note above la is always sung as fa). When the apex of a melodic segment is the leading tone, flatting the pitch removes the impetus towards an upward resolution to the tonic.

Paradigm 2: subject $\hat{1}$ - $\hat{3}$ - $\hat{2}$ - $\hat{1}$; answer $\hat{5}$ - $\hat{7}$ - $\hat{6}$ - $\hat{5}$

Paradigm 2 is based on a stepwise descent to the tonic. Although the initial tonic is not part of the linear progression itself, it is an obligatory part of the formula, clarifying the tonal center and providing a consonant initial note for the answer, which would otherwise begin with the leading note as a structural note (see example 2-4). Paradigm 2 occurs quite frequently, in about eight percent of Bach's fugues. The fact that many of the examples of paradigm 2 are in a simple *stile antico* may be related to the registral restriction of the subject and answer paradigms to the lower and upper tetrachords respectively.

The subject in example 2-17 includes only a single note beyond the paradigm itself. But this added leading tone provides a second voice, $\hat{8}$ - $\hat{7}$ - $\hat{8}$, which supports the main linear progression as a polyphonic melody.[29] The following arpeggiation to $\hat{3}$ gives an expressive diminished fourth in m. 2. Rather than supplying a cadence at the dominant level at the end of the answer, the counterpoint reintroduces f-sharp instead of f-double-sharp, hastening the return to I in preparation for the third entry.

Example 2-17. Bach, Fugue 4 in C-sharp minor (*WTC I*), mm. 1–7

Bach must have been aware that this subject is almost identical to the opening phrase of the well-known advent chorale *Nun komm der heiden Heiland* (see example 2-18) which he himself used in numerous compositions. The chorale melody is itself derived from the plainchant hymn-tune *Veni redemptor gentium*.[30] The plainchant includes the natural form of the leading-tone, which is sometimes found in the chorale tune as well. Others too have adopted this theme: Zarlino employs it for an example of canonic imitation at the octave (*fuga legata*);[31] Benedetto Marcello used the same subject in his Opus 4; Frescobaldi utilized it, but without the raised leading-tone, in *Ricercare 1* (mode 1);[32] Handel, too, borrowed it, but in the major mode, for a fugue in *Solomon*. Although duplication or adaptation—con-

---

[29]This analysis follows that of Schenker, *Free Composition*, Figure 103, 3a.
[30]St. Gall, ms. 438.
[31]See Gioseffo Zarlino, *The Art of Counterpoint*, trans. by Guy A. Marco and Claude V. Palisca (New Haven: Yale University Press, 1968), 129.
[32]*Ricercare et canzoni faranzese... libro primo* (Rome, 1615).

scious or unconscious—may explain the resemblances among this family of subjects, at the same time we must recognize that these extraordinary recurrences grow out of the underlying structural principles embodied in paradigm 2 as it is expanded into a polyphonic melody of two voices.[33] While parody technique has always maintained an important place in traditional western composition, we must recognize that the specific type of parody technique exhibited here has its basis not so much in stylistic aspects but in structural considerations that go far beyond the simple idea of borrowing and reshaping pre-existing materials.

Example 2-18, variants of paradigm 2 with lower neighbor, a, *Nun komm, der Heiden Heiland* (Walther's *Gesangbuchlein*, 1524), b, *Veni redemptor gentium*, c, Zarlino, *The Art of Counterpoint*, p. 129, d, Marcello, Op. 4 *Canzoni Madrigalische*, e, Frescobaldi, Ricercare 1 (*Ricercare et canzoni*, 1615), f, Handel, *Solomon*

Just as paradigm 1 often involves the upper neighbor $\hat{6}$, which aids in forming the tonic chord at the beginning of the answer, so paradigm 2 often uses the upper neighbor $\hat{4}$, which supplies the tonic itself in the answer. Example 2-19 displays this upper neighbor, again in a simple vocal style. Once again the counterpoint to the answer elides the cadence to V and facilitates the motion back to I in preparation for the next subject entry.

---

[33] Chapter 3 illustrates further the importance of the contrapuntal implications of these two voices, $\hat{3}$-$\hat{2}$-$\hat{1}$ and $\hat{8}$-$\hat{7}$-$\hat{8}$, as essential bases for the processes of invertible counterpoint.

Example 2-19. Bach, Fugue 9 in E major (*WTC II*), mm. 1–4

Like the *WTC I* C-sharp minor subject, the *WTC II* E major subject is but one of a whole family of similar subjects in the literature. It occurs in a slightly augmented rhythm in Fischer's *Fuga VIII* in E (example 2-20, (a)).[34] Fux uses the identical subject in both the Phrygian and major modes (b) and (c). Indeed, the first subject used by Fux in *Gradus ad Parnassum* for the demonstration of fugal procedures is simply paradigm 2 itself (d) and (e)). Froberger provides a similar form in *Fantasia 12*[35] (f) but beginning with the answer, and Handel follows Froberger's model in *Israel in Egypt* (g). Not only do these subjects share a family resemblance, but in many cases the countersubjects are also essentially the same as that employed by Bach: a rising scale followed by a leap and a suspension. This remarkable phenomenon of re-utilization has its basis in the structural possibilities inherent in paradigm 2.

Example 2-20, variants of paradigm 2 with upper neighbor, a, Fischer, *Fuga VIII*, b-e, Fux, *Gradus ad Parnassum*, f, Froberger, *Fantasia 12*, g, Handel, *Israel in Egypt*

[34]Johann Caspar Ferdinand Fischer, *Ariadne musica . . . neo organeodum* (Schlackenwerth, 1702).
[35]*Diverse curiose e rare partite musicale* (Mainz, 1696).

Bach's Cantata BWV 29-2 shows a more extended form of paradigm 2 (see example 2-21), but still within the tradition of the vocal style. Chapter 6 illustrates the manner in which this and the other subjects of paradigm 2 provide the basis for a multitude of stretto possibilities.

Example 2-21. Bach, Cantata BWV 29-2, mm. 1–7

Paradigm 2a: subject $\hat{5}$ - $\hat{4}$ - $\hat{3}$ - $\hat{2}$ - $\hat{1}$; answer $\hat{8}$ - $\hat{8}$ - $\hat{7}$ - $\hat{6}$ - $\hat{5}$

Paradigm 2a projects a descending fifth as its main linear progression. Since the first main note is $\hat{5}$, initial tonic, initial arpeggiation, and initial ascent are frequently employed here. The upper neighbor $\hat{6}$ also figures prominently in many cases. The answer is of course tonal, unless $\hat{5}$ is delayed by an initial arpeggiation or initial ascent, and the issues surrounding the melodic alteration of the tonal answer are essentially the same as those for paradigm 1. Paradigm 2a occurs frequently in the literature: in about seventeen percent of Bach's fugues and at least as often in those of his contemporaries.

The subject from Bach's Cantata BWV 21-6 (example 2-22) shows a simple realization of paradigm 2a. It includes the upper neighbor and an arpeggiation of the initial tonic chord. The tonal answer shares the same alteration as for many examples of paradigm 1, where the upper neighbor of the subject becomes a third, c^2–e-flat^2.

Example 2-22. Bach, Cantata BWV 21-6, mm. 43–47

The *WTC I* D-sharp minor subject uses an initial tonic and prolongs $\hat{5}$ by arpeggiation through the tonic chord (see example 2-23)[36]. Once again the upper neighbor provides the harmonic basis of a tonal answer. As for paradigm 1, paradigm 2a provides a basis for subject inversion around the mediant. However, the structural meaning is of course different, as the inversion leads to a conclusion on $\hat{5}$. (see example 2-23 (b)).

Example 2-23. Bach, Fugue 8 in D-sharp minor (*WTC I*), a, mm. 1–6, b, inversion

[36]See also Schenker, *Free Composition*, Fig. 109 e), 5.

SUBJECT AND ANSWER 43

The A minor fugue from *WTC I* illustrates the application of initial ascent to paradigm 2a (see example 2-24). Repetition beautifully integrates the initial ascent within the subject itself: a second ascending passage expands V before the main linear progression descends to $\hat{1}$. The initial ascent gives a real answer, such that the main linear progression of the answer is $\hat{5}$ - $\hat{4}$ - $\hat{3}$ - $\hat{2}$ - $\hat{1}$ in the dominant. This subject also occurs in inversion, based on the same structural pattern as example 2-23.

Example 2-24. Bach, Fugue 20 in A minor (*WTC I*), mm. 1–4

By centering the melodic activity for some time on the $\hat{3}$ - $\hat{2}$ motion in the inner voice, the subject of Bach's Fugue in G minor BWV 578 spins out paradigm 2a at length. Example 2-25 shows how $\hat{5}$ reestablishes itself at the end of m. 4, in preparation for the descent to $\hat{1}$. The answer enters well beyond the end of the subject (no overlap occurs here) and the codetta or link between the two provides for a shift to V at the beginning of m. 6. For this reason there is no necessity for, indeed no reason for, a tonal answer.

Example 2-25. Bach, Fugue in G minor BWV 578, mm.1–7

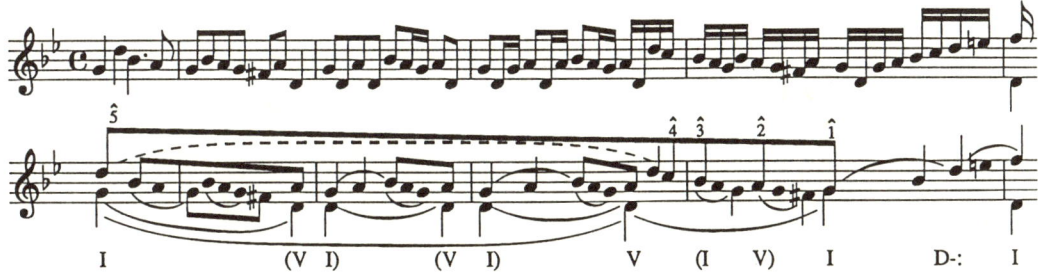

Schenker's analysis of the subject of Bach's Chromatic Fantasy and Fugue in D minor reduces the chromatic subject to a descending fifth, paradigm 2a.[37] It is interesting that this analysis is one of the first examples of a fundamental line in *Free Composition*. Although Schenker cross-

---

[37]*Ibid.*, Fig. 20-2.

references the discussion with Section 1 of chapter 3, "Transference of the Forms of the Fundamental Structure to Individual Harmonies,"[38] he nevertheless makes an explicit connection between the basic structure of a fugue subject (a middleground or foreground phenomenon) and the fundamental line (manifestly a background phenomenon). This important relationship between subject paradigms and fundamental line formations is explored in the context of entire fugues in chapter 7.

A number of paradigm 1 subjects ($\hat{5}$ - $\hat{4}$ - $\hat{3}$) are designed so that they can be converted to paradigm 2a ($\hat{5}$ - $\hat{4}$ - $\hat{3}$ - $\hat{2}$ - $\hat{1}$). This alteration allows a composer, if required by the formal or imitative context, to conclude a bass entry with a root position cadence. Although the subjects of *WTC I*, Fugue 13 in F-sharp major and *WTC II*, Fugue 6 in D minor are clearly forms of paradigm 1, they each include a supplementary motion to $\hat{2}$ before resolving to $\hat{3}$. In each instance the bass entry which concludes the exposition supplants $\hat{3}$ with $\hat{1}$, transforming these subject statements into examples of paradigm 2a. In example 2-26, the upper set of beamed notes shows the original form (paradigm 1) while the lower set shows the altered form of the third entry (paradigm 2a). Clearly these subjects have been constructed in such a way that they are capable of assuming the structure of either paradigm as warranted by the compositional context.

Example 2-26. Paradigm 1 becoming paradigm 2a, a, Bach, Fugue 14 in F-sharp major (*WTC I*), mm. 1–3, b, Bach, Fugue 6 in D minor (*WTC II*), mm. 1–3

Paradigm 2b: subject $\hat{8}$ - $\hat{7}$ - $\hat{6}$ - $\hat{5}$ - $\hat{4}$ - $\hat{3}$ - $\hat{2}$ - $\hat{1}$; answer $\hat{5}$ -(sharp) $\hat{4}$ - $\hat{3}$ - $\hat{2}$ - $\hat{1}$ - $\hat{7}$ - $\hat{6}$ - $\hat{5}$

Compared with paradigms 2 and 2a, the descending octave occurs very rarely as a subject paradigm. The problem of maintaining interest and variety through such a lengthy descent—especially when numerous repeti-

---

[38]*Ibid.*, 34.

tions of the subject are contemplated—may help to explain its rarity. Paradigm 2b occurs only three times in Bach's fugues, in the Toccata and Fugue in D minor BWV 538 (*Dorian*), the Toccata in E major BWV 566, and the Concerto in D minor for two violins BWV 1043. The real answer forms a descending octave from dominant to dominant and cadences in V (see example 2-3). Although the answer is real in terms of its overall progression, in the major mode the second note of the answer may be raised or not, depending on the location at which the dominant becomes the acting tonal center.

The evenly paced descent of Purcell's subject suggests that he consciously developed it from a descending octave in quarter notes (see example 2-27). This is confirmed by the unornamented quarter-note version of the subject found in the thoroughbass part in mm. 5, 11, 17, and 26. Here again we can see the theoretical concept of scale as basis of musical content developed in chapter 1 realized as the basis not simply of a harmonic construct such as Bach's Prelude in C major (*WTC I*) but of an intricate imitative design. In a like manner, earlier composers founded numerous imitative compositions on the ascending hexachord, *ut re mi fa sol la*. Purcell provides interest to the subject through a variety of motives which adorn each step, and greater tension develops as the answer is harmonized by a series of 7-6 suspensions.

Example 2-27. Purcell, Trio Sonata III in D minor, *Canzona*, mm. 1–5

The remarkable subject of Bach's Toccata and Fugue in D minor BWV 538 (*Dorian*) begins with a beautiful initial arpeggiation using reaching over, followed by the descending octave which builds tension through a lengthy chain of suspensions (example 2-28). Bach maintains the expansive style of the subject throughout the entire course of this, the longest of all his organ fugues.

Example 2-28. Bach, Toccata and Fugue in D minor BWV 538 (*Dorian*), fugue, mm. 1–8

In Bach's Concerto in D minor for two violins BWV 1043, the descending octave is expanded through a series of expressive chromatic inflections and wide leaps (see example 2-29). Is it coincidence that all three of these subjects based on paradigm 2b are in D minor, or do we glimpse here a tradition of compositional and possibly improvisational practice in which imitative compositions grow out of the simplest of melodic materials—the descending scale—in the first of keys—mode I as it becomes D minor?

Example 2-29. Bach, Concerto in D minor for two violins BWV 1043-1, mm. 1–4

Paradigm 2c: subject $\hat{1}$ - $\hat{2}$ - $\hat{1}$; answer $\hat{5}$ - $\hat{6}$ - $\hat{5}$

Paradigm 2c shares with paradigm 2b its beginning and ending, but omits the lengthy descent, giving a compact neighbor motion instead.

The subject of the Fugue in D major BWV 580 (ascribed to Bach) projects $\hat{1}$ - $\hat{2}$ - $\hat{1}$ as the upper voice, and also implies two lower voices, $\hat{8}$ - $\hat{7}$ - $\hat{8}$ and $\hat{1}$ - $\hat{5}$ - $\hat{1}$, providing a complete expression of V.[39] The entry of the answer below the subject creates a fourth, but, as example 2-30 shows, this sonority must be understood as I rather than $V^{4-(3)}$ in order to supply the harmonic resolution to the authentic cadence that the subject demands.

Example 2-30. Bach?, Fugue in D major BWV 580, mm. 1–9

Paradigm 2c occurs only rarely, in just three of Bach's fugues.[40] One reason that this paradigm is seldom found is that the elaboration of the main

---

[39]This subject is identical with the countersubject of the *Allabreve* in D major BWV 589, which is also ascribed to Bach.
[40]BWV 580 (attr. Bach), BWV 71-3, and BWV 998-2.

SUBJECT AND ANSWER

linear progression through arpeggiation or neighbor motion above the second note of the scale naturally leads to the aural perception of other paradigms such as paradigm 2. It is appropriate therefore to consider paradigm 2c as a special case of paradigm 2. The subject of Cantata BWV 71-3 exemplifies this case (see example 2-31). This fugue begins with the answer rather than the subject, a procedure not uncommon in vocal fugues that fall within a larger series of interconnected movements. While the embellishment of e and the weak presentation of g in the first statement (answer) leads to a perception of e–f-sharp–e as the basic melodic structure of the answer (paradigm 2c, not 2), the voice exchange which the countersubject and subject form in m. 4 allows the perception of a third-progression, c-B-A, as the main melodic idea of the subject, accompanied by $\hat{8}$-$\hat{7}$-$\hat{8}$ in the counterpoint, i.e. paradigm 2. The theory of paradigms presented here accommodates such cases by construing paradigm 2c as a variant of paradigm 2.

Example 2-31. Bach, Cantata BWV 71-3, mm. 1–5

Paradigm 3: subject $\hat{8}$-$\hat{7}$-$\hat{8}$; answer $\hat{5}$-sharp-$\hat{4}$-$\hat{5}$

The essence of paradigms 3, 3a and 3b is ascending resolution of the leading tone in a basic linear progression. Like paradigm 2c, paradigm 3 is limiting because of its restricted range and motion. That is, any significant degree of motion above the main linear progression is likely to project a different paradigm as primary.[41] Again, such limitations may account for the dearth of examples of paradigm 3 in the literature: it occurs in only five of Bach's fugues.

Although the first part of the subject of Bach's Toccata in G minor BWV 915-4 establishes $\hat{5}$ as a prominent structural note, the prolongation of $\hat{5}$ in the upper voice is suddenly broken off in the midst of an upper neighbor motion, and the cadence completes only the lower $\hat{8}$-$\hat{7}$-$\hat{8}$ voice, which is then affirmed

---

[41]The addition of other notes tends to produce linear progressions which take on greater importance. In example 2-30 above, the $\hat{8}$-$\hat{7}$-$\hat{8}$ motion occurs, but only as an inner voice rather than a guiding outer voice.

through threefold repetition (see example 2-32).[42] The subject of Bach's Fugue in E-flat major BWV 552 (example 2-33), includes an initial arpeggiation of I followed by the paradigm, $\hat{8}$-$\hat{7}$-$\hat{8}$. The answer replicates the arpeggiation through I, followed by the cadence motion $\hat{5}$-sharp-$\hat{4}$-$\hat{5}$. Thus although the paradigm itself is real, the tonal alteration of the answer arises from the harmonic implications of the initial arpeggiation.

Example 2-32. Bach, Toccata in G minor BWV 915, fugue, mm. 1–9

Example 2-33. Bach, Fugue in E-flat major BWV 552 (*Clavier-Übung III*), mm. 1–5

[42]Daniel Harrison explains how the abandonment of e-flat¹ in m. 3 creates a rhetorical problem for which the remainder of the composition provides a solution. See "Rhetoric and Fugue," *Music Theory Spectrum* XII/1 (spring 1990):11–12. Only in rare cases does a subject repeat its cadential pattern. *WTC I*, Fugue 21 in B-flat major is another example.

SUBJECT AND ANSWER

Paradigm 3a: subject $\hat{5}$ - $\hat{6}$ - $\hat{7}$ - $\hat{8}$; answer $\hat{1}$ - $\hat{3}$ -sharp- $\hat{4}$ - $\hat{5}$

Paradigm 3a replaces the initial tonic of paradigm 3 with $\hat{5}$, yielding an ascending fourth as a basic linear expression of I-V-I. The answer gives an ascending fifth with a break in the stepwise continuity, resolving through sharp- $\hat{4}$ to $\hat{5}$. $\hat{5}$ - $\hat{6}$ - $\hat{7}$ - $\hat{8}$ appears only rarely as a basis of fugue subjects.

Example 2-34 shows not only the primary rising fourth of paradigm 3a, but also two supporting progressions, $\hat{1}$ - $\hat{2}$ - $\hat{3}$ and $\hat{3}$ - $\hat{4}$ - $\hat{5}$, which together complete an entire polyphonic expression of the basic harmonic progression.[43] However, the first note of the paradigm itself must be inferred from the context of the initial arpeggiation. The first note of the answer paradigm is actually supplied by the final note of the subject paradigm. The answer thus begins where the subject left off, arpeggiating up to d-sharp[1], which leads on through e-sharp[1] to f-sharp[1]. Although this analysis is based on the assumption of an inferred note (f-sharp in m. 1) as the initiator of the primary linear progression, it is convincing because of the impressive coherence of the combined linear progressions, and it is confirmed by the ensuing exposition, where the apex of the answer (m. 8) actualizes the implied f-sharp[1] of the following subject entry. Thus, *implied* linear-progressions can also be considered as potential foundations of subjects, provided that the context can support such a reading. In an apparent paradox, the subject is in fact real, while the paradigm upon which it is based is tonal. However, it is the omission of the first note of the paradigm ($\hat{5}$) which allows this condition to exist.

Example 2-34. Bach, Fugue 23 in B major (*WTC II*), mm. 1–9

Example 2-35 contains an initial arpeggiation to $\hat{5}$ which is prolonged through a neighbor and a descending third and followed by the stepwise ascent to $\hat{8}$. Since the initial $\hat{5}$ is presented within an initial ascent, a real answer is appropriate, and the answer paradigm becomes $\hat{2}$ - $\hat{3}$ -sharp- $\hat{4}$ - $\hat{5}$, rather than $\hat{1}$ - $\hat{3}$ -sharp- $\hat{4}$ - $\hat{5}$. Nevertheless, the end of the answer is modified in two important ways. First, the second half of the answer occurs in the lower octave, and second, the cadence itself is accelerated in order to provide a continuous motion that prepares for the register of the third entry and leads back to I. The text extends beyond the end of the subject

---

[43]This analysis is based on Schenker's analysis in *Das Meisterwerk in der Musik*, Vol. 1, Fig. 3, p. 97.

proper, but since the subject itself embodies several repetitions of *amen* Handel freely extends the third repetition of amen in order to provide a connection through the cadence of the subject and into the counterpoint to the answer.[44] Although the end of the word *amen* could have coincided with the cadence of the subject, the compressed form of the cadence in the answer does not accommodate the text in the same way.

Example 2-35. Handel, *Amen* (*Messiah*), mm. 1–5

Paradigm 3b: subject $\hat{1}$-$\hat{2}$-$\hat{3}$-$\hat{4}$-$\hat{5}$-$\hat{6}$-$\hat{7}$-$\hat{8}$; answer $\hat{5}$-$\hat{6}$-$\hat{7}$-$\hat{1}$-$\hat{2}$-$\hat{3}$-sharp-$\hat{4}$-$\hat{5}$

The ascending octave is a natural extension of paradigm 3, in analogy with the descending octave of paradigm 2c. However, no example has been found of a Baroque subject which exhibits a complete octave ascent. The broad compass in a single direction easily leads to either crossed parts or excessive separation between parts. Classical examples do exist, however. Haydn's Baryton Trio 81, *Finale*, uses a simple rhythm of one note per bar in the Viennese manner of learned counterpoint, perhaps as a *tonal* reflection of the familiar modal hexachord subject *ut re mi fa sol la*.[45]

---

[44]In case of doubt as to the extent or nature of this subject, the successive tutti statements at mm. 31 and 38 support this analysis.
[45]See Warren Kirkendale, *Fugue and Fugato in Rococo and Classical Chamber Music* (Durham, North Carolina: Duke University Press, 1979), 116.

Paradigm 4: subject $\hat{1}$ - $\hat{5}$ - $\hat{1}$; answer $\hat{5}$ - $\hat{2}$ - $\hat{5}$

Paradigm 4 represents the basic root progression of I–V–I. The answer paradigm is again real, but as example 2-3 shows, the first note of the answer paradigm is in fact the fifth of I, not the root of V. In example 2-36, the interval $\hat{1}$ - $\hat{5}$ of paradigm 4 is filled as a linear progression, giving a melodic character to the subject without altering the essential structure. While the subject presents a melodic aspect, its final three notes can obviously act as a powerful cadential progression when the subject or answer appears in the bass (e.g. m. 9). There is no overlap between subject and answer in this case, since an overlap would have produced an unresolved fourth (I six-four) at the cadence of the subject (compare example 2-30).

Example 2-36. Handel, Suite VIII in F minor, *Fuga*, mm. 1–10

The only example by Bach of paradigm 4 is in Sinfonia 14 in B-flat major BWV 800. The subject fills out the basic paradigm through a descending octave with additional arpeggiation and scalar material (see example 2-37). Although the answer could have been real, Bach modifies the scale passage in the answer so as to introduce at the outset the altered form which is used extensively and in stretto in the later parts (especially mm. 17–21). Despite the modulation to V which the answer form implies, the bass d^1 in m. 3 creates a deceptive cadence to an incomplete chord which is immediately reinterpreted as I six-three in the tonic.

Example 2-37. Bach, Sinfonia 14 in B-flat major BWV 800, mm. 1–3

Paradigm 4a: subject $\hat{5}$ - $\hat{5}$ - $\hat{1}$; answer $\hat{1}$ - $\hat{2}$ - $\hat{5}$

Paradigm 4a substitutes $\hat{5}$ for $\hat{1}$ at the outset, resulting in a tonal answer. In a reversal of roles, it is now the answer that embodies a complete root progression. Like paradigm 4, paradigm 4a is infrequently to be found in the literature. In the absence of the tonic note at the opening of Buxtehude's Toccata in F major BuxWV 157, the a1 helps to project I in the first measure of example 2-38. As in paradigms 1 and 2a, the upper neighbor again facilitates the tonal answer. The delay in the entry of the answer provides time for the first part to move away from the unison f¹ and also promotes a regularity of rhythm.

Example 2-38. Buxtehude, Toccata in F major BuxWV 157, mm. 39–42

The subject of Fischer's *Fuga X* in F major[46] in example 2-39 (a) is almost identical in structure to that in example 2-38. Once again the upper neighbor aids in the formation of the tonal answer. Remarkably, the subject of Handel's C minor fugue (example 2-39 (b)), follows precisely the melodic contour of Fischer's subject, but in a different rhythm and in the minor mode. Bach, in his apparent recomposition of Fischer's subject in the F major fugue of *WTC I* (example 2-39 (c)), ends instead on $\hat{3}$, giving paradigm 1.[47]

Example 2-39. a, Fischer, *Fuga X* in F major, mm. 1–9; b, Handel, Fugue in C minor (*Six grandes fugues*), mm. 1–3; c, Bach, Fugue 11 in F major (*WTC I*), mm. 1–3

---

[46]*Ariadne musicae.*

[47]This alteration, which converts paradigm 4a into paradigm 1 is similar to the alteration which converts paradigm 1 into paradigm 2a (see example 2-26). The Fischer work is known to be a direct antecedent of the *WTC*. See Susan Wollenberg, "Fischer, Johann Caspar Ferdinand," *The New Grove*, 6:609.

SUBJECT AND ANSWER 53

Paradigm 5: subject $\hat{1}$ - $\hat{2}$ - $\hat{3}$; answer $\hat{5}$ - $\hat{6}$ - $\hat{7}$

Although paradigm 5 is based on a simple ascent from tonic to mediant, in practice the ascent is often embellished by reaching over. The answer paradigm, which is real, gives an ascending third progression, $\hat{5}$ - $\hat{6}$ - $\hat{7}$. Paradigm 5 occurs with relative frequency, in about eight percent of Bach's fugue subjects.

In example 2-40, the ascending third occurs in a pattern of reaching-over nested on three levels, as shown by the brackets. The answer is harmonized by an ascent in parallel sixths in the upper part, which continues the ascent initiated by the subject, and establishes a larger ascent to the fifth, d-sharp^2, in m. 9.

Example 2-40. Bach, Fugue 18 in G-sharp minor (*WTC II*), mm. 1–9

Example 2-41 also includes the typical reaching over pattern which assists the primary rising motion of paradigm 5. Although the answer paradigm itself is real, the initial $\hat{5}$ - $\hat{1}$ arpeggiation of the subject demands a tonal response, $\hat{1}$ - $\hat{5}$.

Example 2-41. Bach, *Trauer-Ode* BWV 198-6, mm. 1–7

Extension of the pattern of reaching over as high as $\hat{5}$ yields an interesting situation in which paradigm 5 comes to resemble paradigm 1 with an initial ascent. The two subjects in example 2-42 show this configuration. In Bach's C major fugue (*WTC I*), the simple rising sequential pattern that underlies the subject is shown by the beam beneath the notes. But the apex and its resolution, which could be construed as paradigm 1, are shown by the upper beam. The subject of Corelli's Trio, Op. 1, No. 9-2, follows a similar pattern. These polymorphous subjects contain the potential for two different analytical interpretations, and in the end it is the given contrapuntal context that determines the actual structure at any given point in the fugue.

Example 2-42. a, Bach, Fugue 1 in C major (*WTC I*), mm. 1–2; b, Corelli, Trio Sonata, Op. 1, No. 9-2, mm. 1–2

Paradigm 5a: subject $\hat{5}$ - $\hat{6}$ - $\hat{7}$ - $\hat{1}$ - $\hat{2}$ - $\hat{3}$; answer $\hat{1}$ - $\hat{3}$ - $\hat{4}$ - $\hat{5}$ - $\hat{6}$ - $\hat{7}$

Paradigm 5a is very rarely found. To be considered independent of paradigm 5, the tonic note which occurs in the middle of the progression must be treated in a passing fashion. Otherwise the progression will be heard as an unfolding $\hat{5}$ - $\hat{1}$ followed by paradigm 5. The answer paradigm is tonal. The only example of paradigm 5a to be found in the music of Bach is in the vivace of the Sonata in F minor for violin and clavier BWV 1018 (example 2-43). As with other lengthy subjects, a large stretch of the linear motion is occupied by a sequential progression (harmonized sequentially as well), and it is this sequential character that removes any structural emphasis from the tonic note.

Example 2-43. Bach, Sonata in F minor for violin and clavier BWV 1018-4, mm. 1–9

The five paradigms illustrated here, and their extensions, represent the full complement of subject types that express an underlying I-V-I harmonic progression. Category 1 as a whole accounts for the structure of nearly three of every four baroque fugue subjects.

Subject and Answer Paradigms for Category 2

Modulating subjects occur in about one quarter of Baroque fugues. In this category it is the subject-answer pair that projects a complete harmonic motion, I-V-I, where the subject leads to V through an authentic cadence in V, and the answer, beginning on V, returns to I, replicating the authentic cadence in the tonic. Example 2-44 tabulates the subject and answer paradigms for category 2. Once again, paradigms with identical terminations are identified by letter. Without exception the answer paradigms are tonal, since in every case the answer develops a complementary harmonic expression.

Example 2-44. Subject and answer paradigms for category 2

Paradigm 6: subject $\hat{8}$ - $\hat{8}$ - $\hat{7}$, answer $\hat{5}$ - $\hat{4}$ - $\hat{3}$

Paradigm 6 contains a simple $\hat{8}$ - $\hat{8}$ - $\hat{7}$ motion, ending on the third of V. The answer paradigm, beginning on the dominant, returns to I through the descending third, $\hat{5}$ - $\hat{4}$ - $\hat{3}$.[48] Paradigm 6 seldom occurs. As for paradigm 1, some separation must be introduced between the repeated tonics of the subject so that the alterations in the answer will sound convincing. The subject of Bach's Cantata BWV 50-1 (example 2-45) establishes the tonic through arpeggiation, but d^1 (m. 5) eventually acts as the seventh of V/V, resolving to c-sharp^1 at m. 8. Thus the two structural tonics of the paradigm are separated by time and register. The answer recomposes the octave arpeggio of the subject as a seventh and leads the music back to I through a broad $\hat{5}$ - $\hat{4}$ - $\hat{3}$ progression. Note how the countersubject repeats the ascending 7th of the answer in diminution in m. 12, as shown by the brackets.

Example 2-45. Bach, Cantata 50-1, mm. 1–15

---

[48]The complementary relationships between paradigms 1 and 6 and between other paradigm pairs are illustrated in figure 2-2 at the end of this chapter.

SUBJECT AND ANSWER

Example 2-46 illustrates a real answer for paradigm 6, in which the answer continues through the cirle of fifths to V/V.[49] Why did Bach write a real answer rather than a tonal one? The limitation of the texture to two parts gives an exposition of only two entries, thus preventing any further tonal digression, and the final note of the answer is altered, becoming sharp-$\hat{4}$ in V, rather than $\hat{3}$ in the more distant key of F-sharp minor. Thus in this special case the real answer does not lead to modulation beyond stylistic norms. Further, it is precisely this structure that when transposed and inverted in the subdominant (mm. 20–24) reestablishes I for the conclusion of the composition. Thus it is the larger structure of the fugue, with its systematic use of transposed and inverted repetition, that provides a full explanation of the form of this particular answer.

Example 2-46. Bach, Fugue 10 in E minor (*WTC I*), mm. 1–5

[49]The discussion of paradigm 11 below provides a point of comparison. We will see later how this pattern closely resembles the non-modulating subjects that end on V.

Paradigm 6a: subject $\hat{5}$-$\hat{4}$-$\hat{3}$-$\hat{2}$-$\hat{1}$-$\hat{7}$, answer $\hat{2}$-$\hat{7}$-$\hat{6}$-$\hat{5}$-$\hat{4}$-$\hat{3}$

Paradigm 6a is a logical extension of paradigm 6 to a descent beginning on $\hat{5}$, but no modulating subject displaying this form has yet been located. Consideration of the structure helps to explain why they are rare or indeed non-existent. In particular, the lower tendency-tone $\hat{4}$ in the subject conflicts with its answer counterpart, the upper tendency-tone $\hat{7}$ (see example 2-44). In addition, the opposition of dominant and supertonic at the beginning of subject and answer may project an uncomfortable sense of tonal ambiguity. That is, paradigm 6a may easily suggest a dominant tonality with subsequent modulation to the subdominant at the end of the answer. An initial tonic would help to clarify the tonal structure. A subdominant answer, $\hat{8}$-$\hat{7}$-$\hat{6}$-$\hat{5}$-$\hat{4}$-$\hat{3}$, is another logical solution, provided that the entry of the answer paradigm avoids overlap with the end of the subject and coincides instead with a return to I. However, the result is then essentially paradigm 1a with the order of subject and answer reversed.

Paradigm 7: subject $\hat{8}$-$\hat{7}$-$\hat{6}$-$\hat{5}$, answer $\hat{5}$-$\hat{3}$-$\hat{2}$-$\hat{1}$

Paradigm 7 comprises a simple descending progression connecting the roots of the main harmonies, I and V. Note that $\hat{6}$ is raised in the minor key, functioning as $\hat{2}$ of V. Example 2-44 shows that the initial $\hat{8}$-$\hat{7}$ step of the subject must be treated as a $\hat{5}$-$\hat{3}$ third in the answer paradigm in order to lead back to I. Paradigm 7 is rarely found in the literature.

The unusual answer construction in the fugue of Bach's Cantata BWV 21-II-5 has prompted frequent discussion in the literature.[50] Since the subject begins with an obvious arpeggiation of I, one naturally expects the answer to initiate a corresponding arpeggiation of V. But c¹ replaces d¹ in the answer at the word *Preis* (see example 2-47). Although the principle of alternation of dominant and tonic in subject and answer is often invoked to justify this alteration, a stronger explanation is that the altered form of the answer allows the countersubject to function invertibly at the octave and the twelfth. This counterpoint is exploited in mm. 29–30 and 51–52, where an untransposed countersubject accompanies first the subject and then the answer. However, in terms of paradigm 7, the disputed opening arpeggio is an initial arpeggiation to the first note of the paradigm, and the paradigm itself is simply extended by third arpeggiations and neighbors.

Example 2-47. Bach, Cantata BWV 21-II-5, mm. 12–19

[50]Naldin uses it as an example of the inconsistency with which $\hat{5}$ of the subject is treated in the answer in the case of subjects that arpeggiate the full tonic chord. See *Fugal Answer*, 33.

Paradigm 7a: subject $\hat{5}$ - $\hat{6}$ - $\hat{5}$, answer $\hat{2}$ - $\hat{2}$ - $\hat{1}$

Paradigm 7a concludes in the same manner as paradigm 7, but begins with the fifth rather than the root. As for paradigm 6a, however, the answer form is weakened by beginning on $\hat{2}$, since the beginnings of subject and answer, $\hat{5}$ and $\hat{2}$, set up an opposition which suggests the dominant rather than the tonic. As the examples which follow show, Bach was reluctant to begin the answer on $\hat{2}$, apparently because of this implicit conflict with the primary tonality. A subdominant answer, $\hat{1}$ - $\hat{2}$ - $\hat{1}$, beginning on I, is a reasonable possibility provided that there is no overlap between the end of the subject and the beginning of the answer paradigm. Again, an initial tonic can serve this function, but the result is simply paradigm 2c with the order of subject and answer reversed. There are very few examples of paradigm 7 in the literature.

In example 2-48, Bach provides a bridge which reestablishes I, giving a harmonic context for the tonic note which begins the answer. Thus the subject and answer reverse the order of paradigm 2c. From a compositional aspect, Bach brilliantly integrates this bridge material into the composition through extensive repetition in the episodes of the fugue.

Example 2-48. Bach, Fugue 7 in E-flat major (*WTC I*), mm. 1–4

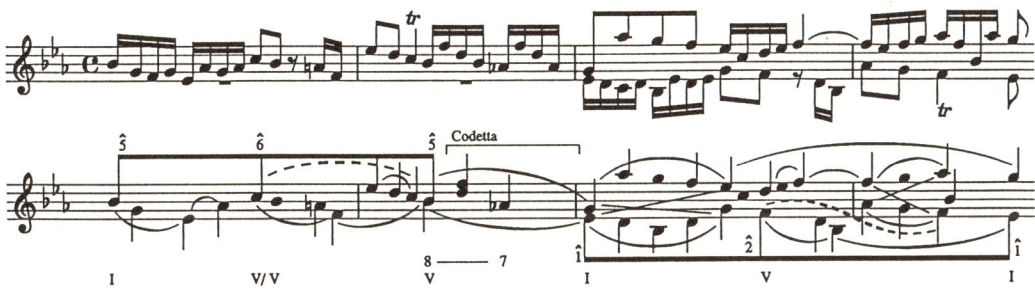

Paradigm 8: subject $\hat{5}$-sharp-$\hat{4}$-$\hat{5}$; answer $\hat{2}$-$\hat{7}$-$\hat{1}$

The essence of paradigm 8 is the upward resolution of the leading tone to the dominant, sharp-$\hat{4}$-$\hat{5}$. A real answer at the fifth ($\hat{2}$-sharp-$\hat{1}$-$\hat{2}$) would lead to II, and a tonal modification which leads back to I results in the answer paradigm $\hat{2}$-$\hat{7}$-$\hat{1}$. Once again this sets up the opposition of $\hat{5}$ and $\hat{2}$ at the beginnning of the subject and answer which can easily disrupt the establishment of the tonality. A subdominant answer ($\hat{8}$-$\hat{7}$-$\hat{8}$) is again an option, provided that the beginning of the answer's linear motion is delayed by an initial tonic or a bridge which removes the overlap. Paradigm 8, too, is infrequently found in the literature.

The Legrenzi subject used by Bach begins with an extensive initial arpeggiation before activating the main linear progression (see example 2-49). Replication of the arpeggiation in the answer delays the statement of the paradigm, allowing it to appear in its subdominant form, $\hat{8}$-$\hat{7}$-$\hat{8}$.[51]

Example 2-49. Bach, Fugue in C minor on a theme by Legrenzi BWV 574, mm. 1–7

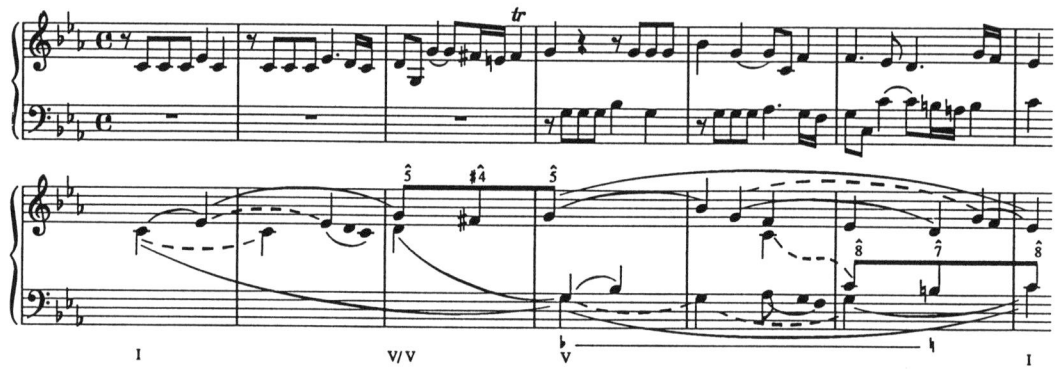

Example 2-50, from the *Sicut locutus est* of Bach's *Magnificat*, follows example 2-49 in all its essentials. In a typical vocal style, the rising profile of the subject's initial ascent is reflected in a rising series of entries which gradually expand the range upwards as the texture thickens. The answer again uses the subdominant form, made possible by the use of an initial ascent.[52]

Example 2-50. Bach, *Magnificat* in D major BWV 243-11, mm. 1–9

[51]See Robert Hill, "Die Herkunft von Bach's 'Thema Legrensianum'," *Bach Jahrbuch*, LXXII (1986): 105–7. See also Handel, Fugue in C Minor (*Six grandes fugues*, No. 6), which echoes this subject and the countersubject that occurs later.

[52]The subject of Bach's Prelude and Fugue in E-flat major for lute BWV 996 is best understood as paradigm 8, but beginning with the answer.

SUBJECT AND ANSWER

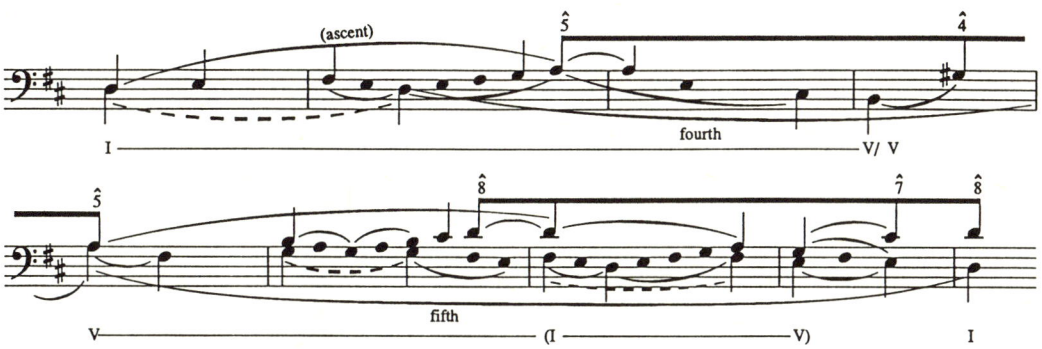

Paradigm 8a: subject $\hat{1}$ - $\hat{2}$ - $\hat{3}$ -sharp- $\hat{4}$ - $\hat{5}$; answer $\hat{5}$ - $\hat{5}$ - $\hat{6}$ - $\hat{7}$ - $\hat{8}$

Paradigm 8a forms a simple rising progression from tonic to dominant through the raised fourth degree. The answer paradigm replicates the subject in an ascent from dominant to tonic. Paradigm 8a is the most common form in which modulating subjects appear; one in three of Bach's modulating subjects follows paradigm 8a. The subject of example 2-51 is based directly on paradigm 8a, and the answer returns to I through a rising fourth. The countersubject continues the motivic work which concludes the subject. The following entries continue the gradual ascent of the first two entries through the remainder of the exposition.

Example 2-51. Bach, Cantata BWV 190-1, mm. 87–93

In addition to the rising fifth, the subject in example 2-52 includes a descending fourth progression which resolves at the first note of the answer. The answer form embodies a rising fourth as well as a descending fifth, the final note of which introduces the third statement, shown by the parenthetical note in m. 3 of the graph.

Example 2-52. Bach, Prelude and Fugue in C major BWV 547, fugue, mm. 1–3

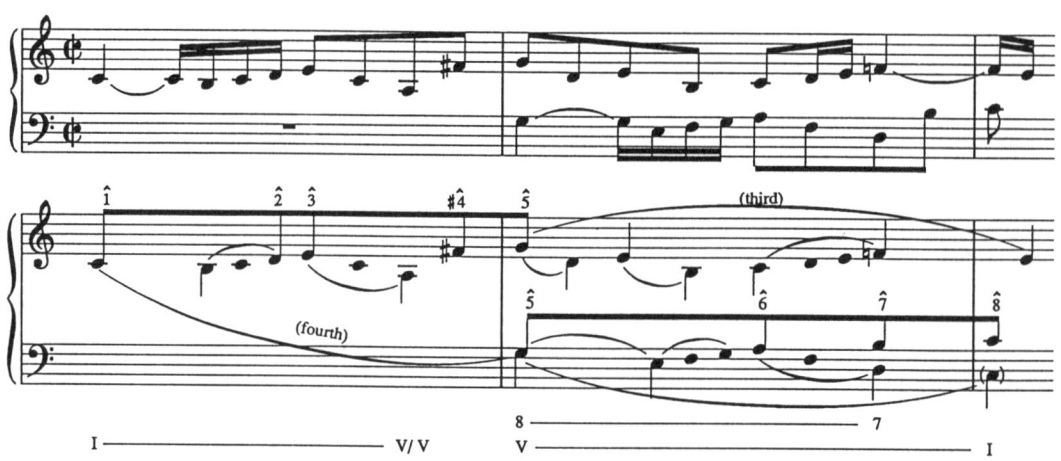

Paradigm 9: subject $\hat{1}$ - $\hat{2}$ - $\hat{5}$; answer $\hat{5}$ - $\hat{5}$ - $\hat{1}$

Paradigm 9 represents the basic structure of modulating subjects founded essentially on a root motion. The corresponding answer paradigm is $\hat{5}$ - $\hat{5}$ - $\hat{1}$. Paradigm 9 occurs infrequently, and in only three of Bach's fugues. In the G-sharp minor fugue of *WTC I*, the initial tonic harmony is prolonged through an ascending fifth, after which the root-motion cadence occurs in a direct manner (see example 2-53). The answer replicates the ascent to the tonic before concluding with the root motion $\hat{5}$ - $\hat{1}$. The strong cadential gesture which characterizes this subject is an important motive in several episodes in this fugue (see example 5-28).

Example 2-53. Bach, Fugue 18 in G-sharp minor (*WTC I*), mm. 1–5

Paradigm 10: subject $\hat{5}$ - $\hat{6}$ - $\hat{7}$; answer $\hat{2}$ - $\hat{2}$ - $\hat{3}$

Paradigm 10 is the final paradigm for modulating subjects. Although subject paradigm 10 can be understood as a modulation from I to V, it requires an initial tonic or other tonic reference in order to prevent the perception of a prolongation of V ($\hat{5}$-$\hat{6}$-$\hat{7}$ in I = $\hat{1}$-$\hat{2}$-$\hat{3}$ in V). Like many of the others in category 2, paradigm 10 requires an answer that begins on $\hat{2}$, thus establishing another conflict with the basic tonality. Again, a subdominant answer is possible ($\hat{1}$-$\hat{2}$-$\hat{3}$), but this may well be thought of as paradigm 5 with the order of subject and answer reversed. While paradigm 10 is a theoretical possibility, no examples have been located in the literature.

Not all modulating subjects so easily project a unified linear or root motion as those illustrated above. Indeed the fact of modulation implies a point of key change, and thus a two part subject, a tonic opening and a dominant conclusion. It is thus possible for a modulating subject to develop two connected linear progressions. Example 2-54, the final subject of *WTC I*, which embodies all twelve pitch-classes, is such a case. The conclusion of the subject is easily perceived as $\hat{3}$-$\hat{2}$-$\hat{1}$ of V, and this is replicated in the answer as $\hat{3}$-$\hat{2}$-$\hat{1}$ of I. This much is clear, and relates to the underlying basis of paradigm 2, with order of entries reversed. The opening of the subject clearly arpeggiates I, and the following chromatic passage is in fact an ascending sequence that leads to V. In a similar manner, the answer begins with a statement of V, followed by the rising sequence leading to I. The subject comprises a melodic ascent $\hat{1}$-$\hat{3}$-sharp-$\hat{4}$-$\hat{5}$ which effects the modulation, followed by a cadential descent, $\hat{3}$-$\hat{2}$-$\hat{1}$ in V; the answer corresponds in its ascent $\hat{5}$-sharp-$\hat{6}$-sharp-$\hat{7}$-$\hat{8}$, followed by $\hat{3}$-$\hat{2}$-$\hat{1}$ in I.

Example 2-54. Bach, Fugue 24 in B minor (*WTC I*), mm. 1–7

Although the answer could have begun on c-sharp¹, b respects the convention of tonic-dominant opposition. But Bach maintains the overlap at the beginning of the answer, so the b with which the answer begins is structurally dependent on the following a to which it resolves.

Subject and Answer Paradigms for Category 3

The third and final group of paradigms contains all those subjects that end on V but which do not modulate. Although several of the subject paradigms in this category follow the contour of those in category 2, the half-cadence with no modulation has different implications for answer construction, hence for exposition structure as well. Example 2-55 illustrates the subject and answer paradigms in category 3. Answer paradigms in category 3 typically occur in two distinct ways. The most common is a direct transposition where the answer ends on a half-cadence in V—a real answer. In this type a bridge usually follows the answer in order to return the music to I for the third entry.[53] The second type of answer, a tonal answer, returns to I via an authentic cadence, much in the manner of the answer to a modulating subject. In this form the subject-answer pair bears the same overall harmonic plan as that of the modulating subject and answer (I-V-I), but whereas the subject ends in a half cadence, the answer ends in an authentic cadence, replacing a symmetry of repetition with a symmetry of complementation. Thus, although the subjects in category 3 do not modulate they bear a distinct relationship to modulating subjects. As the following examples show, despite the fact that real answers occur often enough to be considered normal, the nature of each individual subject determines the possibility of using a tonal answer. Example 2-55 includes both possibilities where appropriate.

Example 2-55. Subject and answer paradigms for category 3

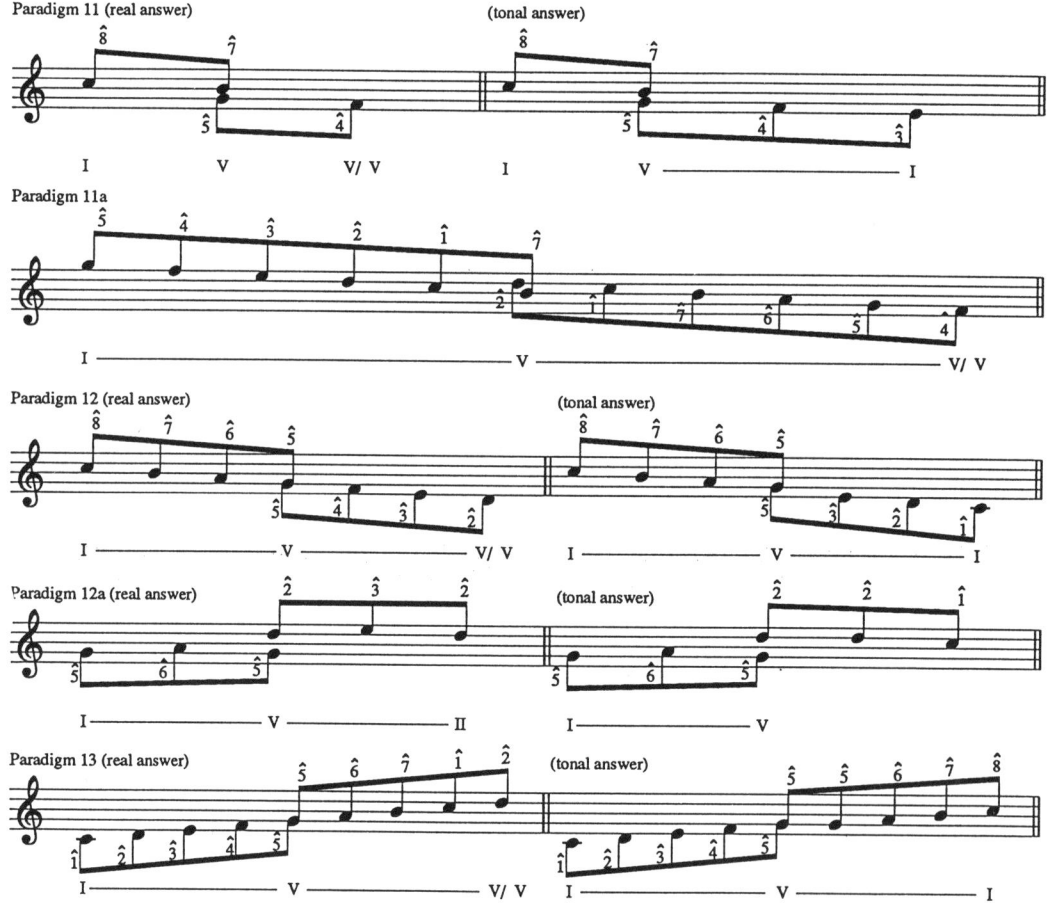

---

[53] V/V at the end of the answer is often reinterpreted as II in the tonic, in order to prepare for the return to I for the next subject entry.

SUBJECT AND ANSWER

Paradigm 11: subject $\hat{8}$ - $\hat{7}$; answer $\hat{5}$ -sharp- $\hat{4}$ or $\hat{5}$ -($\hat{4}$)- $\hat{3}$

Paradigm 11 represents a very simple form of non-modulating subject ending on V. The real answer paradigm is $\hat{5}$ -sharp- $\hat{4}$. The tonal form $\hat{5}$ -($\hat{4}$)- $\hat{3}$ replaces the half cadence with an authentic cadence and returns the music to I. When the tonal answer is considered, paradigm 11 bears an obvious relationship to paradigm 1 with the order of subject and answer reversed.

In example 2-56, the subject expands the initial tonic at great length through an ascending sixth, and falls back by step through the pre-dominants IV and II, cadencing on $\hat{7}$ at m. 5. The accompanying bass supports the subject by a broad fifth-progression, e–B. The answer, a direct transposition, ends on V of V.

Example 2-56. Bach, Sonata in E major for violin and clavier BWV 1016-4, mm. 1–9

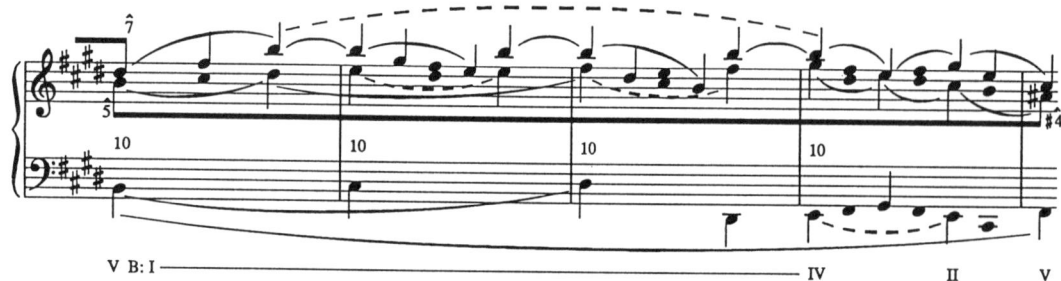

Example 2-57 expands the initial tonic through an octave before moving to $\hat{7}$, at which point the answer enters with $\hat{5}$, harmonizing the leading tone. Frescobaldi takes advantage of the leaps in the subject to recompose the initial octave arpeggiation as a seventh in the answer, giving the tonal response $\hat{5}$ - $\hat{4}$ - $\hat{3}$ (compare example 2-45 above).

Example 2-57. Frescobaldi, Canzona 4 in F (*Capriccio, Ricercare, e Canzoni*, 1626), mm. 1–5

Paradigm 11a: subject $\hat{5}$ - $\hat{4}$ - $\hat{3}$ - $\hat{2}$ - $\hat{1}$ - $\hat{7}$; answer $\hat{2}$ - $\hat{1}$ - $\hat{7}$ - $\hat{6}$ - $\hat{5}$ -sharp- $\hat{4}$

Paradigm 11a expands the descent of the subject to a sixth, in a manner comparable to paradigm 6a, but the answer paradigm is real (see example 2-55). Once again, an initial tonic helps to clarify the tonal structure. The third fugue subject from Böhm's *Capriccio* in D major is the only example found thus far which can be understood as paradigm 11a. In example 2-58 an initial ascent provides an unambiguous statement of I at the beginning. The answer follows paradigm 11a, and would have ended on V/V if G-sharp were introduced. One could also consider this subject as simply paradigm 11 rather than 11a. In this case the ascent and following descent would be considered as a prolongation of I. This theory recognizes the legitimacy of such varying interpretations by considering paradigm 11a as a variant of paradigm 11.

Example 2-58. Böhm, *Capriccio* in D major, mm. 96–99

Paradigm 12: subject $\hat{8}$ - $\hat{7}$ - $\hat{6}$ - $\hat{5}$; answer $\hat{5}$ - $\hat{4}$ - $\hat{3}$ - $\hat{2}$ or $\hat{5}$ - $\hat{3}$ - $\hat{2}$ - $\hat{1}$

Paradigm 12 is the category 3 cognate of paradigms 2a and 7. The subject paradigm moves down by step from tonic to dominant. The real answer replicates this motion beginning on the dominant. A tonal answer is possible as well, as example 2-55 illustrates. Paradigm 12 occurs rarely, yet it has historical significance since its underlying idea is an imitative treatment of the descending tetrachord, the basis of any number of baroque variation movements. In the major mode the $\hat{6}$ - $\hat{5}$ motion of the subject can imply either a half-cadence in I or an authentic cadence in V (paradigm 7), but in the minor mode the lowered sixth degree clarifies the tonality of the cadence. The final fugue of Bach's Toccata in F-sharp minor BWV 910 is a good example of paradigm 12. In example 2-59, chromatic motion embellishes the descending fourth. As the example shows, the answer is real, expressing a descending fourth, $\hat{5}$ - $\hat{4}$ - $\hat{3}$ - $\hat{2}$, harmonized sequentially by the countersubject. At the end of the answer, g-sharp[1] is reinterpreted as the fifth of V rather than as the root of V/V, leading quickly back to I at the end of the excerpt.

Example 2-59. Bach, Toccata in F-sharp minor BWV 910, mm. 135–138

In example 2-60 the independent continuo part provides a sequential support for the simple subject structure. The third entry anticipates the end of the second entry in a simple stretto configuration.[54]

---

[54]Handel's Concerto Grosso, Op. 6, No. 6-2, contains another example of paradigm 12. See Schenker, *Free Composition*, Fig. 102-4.

Example 2-60. Bach, Cantata BWV 172-1, mm. 76–84

Paradigm 12a: subject $\hat{5}$ - $\hat{6}$ - $\hat{5}$; answer $\hat{2}$ - $\hat{3}$ - $\hat{2}$ or $\hat{2}$ - $\hat{2}$ - $\hat{1}$

Paradigm 12a is similar in profile to paradigm 7a discussed above, but its harmonic implication is of course different. The $\hat{6}$ implies a predominant rather than a secondary dominant, and the following V completes a half-cadence in the tonic, not an authentic cadence in the dominant. The real answer paradigm is $\hat{2}$ - $\hat{3}$ - $\hat{2}$, ending on V/V. A tonal answer is possible, as example 2-55 illustrates. Bach's Passacaglia and Fugue in C minor BWV 582 illustrates paradigm 12a (see example 2-61). The single measure separating the subject and answer effects a modulation to V, permitting the answer to function as a direct transposition of the subject.

Example 2-61. Bach, Passacaglia and Fugue in C minor BWV 582, *Thema fugatum*, mm. 1–9

In example 2-62, the tonal alteration of the first paradigm note of the answer (a-flat instead of b-flat) must be seen as an alteration of detail, not of structure, for Bach does not take advantage of the alteration to provide a subdominant answer form ($\hat{1}$ - $\hat{2}$ - $\hat{1}$). Rather, he bows to the principle of opposition between dominant and tonic notes at the beginning of subject and answer. By emphasizing a-flat, the counterpoint to the answer maintains the tonic key rather than moving to the dominant.

Example 2-62. Bach, Fugue 17 in A-flat major (*WTC I*), mm. 1–3

Paradigm 13: subject $\hat{1}$ - $\hat{2}$ - $\hat{3}$ - $\hat{4}$ - $\hat{5}$; answer $\hat{5}$ - $\hat{6}$ - $\hat{7}$ - $\hat{1}$ - $\hat{2}$ or $\hat{5}$ - $\hat{5}$ - $\hat{6}$ - $\hat{7}$ - $\hat{8}$

Like the descending fourth of paradigm 12 ($\hat{8}$ - $\hat{7}$ - $\hat{6}$ - $\hat{5}$), the rising fifth can be understood as a linear expression of the essential root motion I-V. In contrast to paradigm 8a ($\hat{1}$ - $\hat{2}$ - $\hat{3}$ -sharp- $\hat{4}$ - $\hat{5}$), the natural- $\hat{4}$ precludes any sense of modulation to V in paradigm 13. On account of the continuous conjunct motion, the answer paradigm is usually real. The subject of Bach's Fugue 6 in D minor (*WTC I*) employs reaching-over in the ascent to $\hat{5}$. Example 2-63 shows how the answer replicates the half cadence at the dominant level, ending on e¹, which is interpreted as II in the tonic key, preparing the return to I for the third entry.[55]

---

[55]Schenker's analysis of this subject highlights the underlying fifth-progression which the reaching-over obscures on the surface. See *Free Composition*, Figs. 53-5 and 156-1.

Example 2-63. Bach, Fugue 6 in D minor (*WTC I*), a, mm. 1–5, b, inversion

Example 2-63 (b) illustrates how the simple rising fifth of paradigm 13 can be readily inverted into the descending fifth of paradigm 2b. The upper neighbor to $\hat{5}$ and lower neighbor to $\hat{1}$ switch roles, as in examples 2-13 and 2-14.

Paradigm 14: subject $\hat{1}$ - $\hat{5}$; answer $\hat{5}$ - $\hat{1}$ or $\hat{5}$ - $\hat{2}$

Paradigm 14 is the simple root motion $\hat{1}$ - $\hat{5}$. Since this paradigm is a leap, the tonal answer $\hat{5}$ - $\hat{1}$ is usually convenient. The real answer $\hat{5}$ - $\hat{2}$, which continues the cycle of fifths, is also possible but rarely found. Example 2-64 is typical of paradigm 14. The subject is based on a prolongation of I, followed by a leap to $\hat{5}$ and a change of harmony. In corresponding fashion, the answer prolongs V before leaping back to $\hat{1}$ and returning to the tonic harmony. Paradigm 14 is also to be found in several of Bach's short invention themes, such as the inventions in C major and E minor.

Example 2-64. Bach, Cantata BWV 136-1, mm. 10–12

SUBJECT AND ANSWER

Paradigm 15: subject $\hat{5}$ - $\hat{6}$ - $\hat{7}$; answer $\hat{2}$ - $\hat{3}$ -(sharp)- $\hat{4}$ or $\hat{2}$ - $\hat{2}$ - $\hat{3}$

Paradigm 15 occurs very infrequently, perhaps because neither the subject nor the answer gives significant expression of the tonic (see example 2-55). Indeed, an initial tonic or arpeggiation of I is necessary to establish the tonality. The real answer is a stepwise ascent to (sharp)-$\hat{4}$, the third of II or the leading tone of V. Again a tonal answer ($\hat{2}$ - $\hat{2}$ - $\hat{3}$) can lead back to I. Example 2-65 illustrates paradigm 15 with two of Frescobaldi's *canzoni*. Both subjects embellish the linear progression with arpeggios of tonic harmony and an upper neighbor. Although paradigm 15 can be answered at the dominant without contrapuntal difficulty, in both cases Frescobaldi imitates at the octave, harmonizing the leading tone with the root of V. Perhaps Frescobaldi felt that the second entry should assist in projecting the weakly established tonic. No examples have been located in which paradigm 15 is imitated at the fifth.

Example 2-65. Frescobaldi, a, Canzona 1, mm. 1–2; b, Canzona 5, mm. 1–2

Paradigm 16: subject $\hat{5}$ - $\hat{4}$ - $\hat{3}$ - $\hat{2}$; answer $\hat{2}$ - $\hat{1}$ - $\hat{7}$ - $\hat{6}$ or $\hat{2}$ - $\hat{7}$ - $\hat{6}$ - $\hat{5}$

Ending on the supertonic as fifth of V precludes any sense of modulation in paradigms 16 and 17. The real answer for paradigm 16 is $\hat{2}$ - $\hat{1}$ - $\hat{7}$ - $\hat{6}$, and the tonal answer is $\hat{2}$ - $\hat{7}$ - $\hat{6}$ - $\hat{5}$, leading back to I. Once again, some initial arpeggiation is necessary in order to establish the tonality. In example 2-66, from Bach's Trio Sonata 5 for organ, the bass clarifies the role of the subject's g^2 in mm. 2–3 as a passing note within the third a^2–f^2, rather than as a return to the opening g^2. The answer begins on c^2, not d^2, once again conforming with the traditional opposition of tonic and dominant notes. However, in structural terms the c^2 at the beginning of the answer is a passing note in the motion d^2–c^2–b^1 which begins with the last note of the subject.

Example 2-66. Bach, Trio Sonata 5 for organ BWV 529-3, mm. 1–9

Paradigm 17: subject $\hat{1}$ - $\hat{2}$; answer $\hat{5}$ - $\hat{6}$

Paradigm 17, the final paradigm, is rarely found in the literature. It calls for a real answer paradigm, $\hat{5}$ - $\hat{6}$. The subject of Reinken's Sonata VI, Allegro (*Hortus Musicus*) (BWV 954) illustrates paradigm 17 (see example 2-67). The initial tonic is prolonged through arpeggiation and linear progressions covering a full octave before rising through a ninth to its conclusion on c^3. One might consider the first b-flat^1 of m. 4 as the conclusion to a subject based on paradigm 2a ($\hat{5}$ - $\hat{4}$ - $\hat{3}$ - $\hat{2}$ - $\hat{1}$), in which case m. 4 would be understood as a link to the beginning of the answer. Yet the continuing sixteenth-note motion and the registral connection, not to mention later repetitions, aid in the perception of the subject as extending to the beginning of m. 5. The answer is a direct transposition down a fourth.

Example 2-67. Reinken, Sonata 6, Allegro (*Hortus Musicus*) (BWV 954), mm. 1–5

Bach's Duet in F major BWV 803 is another example of paradigm 17. In example 2-68 the subject arpeggiates the tonic for three measures and then approaches $\hat{2}$ through reaching-over. The answer progresses similarly from c to d^1, but once again Bach bows to tradition: the opening $\hat{5}$ of the subject is answered as $\hat{1}$ (compare example 2-47). Although the answer paradigm is real, this particular elaborative detail is tonal.

Example 2-68. Bach, Duet 2 in F major BWV 803 (*Clavierübung III*), mm. 1–8

Paradigms in Perspective

Categorization, by its very nature, is a process of limitation which recognizes similarities but downplays unique characteristics. While most baroque fugue subjects accommodate themselves very well to the system of paradigms outlined here, it is inevitable that some subjects conform uneasily or indeed resist such analysis. However, by and large the series of paradigms presented here does account systematically for all but a minuscule portion of baroque fugue subjects and answers.

The Fugue in E minor BWV 945, attributed to Bach, illustrates one of the very few subjects that does not conform to any of the paradigms given above. In example 2-69 the beginning of the subject establishes a descent from $\hat{5}$ which could easily end on $\hat{1}$, giving paradigm 2a (see the recomposed version in example 2-69 (b)), but the cadence instead redirects the subject to IV. Thus the subject suggests a basic harmonic expression I–IV, and the answer provides a transposition, V–I which completes a harmonic cycle. It is thus a rearrangement of the standard harmonic pattern that accounts for the unique structure of this subject.

Example 2-69. Bach?, Fugue in E minor BWV 945, a, mm. 1–8; b, recomposition

Other nonconforming subjects are *prius factus* phrases of chorales which are adopted as *fugato* themes for chorale preludes. For example, the subject of Bach's *Manualiter "Kyrie, Gott Vater in Ewigkeit"* BWV 672, in E Phrygian, is $\hat{3}$ - $\hat{4}$ - $\hat{5}$, and the answer is $\hat{7}$ - $\hat{1}$ - sharp - $\hat{2}$. As example 2-70 shows, this configuration produces an exposition that prolongs G, rather than the modal *finalis*, E.[56]

Example 2-70. Bach, *Kyrie, Gott Vater in Ewigkeit* BWV 672, mm. 1–3

Example 2-41 illustrated the further possibility that any single subject may contain elements of more than one paradigm, or even contain two complete paradigms. Schenker's analysis of the fugue subject in Handel's *Suite 2* in F for Harpsichord is similar to those in example 2-41: $\hat{5}$ - $\hat{4}$ - $\hat{3}$ and $\hat{1}$ - $\hat{2}$ - $\hat{3}$ again converge on the final note of the subject.[57] Although the descending progression seems to predominate in Handel's subject, the ascending progression could easily assume a primary structural role, particularly in a bass entry of the subject such as in mm. 37–39. The following chapters, which place the paradigms in the context of multi-voice counterpoint, will help to clarify the significance of subjects such as these. Examples 2-18, 2-20 and 2-42 are other instances in which a single subject paradigm is the basis of several similar subjects by different composers. As the following chapters show, composers have developed many subjects from a limited number of paradigms precisely because it is these paradigms that reflect the underlying principles of voice-leading inherent in Baroque contrapuntal practice. This is not to deny, however, instances of parody and borrowing, such as in Bach's Prelude and Fugue in D major BWV 532, the subject of which has parallels to Pachelbel, Buxtehude and Reinken, and the Fantasy and Fugue in G minor BWV 542, which seems to have developed from the subject of an improvisation competition.[58]

---

[56] William Renwick, "Modality, Imitation and Structural Levels: Bach's *Manualiter* "Kyries" from *Clavierübung III*," *Music Analysis* XI/1 (March, 1992): 55–74, explores this topic in some detail.
[57] Schenker, *Free Composition*, Fig. 92.
[58] See Williams, *The Organ Music of J. S. Bach* 1:64 and 119.

The theory of subject paradigms presented here provides a basis for the comparative studies of several kinds. Figure 2-2 summarizes all of the paradigms discussed in chapter 2. Column one gives the paradigm number, and columns two and three give the subject and answer paradigms. The fourth column identifies cognates between paradigms of different categories, showing that most of the subject paradigms in each category are reflected in the subject or answer paradigms of the other two categories. For example, paradigm 1 is similar to paradigms 6 and 11, except the order of subject and answer is reversed. This correspondence results from the basic harmonic framework of I and V that each category represents. As noted above, however, paradigms 16 and 17 have no cognates in the other categories. They result from the special circumstance that the subject can end on $\hat{2}$ as the fifth of V in an imperfect cadence. Column five in Figure 2-2 identifies the answer paradigms as real or tonal. The final columns give the number of occurrences and percentages of each paradigm in the fugal works of Bach.[59]

Figure 2-2. Paradigms and their frequency in Bach's fugues

Paradigm	Subject	Answer	Cognates	(Tonal/Real)	Number in Bach	Percentage in Bach
Category 1						
1	$\hat{5}$-$\hat{4}$-$\hat{3}$	$\hat{8}$-$\hat{8}$-$\hat{7}$	6,11	T	122	41
1a	$\hat{8}$-$\hat{7}$-$\hat{6}$-$\hat{5}$-$\hat{4}$-$\hat{3}$	$\hat{5}$-(#)$\hat{4}$-$\hat{3}$-$\hat{2}$-$\hat{1}$-$\hat{7}$	6b, 11	R	5	2
2	$\hat{1}$-$\hat{3}$-$\hat{2}$-$\hat{1}$	$\hat{5}$-$\hat{7}$-$\hat{6}$-$\hat{5}$		R	24	8
2a	$\hat{5}$-$\hat{4}$-$\hat{3}$-$\hat{2}$-$\hat{1}$	$\hat{8}$-$\hat{8}$-$\hat{7}$-$\hat{6}$-$\hat{5}$	7, 12	T	50	17
2b	$\hat{8}$-$\hat{7}$-$\hat{6}$-$\hat{5}$-$\hat{4}$-$\hat{3}$-$\hat{2}$-$\hat{1}$	$\hat{5}$-(#)$\hat{4}$-$\hat{3}$-$\hat{2}$-$\hat{1}$-$\hat{7}$-$\hat{6}$-$\hat{5}$		R	3	1
2c	$\hat{1}$-$\hat{2}$-$\hat{1}$	$\hat{5}$-$\hat{6}$-$\hat{5}$	7a, 12a	R	3	1
3	$\hat{8}$-$\hat{7}$-$\hat{8}$	$\hat{5}$-#$\hat{4}$-$\hat{5}$	8	R	5	2
3a	$\hat{5}$-$\hat{6}$-$\hat{7}$-$\hat{8}$	$\hat{1}$-$\hat{3}$-#$\hat{4}$-$\hat{5}$	8a, 13	T	5	2
3b	$\hat{1}$-$\hat{2}$-$\hat{3}$-$\hat{4}$-$\hat{5}$-$\hat{6}$-$\hat{7}$-$\hat{8}$	$\hat{5}$-$\hat{6}$-$\hat{7}$-$\hat{1}$-$\hat{2}$-$\hat{3}$-#$\hat{4}$-$\hat{5}$		R	0	0
4	$\hat{1}$-$\hat{5}$-$\hat{1}$	$\hat{5}$-$\hat{2}$-$\hat{5}$		R	1	.3
4a	$\hat{5}$-$\hat{5}$-$\hat{1}$	$\hat{1}$-$\hat{2}$-$\hat{5}$	9, 14	T	2	.7
5	$\hat{1}$-$\hat{2}$-$\hat{3}$	$\hat{5}$-$\hat{6}$-$\hat{7}$	10	R	23	8
5a	$\hat{5}$-$\hat{6}$-$\hat{7}$-$\hat{1}$-$\hat{2}$-$\hat{3}$	$\hat{1}$-$\hat{3}$-$\hat{4}$-$\hat{5}$-$\hat{6}$-$\hat{7}$	8	T	1	.3
Total					244	83

---

[59]The identification of precisely 295 works of Bach as fugal is necessarily interpretive. I have in each case tried to establish whether a movement is founded upon the general principles of fugal exposition.

Paradigm	Subject	Answer	Cognates	(Tonal/Real)	Number in Bach	Percentage in Bach
Category 2						
6	$\hat{8}$-$\hat{8}$-$\hat{7}$	$\hat{5}$-$\hat{4}$-$\hat{3}$	1, 11	T	5	2
6a	$\hat{5}$-$\hat{4}$-$\hat{3}$-$\hat{2}$-$\hat{1}$-$\hat{7}$	$\hat{8}$-$\hat{7}$-$\hat{6}$-$\hat{5}$-$\hat{4}$-$\hat{3}$	1a, 11a	T	0	0
7	$\hat{8}$-$\hat{7}$-$\hat{6}$-$\hat{5}$	$\hat{5}$-$\hat{3}$-$\hat{2}$-$\hat{1}$	2a, 12	T	1	.3
7a	$\hat{5}$-$\hat{6}$-$\hat{5}$	$\hat{2}$-$\hat{2}$-$\hat{1}$	2c, 12a	T	3	1
8	$\hat{5}$-#$\hat{4}$-$\hat{5}$	$\hat{2}$-$\hat{7}$-$\hat{1}$	3	T	7	2.4
8a	$\hat{1}$-$\hat{2}$-$\hat{3}$-#$\hat{4}$-$\hat{5}$	$\hat{5}$-$\hat{5}$-$\hat{6}$-$\hat{7}$-$\hat{8}$	3a, 13	T	9	3
9	$\hat{1}$-$\hat{2}$-$\hat{5}$	$\hat{5}$-$\hat{5}$-$\hat{1}$	4a, 14	T	2	.7
10	$\hat{5}$-$\hat{6}$-$\hat{7}$	$\hat{2}$-$\hat{2}$-$\hat{3}$	5	T	0	0
Total					27	9
Category 3						
11	$\hat{8}$-$\hat{7}$	$\hat{5}$-(#)$\hat{4}$ ($\hat{5}$-$\hat{4}$]-$\hat{3}$)	1, 6	R [T]	7	2.4
11a	$\hat{5}$-$\hat{4}$-$\hat{3}$-$\hat{2}$-$\hat{1}$-$\hat{7}$	$\hat{2}$-$\hat{1}$-$\hat{7}$-$\hat{6}$-$\hat{5}$-(#)$\hat{4}$	1a, 6b	R	0	0
12	$\hat{8}$-$\hat{7}$-$\hat{6}$-$\hat{5}$	$\hat{5}$-$\hat{4}$-$\hat{3}$-$\hat{2}$ ($\hat{5}$-$\hat{3}$-$\hat{2}$-$\hat{1}$)	2a, 7	R [T]	4	1.4
12a	$\hat{5}$-$\hat{6}$-$\hat{5}$	$\hat{2}$-$\hat{3}$-$\hat{2}$	2c, 7a	R	2	.7
13	$\hat{1}$-$\hat{2}$-$\hat{3}$-$\hat{4}$-$\hat{5}$	$\hat{5}$-$\hat{6}$-$\hat{7}$-$\hat{1}$-$\hat{2}$	3a, 8a	R	2	.7
14	$\hat{1}$-$\hat{5}$	$\hat{5}$-$\hat{2}$ ($\hat{5}$-$\hat{1}$)	4a, 9	R [T]	7	2.4
15	$\hat{5}$-$\hat{6}$-$\hat{7}$	$\hat{2}$-$\hat{3}$-(#)$\hat{4}$	5, 10	R	0	0
16	$\hat{5}$-$\hat{4}$-$\hat{3}$-$\hat{2}$	$\hat{2}$-$\hat{1}$-$\hat{7}$-$\hat{6}$		R	2	.7
17	$\hat{1}$-$\hat{2}$	$\hat{5}$-$\hat{6}$		R	0	0
Total					24	8
Unclassified subjects					2	.7
Grand total					295	100

The figures in column six are open to a degree of revision since the classification of any subject to a given paradigm is inevitably based on an analytical interpretation. It has already been shown that certain subjects can suggest more than one paradigm as fundamental. However, the figures in column six do provide a basis for evaluating Bach's usage of the basic structures which the paradigms represent. First, an overwhelming proportion of Bach's subjects fall within category one, and less than ten percent fall in each of the other two categories. Within category 1, fully half of the subjects represent paradigm 1, and another fifth are based on paradigm 2a.[60] Paradigms 2 and 5 each represent approximately one tenth

---

[60]Walter Schenkman has recognized the pervasiveness of paradigms 1 and 2a in Bach's fugue subjects, but accounted for it in different terms. By including the upper neighbor as the high point, and the terminus on $\hat{3}$ or $\hat{1}$ as the low point, he has identified $\hat{6}$-$\hat{5}$-$\hat{4}$-$\hat{3}$-$\hat{2}$-$\hat{1}$ and $\hat{6}$-$\hat{5}$-$\hat{4}$-$\hat{3}$ as common patterns. Although he further connects these patterns with the ancient tradition of solmization subjects, where compositions were based *on ut re mi fa sol la*, it should be clear that these patterns in fact grow out of principles of tonal voice-leading. See "The Influence of Hexachordal Thinking in the Organization of Bach's Fugue Subjects," Bach VII (1976):10–11. Robert Gauldin refers to $\hat{5}$-$\hat{6}$-$\hat{5}$-$\hat{4}$-$\hat{3}$ with an optional final descent to the tonic as a "scarlet thread" running throughout the literature of Baroque fugue subjects. See *A Practical Approach to Eighteenth Century Counterpoint* (Englewood Cliffs, New Jersey: Prentice Hall, 1988), 212.

of the subjects in category 1. All the other paradigms in category 1 appear seldom, except paradigm 3b which occurs not at all. In category two, paradigms 8, 8a and 6 predominate, and in category 3, paradigms 11 and 14 are most frequently found.

Of the thirty paradigms identified here, only about ten occur with enough frequency in the literature to be considered as important repetitive patternings. Yet the entire complement is necessary in order to account for the full range of theoretical possibilities implicit in the original limiting factors of harmonic and melodic coherence set forth by Schenker. One might well have expected a more balanced representation of the various structural possibilities in Bach's fugues. However, as the discussion has already suggested, some paradigms fulfill Schenker's criteria of self-substantiation and directed motion better than others, and some paradigms are more amenable to convincing answer construction.

A comparison of Bach's use of paradigms in *WTC I* and *WTC II* illustrates an interesting facet of his compositional development. As Figure 2-3 indicates, *WTC II* exhibits a much more consistent use of a limited number of paradigms and contains a truly extraordinary proportion of subjects based on paradigm 1. Further, Bach favor of subjects that end on $\hat{3}$ in *WTC II* almost to the complete exclusion of other types. These observations may relate to two additional interrelated aspects of differentiation between the two books. First, *WTC II* exhibits a more consistent use of dance idioms and less vocal style, and second, a greater proportion of the fugues in *WTC II* are in three parts. The contrast between the two sets which Figure 2-3 shows may reflect the degree of compositional development and stylistic consistency that Bach achieved in the twenty-two year period between the completion of *WTC I* and *WTC II*.

Figure 2-3. Subject paradigms in *WTC I* and *WTC II*

Subject paradigm		Number of occurrences		
		WTC I	*WTC II*	*WTC I & II*
1	$(\hat{5}\text{-}\hat{4}\text{-}\hat{3})$	6	17	23
2	$(\hat{1}\text{-}\hat{3}\text{-}\hat{2}\text{-}\hat{1})$	2	1	3
2a	$(\hat{5}\text{-}\hat{4}\text{-}\hat{3}\text{-}\hat{2}\text{-}\hat{1})$	5	1	6
3a	$(\hat{5}\text{-}\hat{6}\text{-}\hat{7}\text{-}\hat{8})$	0	1	1
5	$(\hat{1}\text{-}\hat{2}\text{-}\hat{3})$	3	4	7
6	$(\hat{8}\text{-}\hat{8}\text{-}\hat{7})$	1	0	1
7a	$(\hat{5}\text{-}\hat{6}\text{-}\hat{5})$	1	0	1
8	$(\hat{5}\text{-}\#\hat{4}\text{-}\hat{5})$	1	0	1
9	$(\hat{1}\text{-}\hat{2}\text{-}\hat{5})$	1	0	1
8a + 2 (see Ex. 2-54)		1	0	1
12a	$(\hat{5}\text{-}\hat{6}\text{-}\hat{5})$	1	0	1
13	$(\hat{1}\text{-}\hat{2}\text{-}\hat{3}\text{-}\hat{4}\text{-}\hat{5})$	2	0	2

Subject and answer are the basis of all contrapuntal procedures in fugue. Chapter 2 has shown how fugue subjects and answers present basic voice-leading and harmonic structures that convey unity and directed motion. The following chapters, which consider how the structural aspects of fugue subjects and answers form the basis of the contrapuntal, imitative and formal procedures of entire fugues, will make more readily apparent why some paradigms promote more fruitful contrapuntal combinations and others are comparatively barren.

CHAPTER 3

Invertible Counterpoint

The fact that Schenker had little use for invertible counterpoint is at first glance surprising. After all, he dealt with the abstract nature of counterpoint at great length in his highly systematic two-volume study *Counterpoint*, and analyzed a number of compositions in which invertible counterpoint figures prominently, most notably the C minor fugue from *WTC I*.[1] Nevertheless, invertible counterpoint is seldom a topic of discussion in his theoretical or analytical work. Indeed, in *Free Composition* Schenker rejects the concept of invertible counterpoint:

> Double counterpoint therefore takes its place in the ranks of such fallacious concepts as the ecclesiastical modes, sequences, and the usual explanation of consecutive fifths and octaves.[2]

Example 3-1, from Bach's unfinished Fugue in C minor BWV 906, is the only example of invertible counterpoint in *Free Composition*. Yet it is introduced within the discussion of "The Combination of Two or More Linear Progressions" where it serves to diminish the importance of double counterpoint as it reinforces the concept of "leader" and "follower":

> In the light of this evaluation, the specific teachings of double counterpoint become somewhat less significant.[3]

The specific problem that Schenker isolates here is that the concept of the equality of the individual voices of invertible counterpoint is invalid, since in any polyphonic construct one of the several linear progressions serves as the leader and represents the underlying linear basis of the passage.

Example 3-1. Bach, Fugue in C minor BWV 906, a, mm. 7–8, 16–17, 12–13; b, Schenker, *Free Composition*, Fig. 99-1

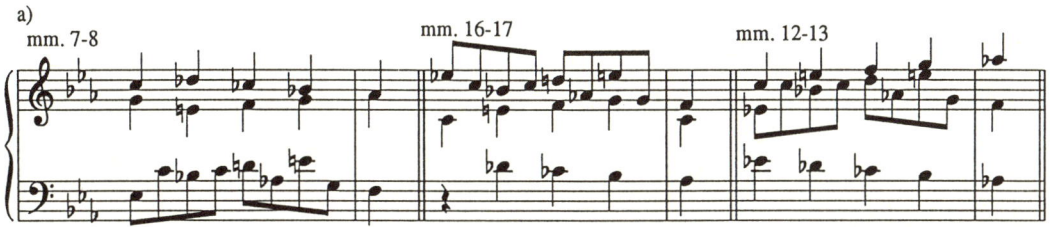

---

[1]Schenker, *Counterpoint*, trans. by John Rothgeb and Jürgen Thym, 2 vols. (New York: Schirmer, 1987); Schenker, "Das Organische der Fuge," *Das Meisterwerk in der Musik*, 2:55–95.

[2]*Free Composition*, 78.

[3]*Ibid.*, 82.

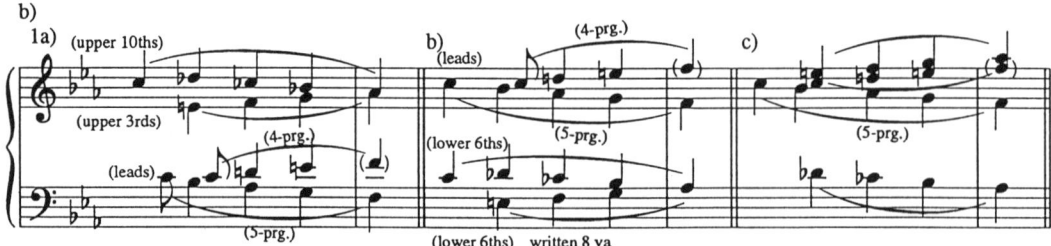

Schenker's mistrust of invertible counterpoint apparently stems from a philosophical aversion to any form of systematic composition whatsoever. Since his starting point is the organic whole and his emphasis is on the unique aspects of each masterwork, it follows that a technique which smacks of formula or appears mechanically constructed is anathema. Schenker had little patience for pedagogues who perpetuated note-by-note and chord-by-chord approaches to composition and who could not perceive the more fundamental aspects of the tonal system that he was discovering and codifying. No doubt Schenker's impatience with such contrapuntal effects as invertible counterpoint was fueled by his intolerance of those who championed counterpoint for counterpoint's sake. We may consider his attack on Reger in "Ein Gegenbeispiel: Max Reger, Op. 81: *Variationen und Fuge uber ein Thema von Joh. Seb. Bach fur Klavier*" as an example of this.[4] But more important is his stand against imitative counterpoint exhibited in *Counterpoint*. Schenker's identification of counterpoint here as an abstract, pre-compositional study of voice-leading entirely divorced from considerations of harmony, form, motive, or imitation, may well have predisposed him in his later work to slight contrapuntal techniques that lay outside the confines that he had previously established in *Counterpoint*.

Yet invertible counterpoint is fundamental to polyphonic composition, and therefore it remains surprising that Schenker would dismiss a technique so frequently used by his greatest idols—not only Bach and Handel but even Beethoven and Brahms—in ingenious, indeed brilliant ways. Invertible counterpoint plays a major role in the subject-countersubject complex, in many sequences, and very frequently in stretti and canons as well. For these composers, invertible counterpoint was not simply a contrapuntal artifice, but a special means of developing coherence and complexity. Treated properly, invertible counterpoint is one of the most profound means of achieving organic unity in musical composition.

In order to reconcile Schenker's theory of structural levels with the practice of the masters in invertible counterpoint, chapter 3 approaches invertible counterpoint not in the traditional manner, through intervals and their inversions (a relic of the compositional practice of the pre-figured-bass era which still holds the place in classroom and textbook with which Zarlino endowed it), but as an outgrowth of Schenker's own theory of

---

[4]*Das Meisterwerk in der Musik*, 2:171–92; trans. in Kalib, "Thirteen Essays from the Three Yearbooks," 2:451–90.

voice-leading and harmony. Rather than building from the atomic basis of intervals and their inversions, it begins from Schenker's global concepts of harmony and voice-leading, and views invertible counterpoint as a manifestation of structural levels and tonal voice-leading.

The Voice-leading Matrix

Schenker's theory of structural levels makes an absolute distinction between the roles and structures of melody and bass in tonal music. Melody expresses tonality through stepwise linear progressions, primarily ones which unfold the tonic chord. The bass, on the other hand, expresses tonality through a combination of leaps and steps which support the melody and give definition to the harmonic progressions, often through chordal roots. In most tonal music, melody and bass are clearly differentiated in style and aspect, as they are in function. But what of invertible counterpoint? How are the norms and conditions of tonality, prolongation and progression expressed and interpreted in music where the melody *becomes* the bass and vice versa.

Example 3-2 reproduces Schenker's *fundamental structure* as given in *Free Composition*.[5] As the structural basis for an entire musical composition, it contains harmonic prolongation and melodic progression; a complete I–V–I harmonic movement and a full melodic resolution to the tonic. The fundamental structure is a model of tonal coherence, not only at the background level, but also at higher levels, including the foreground, as understood through the concept of "transference of the fundamental structure to individual harmonies"[6], and it is this model that provides a theoretical basis for the development of a *structural* theory of invertible counterpoint presented here. If we approach the problem of invertible counterpoint from this basis of tonal structure, the question is how can Schenker's fundamental structure be realized in the format of invertible counterpoint?

Example 3-2. Schenker, *Free Composition*, Fig. 1

Example 3-3 (a) works out in full the voice-leading implications of Schenker's $\hat{3}$-$\hat{2}$-$\hat{1}$ fundamental structure, utilizing root motion in the bass and scalar and common-tone connections in the upper parts. As a fundamental expression of tonal voice-leading, a primal basis for unlimited expansion and development, I refer to it as a *voice-leading matrix*. Examples 3-3 (b) and (c) show more elaborate forms that include pre-dominant harmony as well.

---

[5]*Free Composition*, Fig. 1.
[6]*Ibid.*, 87.

Example 3-3. Voice-leading matrix

Although the voice-leading matrix is based on the fundamental structure, its meaning is different. The matrix presents a kind of fundamental voice-leading structure for tonal music at the foreground and middleground levels. Further, and most important for the study of invertible counterpoint, the matrix idealistically places equal importance on each of the moving voices and assumes that the vertical ordering of the upper voices is flexible. The several melodic strands of the voice-leading matrix replicate the primary subject paradigms 1, 2, 3, and 4, and it will become clear that this has important implications for the combination of subjects and countersubjects.

While Schenker's fundamental structure is an original creation, the matrix of example 3-3 is by no means unique in music theory. Example 3-4 illustrates how Rameau conceived of tonal voice-leading in a similar manner in his *Treatise on Harmony* as an abstract series of step-wise voices supported by a fundamental bass. Rameau's formula is a *schema* of the way that voices progress naturally through a basic chord progression. Like the voice-leading matrix, Rameau's conception of voice-leading in a basic har-

Example 3-4. Rameau, *Treatise on Harmony*, 117

monic progression also ignores the specificity of given soprano and bass voices, and in this sense Rameau's formulation is more abstract than Schenker's.

The Voice-leading Complex

What potential does the voice-leading matrix of example 3-3 have as a basis of invertible counterpoint? Any of the four upper voices could appear in the highest part at a middleground level. However the root movement of the bass voice (paradigm 4) properly belongs in the lowest part. Indeed, this root movement loses its significance when placed among the higher parts, for its notes simply double those of other voices. In contrast, among the higher voices, $\hat{5}$-$\hat{4}$-$\hat{3}$, $\hat{3}$-$\hat{2}$-$\hat{1}$, and $\hat{8}$-$\hat{7}$-$\hat{8}$ (paradigms 1, 2, and 3) can successfully function in the bass, giving inverted progressions, but the voice which sustains the dominant—shown as the tenor—is inappropriate for the bass since its conclusion implies an unresolved second-inversion tonic chord. Thus, of the five voices, only three, $\hat{8}$-$\hat{7}$-$\hat{8}$, $\hat{3}$-$\hat{2}$-$\hat{1}$, and $\hat{5}$-$\hat{4}$-$\hat{3}$ can be distributed in any order and at the same time maintain a good expression of tonal voice-leading as a prolongation of the tonic chord. That these three lines represent three of the most frequently occurring subject paradigms is not without significance. Indeed, it is precisely their ability to simultaneously convey tonal and melodic coherence within the limitations of invertible counterpoint that accounts for their overwhelming predominance in the literature.

When we begin to consider the rearrangement of the voices of the matrix in relation to one another, in particular the substitution of an upper voice for the bass, we are dealing with invertible counterpoint at the octave in its elementary structural form. Example 3-5 presents the six possible permutations of the set of three invertible voices, paradigms 1, 2, and 3, and eliminates the sustained dominant and the root motion, the two voices that are not susceptible to inversion. Each arrangement in example 3-5 prolongs the tonic chord while at the same time expressing movement and resolution, thus fulfilling the essentials of tonality and directed motion inherent in the fundamental structure. Note, however, that in the absence of a larger context the second inversions which begin examples 3-5 (a)-5 and (a)-6 imply V–I rather than I–V–I. Example 3-5 thus represents the manner in which three structural voices of the voice-leading matrix can be arranged in invertible counterpoint. As a series of permutations of basic voices in an abstract "pitch-class space," I refer to example 3-5 as a *voice-leading complex*.[7] example 3-5 thus represents a voice-leading model of the most fundamental tonal structure upon which invertible counterpoint can be based. The second line of Example 3-5 shows how the basic progression of the voice-leading complex can be expanded to include two of the most common

---

[7] Related issues are developed by Patrick McCreless in "Syntagmatics and Paradigmatics: Some Implications for the Analysis of Chromaticism in Tonal Music," *Music Theory Spectrum* XIII/8 (fall, 1991):147–78 (especially 157–59).

prolongation techniques seen in chapter 2, predominant harmony and the upper neighbor motions $\hat{5}$-$\hat{6}$-$\hat{5}$ and $\hat{3}$-$\hat{4}$-$\hat{3}$.

Example 3-5. Voice-leading complex, a, simple forms, b, extended form

Like the voice-leading matrix, the voice-leading complex has precedents in music theory. In *Studies on the Origin of Harmonic Tonality*, Carl Dahlhaus isolates the same voices as the essentials of the discant-tenor *clausula* of the *prima prattica* (example 3-6). While the relationship of this ancient formula to Schenker's concepts of structure may seem trivial, Dahlhaus himself makes a direct connection:

> Schenker's hypothesis [regarding the I–IV–V–I cadence] seems to be supported by the memory of one of the proto-forms of the I–IV–V–I cadence. The *Terzzug* (third progression) $\hat{3}$-$\hat{2}$-$\hat{1}$ is the tenor formula of the discant-tenor clausula.[8]

Example 3-6. Discant clausula (after Dahlhaus)

A similar voice-leading structure can be found in the *clausulae* of Andreas Werckmeister. Example 3-7 shows several examples in which the same set of voices is inverted, first in the three upper parts of a four-part texture, and then in a corresponding three-part setting.[9] Werckmeister's fourth voice (paradigm 4), does not enter into the inversion scheme but remains in the bass, because for Werckmeister this voice is the given, the foundation of his polyphony.

---

[8] Carl Dahlhaus, *Studies on the Origin of Harmonic Tonality*, trans. Robert O. Gjerdingen (Princeton: Princeton University Press, 1990.), 39, 46, and 235.

[9] Andreas Werckmeister, *Harmonologia musica* (1702), 48–49. In our own time, William Benjamin has formulated a theory of "pitch-class counterpoint" that considers the structure of music as a counterpoint of pitch-class lines. See William Benjamin, "Pitch-class Counterpoint in Tonal Music," in *Music Theory: Special Topics*, ed. Richmond Brown (New York: Academic Press, 1981), 1–32. While Benjamin's formulations are based on the generative force of the descending fifth rather than the linear progression, the underlying model that he creates is similar to those under discussion here.

INVERTIBLE COUNTERPOINT

Example 3-7. Werckmeister's *clausulae* (*Harmonologia Musica*, 1702)

The voice-leading matrix provides a means of linking the subject paradigms of chapter 2 with the underlying voice-leading patterns of invertible counterpoint. Example 3-8 provides a complete theoretical basis for invertible counterpoint in subjects and answers by developing voice-leading matrices for subject and answer paradigms for each of the three categories. Bearing in mind the cognitive relationships among paradigms of different categories, the possibilities are quite limited.

Example 3-8. Voice-leading matrices, a, category 1; b, category 2; c, category 3

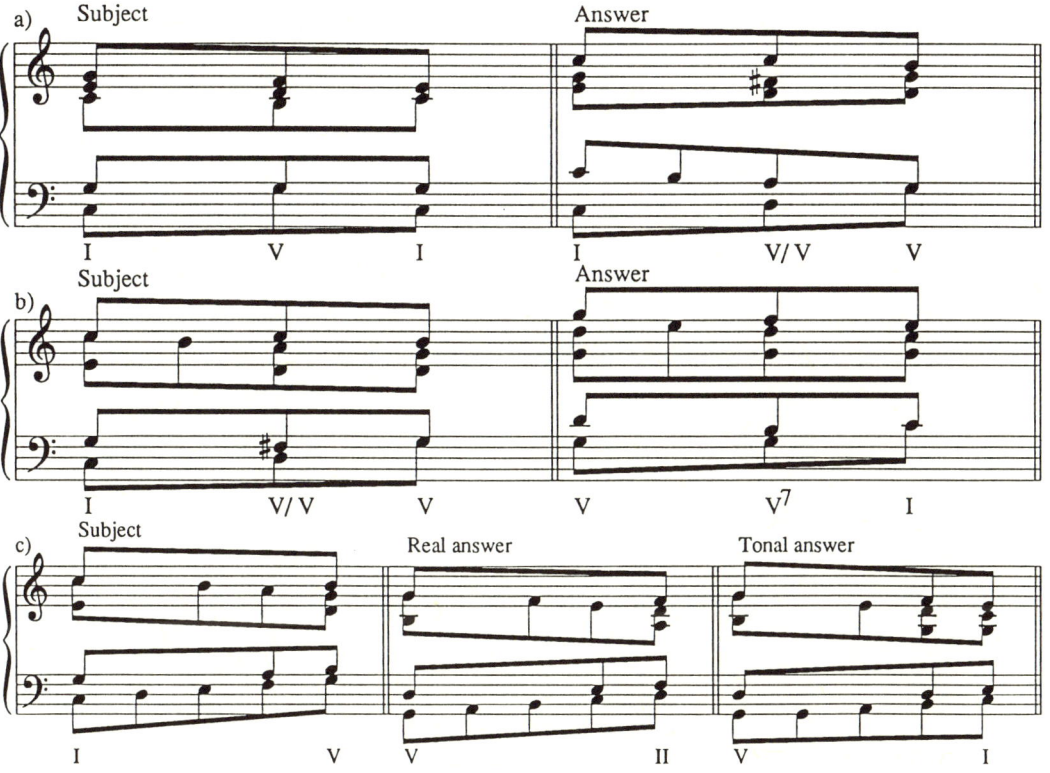

Invertible counterpoint for the answer is essentially founded on direct transposition, except in the case of tonal answers for category 3, where the cadential structure of the answer is significantly altered. For category 1, changes in voice-leading arise from the fact that the beginning of the answer expresses I rather than V, but in practice, as shown in chapter 2, this too can be modified through initial tonic, initial arpeggiation, or initial ascent. For category 2 answers, the same situation obtains with the roles reversed: the bulk of the subject follows the answer structure of category 1, but beginning with the tonic harmony. The answer is a transposition to I, connected to a beginning on V. For category 3, of course, there are two distinct underlying voice-leading patterns: that which ends on V/V (II) uniquely contains a strict transposition of the voice-leading of the subject. That which ends on I contains an essentially different voice-leading pattern since it responds to the half cadence of the subject with an authentic cadence in the answer.[10]

The following examples illustrate how the essential voice-leading progressions of several passages of invertible counterpoint realize the voice-leading matrices of example 3-8 at a middleground level and use it as a structural basis. In accord with Schenker's notions of strict counterpoint at deeper levels, the underlying proposition here is that the level at which invertible counterpoint is truly functional is not so much the surface but the higher middleground levels.

Invertible Counterpoint for Category 1 Subjects

Double Counterpoint

Example 3-9 illustrates a simple two-voice invertible counterpoint by Bach, taken from *WTC II*.[11] The subject is paradigm 1 (see example 2-5). The countersubject takes the form of a descending fifth articulated as two third-progressions. The first of these forms a voice exchange with the beginning of the subject and prolongs the tonic chord, and the following $\hat{3} - \hat{2} - \hat{1}$ progression forms the cadence. Thus although the countersubject is based on paradigm 2a ($\hat{5} - \hat{4} - \hat{3} - \hat{2} - \hat{1}$), the essential structure of the countersubject in relation to the subject is paradigm 2, $\hat{3} - \hat{2} - \hat{1}$, which combines in invertible counterpoint with the main linear progression of the subject.[12] The parallel sixths of the first form become parallel thirds (tenths) in the inversion, and two of the voices of the voice-leading complex form the basis of this counterpoint. Before leaving example 3-9, the role of the C in the subject should be noted. Although this tonic does not participate in any explicit

---

[10]Chapter 3 does not address directly the question of invertible counterpoint in relation to answers. It is chapter 4 that illustrates how subject and answer paradigms and countersubjects utilize voice-leading complexes in the context of fugal expositions.

[11]For the purposes of comparative analysis, examples in chapter 3 are abstracted from actual compositions and presented in the tonic key.

[12]This alteration of interpretation points up the close association among paradigms of the same number, as suggested in chapter 2.

linear motion, it provides a root for the tonic chord when the subject is in the bass, thus negating any implication of the second inversion at this point.

Example 3-9. Bach, Fugue 2 in C minor (*WTC II*), invertible counterpoint

While example 3-9 projects only two voices of the voice-leading complex, example 3-10, taken from a keyboard fugue of Padre Martini, contains all three voices in specific registers. The subject, based on paradigm 1, contains a second voice, $\hat{3}$-$\hat{2}$-$\hat{1}$, but the final tonic, shown in parentheses, is omitted. The countersubject expresses the lower neighbor motion $\hat{8}$-$\hat{7}$-$\hat{8}$ (paradigm 3). Thus, although only two parts are inverted here (subject and countersubject), three voices are involved, of which only $\hat{8}$-$\hat{7}$-$\hat{8}$ and $\hat{3}$-$\hat{2}$-$\hat{1}$ take the role of bass lines. The main linear progression of the subject, $\hat{5}$-$\hat{4}$-$\hat{3}$, never appears as a structural bass voice. Martini's invertible counterpoint thus expands upon patterns (a)-1 and (a)-3 of the voice-leading complex in example 3-5.

Example 3-10. Martini, Fugue in C major, invertible counterpoint

The concept of basing multiple invertible counterpoints upon a simple underlying basis is exemplified by C. P. E. Bach in his essay "An invention by which six measures of double counterpoint can be written without a knowledge of the rules."[13] Here Bach creates a dice game in which the player selects six separate measures each of treble and bass and then combines them into an invertible counterpoint. Example 3-11, which gives one of the 282,429,536,481 possibilities, illustrates how the underlying structural basis of the passage is a nesting of two statements of the voice-leading matrix. The upper part implies paradigms 1 and 2, and the bass uses paradigm 3. Indeed, it is only by means of repeating a simple underlying structure such as this that Bach is enabled to let any treble harmonize with any bass.

Example 3-11. C. P. E. Bach, invertible counterpoint

Example 3-12 adds a further level abstraction. Here the notion of *voice* is separated from that of *part*. The subject itself (paradigm 1) includes as well the cadential motion A–G, the final notes of the descending third, $\hat{3}$ - $\hat{2}$ - $\hat{1}$ (paradigm 2). But the $\hat{3}$ that initiates this progression is contained in the countersubject, as the graph shows. Likewise, the countersubject is based on the motion $\hat{8}$ - $\hat{7}$ - $\hat{8}$ (paradigm 3), but the initial $\hat{8}$ is contained in the subject rather than the countersubject. Once again, although paradigm 1 is a guiding linear progression in the structure, only the notes $\hat{3}$, $\hat{2}$ and $\hat{1}$ occur as structural bass notes because of the way the structural notes are deployed between the two voices. In summary, the three essential voices of the voice-leading complex are distributed among two invertible parts, subject and countersubject.

---

[13]"Einfall, einen doppelten Contrapunct in der Octave von sechs Tacten zu machen, ohne die Regeln davon zu wissen," in Friedrich Wilhelm Marpurg, *Historisch-kritische Beyträge zur Aufnahme der Musik* III (1757):167–74. Translated in Eugene Helm, "Six Random Measures of C. P. E. Bach," *Journal of Music Theory* X (1966):139–51.

INVERTIBLE COUNTERPOINT

Example 3-12. Bach, Fugue 16 in G minor (*WTC I*), invertible counterpoint

Example 3-13, from *WTC II*, also contains three voices in only two parts. This example shows how an initial ascent functions to prolong the opening tonic chord in the same basic progression. The subject is a lengthy initial ascent concluded by paradigm 1. But the subject also contains a subordinate $\hat{3}$-$\hat{2}$-$\hat{1}$ linear-progression which is completed by the notes in parentheses that follow the end of the subject proper (see example 2-12). The countersubject has a corresponding ascent of a sixth from third to tonic, after which it proceeds to the cadence through paradigm 3 ($\hat{8}$-$\hat{7}$-$\hat{8}$). Once again, the same underlying voice-leading structure is at the root of this example of invertible counterpoint.

Carl Schachter has noted how the subject unfolds a series of rising fourths in half notes and then in eighths at the surface level, as the brackets show.[14] But the countersubject reinforces this motivic structure in an ingenious way through its rising chromatic motion in quarter notes, the second of which also unfolds a rising fourth. It should be noted that the final B-flat of the countersubject represents the implied conclusion. In the music itself the lowered seventh A-flat appears instead, eliding the expected cadence in the manner of *inganno*[15] and pressing on through a secondary dominant to the next part of the piece.

---

[14]Carl Schachter, "Rhythm and Linear Analysis: A Preliminary Study," *The Music Forum* IV (1976):329.

[15]*Inganno* (It. deception) refers here to the change of trajectory in which the leading tone is lowered and transformed into the seventh of a dominant chord, avoiding the expected resolution and typically leading the music back from the dominant key area to the tonic. See also example 2-19.

Example 3-13. Bach, Fugue 22 in B-flat minor (*WTC II*), invertible counterpoint

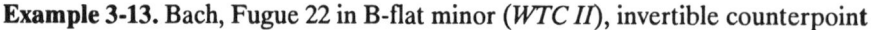

Example 3-14, also from *WTC II*, illustrates another manner of realizing the same basic voice-leading. As shown in example 2-11, the subject contains the primary descent $\hat{5}$ - $\hat{4}$ - $\hat{3}$ (paradigm 1) as its upper voice and $\hat{8}$ - $\hat{7}$ - $\hat{8}$ (paradigm 3) as its lower voice. The countersubject contains a $\hat{3}$ - $\hat{2}$ - $\hat{1}$ descent (paradigm 2) as well as the $\hat{8}$ - $\hat{7}$ - $\hat{8}$ motion formed by its lower notes. Thus the subject and the countersubject both contain the same structural bass, paradigm 3. As a result, although double counterpoint occurs at the surface of the music and is perceived as a motivic inversion, at the middleground level no real harmonic inversion takes place, since the bass remains the same in either arrangement. At several points in the composition Bach takes advantage of the compound structure of the countersubject and divides it between two parts, giving a three-part texture. But of course this textural change makes no difference to the voice-leading structure.[16]

---

[16] See mm. 13 and 24.

INVERTIBLE COUNTERPOINT

Example 3-14. Bach, Fugue 10 in E minor (*WTC II*), invertible counterpoint

Triple Counterpoint

Critical to a unified theory of invertible counterpoint is that a single set of principles and voice-leading patterns underlie not only double counterpoint, but also triple and quadruple counterpoint. As one can adduce from the three-voice structure of the voice-leading complex, the same structure can easily form the basis of triple invertible counterpoint at the octave.

Example 3-15 shows the three subjects of the five-voiced Fugue in C-sharp minor from *WTC I*. Subject 1, in long notes, is paradigm 2 ($\hat{3}$ - $\hat{2}$ - $\hat{1}$) expanded by an unfolding of the third C-sharp–E at the beginning (see example 2-17). Countersubject 1, introduced in measure 35, is a running figure of eighth notes that traverses a descending third $\hat{5}$ - $\hat{4}$ - $\hat{3}$ (paradigm 1). Countersubject 2, first presented in measure 49, is based on paradigm 3 ($\hat{8}$ - $\hat{7}$ - $\hat{8}$), elaborated by a decorated suspension. Bach gives each subject a unique rhythmic and motivic treatment, and begins each at a different time, emphasizing the melodic independence of the three themes. Yet they can be reduced to a strict three-part note-against-note counterpoint that works out the voice-leading complex. Example 3-15 shows only three of the six possible arrangements, each with a different theme in the bass. In the fugue, Bach uses five of the six possible combinations, and omits the arrangement in ascending order: countersubject 1, subject, countersubject 2. The five permutations that Bach does employ occupy the middle section of the fugue, from measures 49 through 88. The final section of the fugue dispenses with the first countersubject and instead works out various stretti of the subject and the second countersubject.

Example 3-15. Fugue 4 in C-sharp minor (*WTC I*), invertible counterpoint

Example 3-16 shows a comparable triple counterpoint in Bach's four-part organ fugue in B minor BWV 544. The subject, presented as an even series of stepwise eighth-notes, is based on paradigm 1 (see example 2-10). The initial ascent of the subject provides the basis of a tonic prolongation that is supported by arpeggiation in the two countersubjects. Countersubject 1, used in the opening and closing sections of the fugue, is essentially paradigm 3 ($\hat{8} - \hat{7} - \hat{8}$), filled out by arpeggiation and a suspension. Countersubject 2, used only in the final section, is based structurally on the descending third $\hat{3} - \hat{2} - \hat{1}$ (paradigm 2), but motivically on the opening of the principle subject. Thus all three themes are motivically unified through the shared pattern B–A-sharp–B.[17] Once again, the combination of the three lines yields the same underlying structure seen in the previous example. But the arpeggiations of the opening measure provide a remarkable breadth of register that is absent from the C-sharp minor fugue. In this fugue, only four of the six possible inversions of this triple counterpoint occur. Bach's limitation in this case is the proportions of the fugue. Exposing all six forms would unduly prolong the final section of the fugue.

---

[17]The central section of the fugue includes several statements of yet another countersubject which however is never combined with these.

INVERTIBLE COUNTERPOINT

Example 3-16. Bach, Fugue in B minor BWV 544, invertible counterpoint

The *fugato* from Mozart's *Musical Joke* is another simple example of triple counterpoint based on the voice-leading complex. Example 2-3 illustrates how this pattern is worked out through an entire exposition. The subject is paradigm 2, countersubject 1 is paradigm 3, and countersubject 2 is paradigm 1.

In terms of triple counterpoint, examples 3-15 and 3-16 are quite simple. Example 3-17, from *WTC I*, is more complex, since the underlying structure of each theme is itself more complex (see example 2-1). The subject (paradigm 1) is ornamented by the upper neighbor, a-flat, and by a second linear motion that circles around the tonic but does not resolve explicitly. The first countersubject outlines the descending third $\hat{3}$ - $\hat{2}$ - $\hat{1}$ (paradigm 2), but this too is expanded by an upper neighbor, f², final note in the first measure of example 3-16, and by a series of third progressions. But countersubject 2 really lacks a distinct or independent linear structure of its own. Instead it acts more as a harmonic filler, doubling the essential notes of the other parts. The subject and first countersubject clearly project two voices of the voice-leading complex, $\hat{5}$ - $\hat{4}$ - $\hat{3}$ and $\hat{3}$ - $\hat{2}$ - $\hat{1}$, extended by upper neighbors in the manner of example 3-5 (a)-2. However, the third voice of the voice-leading complex, $\hat{8}$ - $\hat{7}$ - $\hat{8}$, must be synthesized by combining the initial tonic of the subject with the concluding notes of countersubject 1, as shown by the analysis. What is most significant about this construction, as with example 3-12, then, is that the linear motion $\hat{8}$ - $\hat{7}$ - $\hat{8}$, is realized only through the combination of subject and countersubject.

That is, the voice-leading complex is one step further removed from the part writing here.

Example 3-17. Bach, Fugue 2 in C minor (*WTC I*), invertible counterpoint

Bach uses five of the possible six inversions in this fugue. But it must be noted that countersubject 2 never occurs in the bass in its original form. Rather, its ending is always altered to form a root movement to the tonic. That is, when countersubject 2 assumes a structural role it also assumes a structural characteristic, paradigm 4a.

Example 3-18 shows the triple counterpoint of Bach's F-sharp minor fugue from *WTC II*, this time using a subject of paradigm 2a ($\hat{5}$-$\hat{4}$-$\hat{3}$-$\hat{2}$-$\hat{1}$). The first part of the fugue deals exclusively with the subject itself, which clearly expresses the descending fifth. At m. 20, a new point of imitation introduces countersubject 1, which is essentially the neighbor motion $\hat{8}$-$\hat{7}$-$\hat{8}$ (paradigm 3).[18] In mm. 28–35 subject and countersubject 1 are combined. In m. 36 a third point of imitation exposes countersubject 2, a stepwise descending motion of a third which is simple enough to be able to be used as paradigm 1 or paradigm 2. Beginning at m. 55, all three subjects are combined for the last third of the piece. The analysis in example 3-18 shows how the three subjects combine together. While each subject retains its essential melodic structure, the combination of all three yields an important new and deeper level of structure. It is really the underlying harmonic motion that governs the passage. Countersubject 2 is extended sequentially to a full descending sixth, $\hat{8}$-$\hat{7}$-$\hat{6}$-$\hat{5}$-$\hat{4}$-$\hat{3}$. The lengthy descending motions of subject and countersubject 2 must be seen partly as composing out of voice exchanges between the parts, in such a way that the deeper structure once again reduces to the voice-leading complex, but with voice-exchange applied as

---

[18]One might wish to distinguish between second subject and countersubject on the basis of their differing formal functions; that a second subject stands on its own as the basis of an independent section of a fugue. But in terms of the contrapuntal structure, and of invertible counterpoint in particular, the distinction is unimportant.

INVERTIBLE COUNTERPOINT

well (shown by the diagonal beams. That is, while the melodic shapes in and of themselves express extensive descents, in combination these motions are reduced somewhat to composing-out of more basic motions through voice-exchange. In particular, the fifth progression of the subject is broken up in such a way that the $\hat{3}$ is heard as a lower level passing note within an extended V.

In this fugue, only three of the six combinations appear: m. 55, subject, countersubject 1, countersubject 2, reading down; m. 60, countersubject 2, countersubject 1, subject; m. 67, subject, countersubject 2, countersubject 1. In this instance, like the B minor organ fugue, it is the restrictions of the formal proportions that limit the number of combinations. A full presentation would unnecessarily prolong the final section of this fugue, which itself is already stretched to the limit by including separate expositions for each of the three subjects.

Example 3-18. Fugue 14 in F-sharp minor (*WTC II*), invertible counterpoint

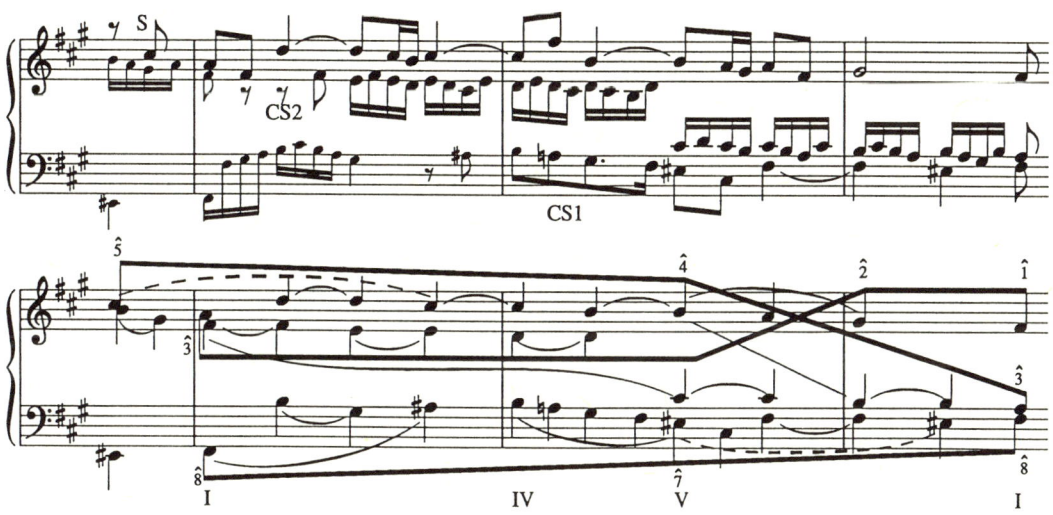

It is interesting to note that countersubject 2 is similar to countersubject 1 of example 3-14 and countersubject 1 is similar to countersubject 2 of the same example, not only in structure, but also in rhythmic detail. Obviously this was a pattern with which Bach was quite satisfied.

The sole example of triple counterpoint in Luigi Cherubini's treatise *Counterpoint and Fugue*,[19] example 3-19, is once again based on the voice-leading complex. It is not simply coincidence that Cherubini's triple counterpoint realizes the same basic structure as the voice-leading complex. Rather it shows a recognition of the naturalness and logic inherent in this particular progression.

---

[19]Luigi Cherubini, *Counterpoint and Fugue*, 2 vols., trans. J. A. Hamilton (London: Cocks and Co., 1837), I:253 and 255. Although Cherubini is credited as author, this is apparently the work of Halévy.

Example 3-19. Cherubini, Counterpoint and Fugue, 253

Quadruple Counterpoint

Even more interesting is the quadruple counterpoint from the same volume, example 3-20, for here a fourth part that moves through paradigm 5 is added to the three parts of the triple counterpoint. This added part is entirely compatible with the others since it simply doubles existing notes and proceeds in contrary motion to the existing parts. However, the fourth part adds nothing new to the tonal structure. It is a synthetic part, in the sense that it is formed through doublings of the other three. Thus even this quadruple counterpoint, like the double and triple before, is based on the same underlying voice-leading complex. Examples 3-19 and 3-20 make explicit the unity of triple and quadruple counterpoint by basing the quadruple on the triple counterpoint. Other quadruple counterpoints typically work along similar lines as these or follow a simple pattern in which the fourth part doubles and alternates with notes of other parts in a similar manner.

Example 3-20. Cherubini, *Counterpoint and Fugue*, 255

INVERTIBLE COUNTERPOINT

Bach's quadruple counterpoints appear most often in his vocal fugues, where four parts is presumed and where independence and equality of parts is more important than in keyboard fugues. The necessity of setting text naturally leads to the development of fugues with multiple countersubjects, since free counterpoint does not provide the same rigor of text-music association. The *Choral-einbau* fugue provides a conceptual model. In the *Choral-einbau* fugue the formal basis is a four-part contrapuntal scheme arranged into an imitative texture. Figure 3-1 illustrates how a vertical arrangement of four-part counterpoint can be converted into an imitative, even canonic structure of horizontal counterpoint.[20]

Figure 3-1. *Choral-einbau* schema of motivic material

S:	A	A	B	C	D
A:	B		A	B	C	D
T:	C becomes			A	B	C	D
B:	D				A	B	C	D

Example 3-21 shows one of Bach's quadruple counterpoints, from Cantata BWV 105-1. In example 3-21, each of the four lines is analyzed independently. Each theme exhibits a simple paradigm structure, but interestingly, two are paradigm 2a ($\hat{5} - \hat{4} - \hat{3} - \hat{2} - \hat{1}$). However, it is important to note that countersubject 1 descends earlier than countersubject 2 and continues to the leading tone before resolving to the tonic. Thus in combination countersubject 2 and countersubject 1 form a chain of parallel thirds with suspensions. Countersubject 3 simply doubles notes of countersubject 1 and countersubject 2 in alternation. This gives countersubject 3 a semblance of independence without however introducing any additional pitches. Here countersubject 3 could be considered a synthetic voice, since it is not really independent.

Example 3-21. Bach, Cantata BWV 105-1, invertible counterpoint

[20]See Werner Neumann, *J. S. Bach's Chorfuge* (Leipzig: F. Kistner, 1938). Daniel Harrison develops this type of patterning into a theory of permutations of triple counterpoint and relates it to issues of formal structure in "Some Group Properties of Triple Counterpoint and their Influence on Compositions by J. S. Bach," *Journal of Music Theory* XXXII/1 (spring 1988):22–49.

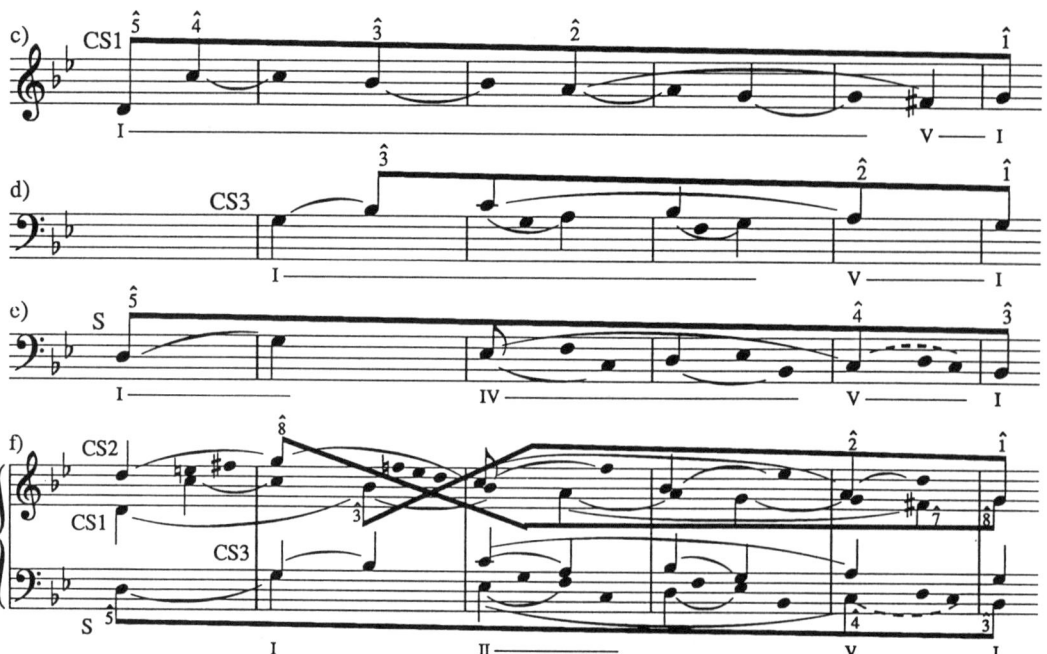

When the four counterpoints are considered in combination, as they were presumably conceived, a different picture emerges. The harmonic implications of the entire structure tends to reduce the importance of the descending fifths of countersubject 1 and countersubject 2 in favor of a simpler realization that once again comes back to the voice-leading complex in example 3-5. The subject maintains its fundamental pattern of paradigm 1, but the other lines can easily be perceived now as involving a voice exchange among the parts as shown by the crossing beams. When the voice-exchange is introduced, the whole can be reduced a further level to simple $\hat{3}$-$\hat{2}$-$\hat{1}$ and $\hat{8}$-$\hat{7}$-$\hat{8}$ voices prolonged by stepwise movements in the parts. Countersubject 3 of course simply doubles the $\hat{3}$-$\hat{2}$-$\hat{1}$ motion of the other countersubjects. Thus in essence the sequential aspect of this passage is reduced at the middleground level to a more basic I–V–I harmonic underpinning expressed fundamentally by the voice-leading complex.

What is quite interesting here is how the combination of paradigms leads to reinterpretations. While the melodic structures of the paradigms remain valid as expressions of tonality, in combination they are subsumed under a more fundamental voice-leading pattern at a deeper level that harks back again to the voice-leading matrix as a fundamental basis of voice leading. And this is the means by which a great variety of melodic structures can still express the basic requirements of tonal music in the same way—*semper idem sed non eodem modo*! Another important element in these subjects is that in each case the only really important structural note in the first measure is D, the dominant. This limitation in fact permits the elision at the entry of the answer, as well as for the entry of the subject after the answer through elision. In the first case the tonal alteration gives G as the beginning of the answer and its first and second countersubjects, harmoniz-

INVERTIBLE COUNTERPOINT

ing with the end of the subject and its countersubjects. In the second case, the Ds act as root of the V which ends the answer and its countersubjects.[21]

It is worthwhile comparing the above to an example of quadruple counterpoint in a keyboard fugue, a rare occurrence. Example 3-22 shows the quadruple counterpoint from the F minor fugue of *WTC I*. Once again, each of the four strands is analyzed individually for its structural implications. The subject is paradigm 2a; countersubject 1 is essentially paradigm 3; countersubject 2 is essentially paradigm 1, and countersubject 3 is simply a prolongation of $\hat{5}$. When the four themes are combined, the subject continues to project a fifth descent. The chromatic motion of m. 2 provides in essence a prolongation of I. In other respects, the basic voice-leading retains its meaning. However, what may be contentious here is that the $\hat{3}$ of the subject is "unsupported." It is part of a six-four construction over V.[22]

Example 3-22. Bach, Fugue 12 in F minor (*WTC I*), invertible counterpoint

[21] This procedure has important compositional and practical consequences. Such fugues typically remain within the tonic-dominant orbit, and thus cannot be developed into lengthy choral fugues. On the other hand, they can be learned extremely quickly. The four themes can be leaned sequentially in unison, and then the fugue can be easily sung with minimal tonal modifications.

[22] The issue of the unsupported stretch has been the subject of a recent debate. See Carl Schachter, "A Commentary on Schenker's *Free Composition*," *Journal of Music Theory* XV/1 (spring, 1981):125–26, and David Neumeyer, "Fragile Octaves, Broken Lines: On Some Limitations in Schenkerian Theory and Practice," *In Theory Only* XI/3 (July, 1989):13–30.

In quadruple counterpoint it is virtually impossible to avoid a profusion of crossed parts. This problem limits the practicality of quadruple counterpoint at the keyboard. In this fugue only two of the theoretically possible permutations actually occur (mm. 13 and 27). In addition, in order to make performance possible, the order of themes remains the same in both instances: countersubject 2, countersubject 3, and countersubject 1 are arranged in descending order, with subject either in the soprano or the bass. Of course, as explained above, countersubject 3 in its stated form is in fact ineligible as a functioning bass voice since it simply prolongs $\hat{5}$. Nevertheless, that should not disqualify this music entirely as quadruple counterpoint, since the final note of countersubject 3 could easily be altered to F to provide the necessary resolution, yielding paradigm 4a, in accordance with Bach's practice in the *WTC I* C minor fugue.

Invertible Counterpoint for Category 2 Subjects

Thus far the examples have been restricted to subjects of category 1, those that end on I. But invertible counterpoints work along the same lines for the other two categories as well. Example 3-8 (b) illustrates the voice-leading matrix that underpins the structure of modulating subjects and their counterpoints. It should be borne in mind that the underlying harmonic and voice-leading structure of the modulating subject is almost identical to that of the answer for category 1, which itself is a transformation of the structure of the category 1 subject. Thus, we are really looking at the same basic tonal structure deployed in a different relationship to the imitative elements.

Example 3-23 shows the voice leading for the invertible counterpoint of Bach's Cantata BWV 21-II-5. At first glance this choral fugue appears to be in quadruple counterpoint. However, countersubjects 2 and 3, the inner parts of example 3-23 (a), are in fact treated too freely to be considered invertible countersubjects. A comparison of these elements in examples 3-23 (a) and 3-23 (b) will reveal how Bach redraws these counterpoints to strengthen the tonal meanings of the more important motivic elements, subject and countersubject 1, paradigms 7 and 8. The alto of example 3-23 (a) represents paradigm 9, but its ending is altered in example 3-23 (b) so as to form the answer for paradigm 6, $\hat{5} - \hat{4} - \hat{3}$.[23]

---

[23]Similar alterations to subjects are illustrated in example 2-26.

INVERTIBLE COUNTERPOINT

Example 3-23. Bach, Cantata BWV 21-II-5, invertible counterpoint

Invertible Counterpoint for Category 3 Subjects

Category 3 subjects present their own problems as regard invertible counterpoint (see example 3-8 (c)). Regardless of paradigm, the underlying subject structure is a motion to a half cadence. Of course, there are two possible forms for the answer, one a direct transposition, which of course poses no additional issues for invertible counterpoint, and the tonal answer that returns to I and thus demands significant alterations in voice leading.

Example 3-24, from the D minor fugue of *WTC I*, shows the invertible counterpoint upon which the subject and countersubject are based. As noted in example 2-63, the subject expresses a rising fifth, paradigm 13. The countersubject acts to reinforce the initial tonic harmony through an arpeggiation of d^2, a^1, and f^2, before proceeding down to c-sharp^2, giving an underlying $\hat{8}$ - $\hat{7}$ progression, paradigm 11. At each step along the way, consonant thirds and sixths fill out the progressions. The answer being real, there are no structural alterations to be considered in the transposed form.

Example 3-24. Bach, Fugue 6 in D minor (*WTC I*), invertible counterpoint

Invertible Counterpoint at the Tenth and Twelfth

So long as the interval of inversion is the octave and its multiples, invertible counterpoint retains its essential harmonic meaning. That is, each scale degree of the original is retained in the inversion, and the tonal meaning of the passage remains unaltered in its fundamental meaning. It is simply a reordering of the same pitch classes. But when the interval of inversion is the tenth or twelfth (or any other interval, for that matter), we are dealing with a quite different problem. Under inversion new pitch classes are introduced, representing different scale degrees. That invertible counterpoint at the tenth and twelfth is in a different class altogether than invertible counterpoint at the octave, seems to have been clearly recognized by Zarlino, for he considers inversion at the octave to be essentially the same as the original, but notes that double counterpoint takes on unique qualities when it introduces different pitch classes.[24] It is this aspect that evidently concerned Schenker most when he denounced double counterpoint:

> From the concept of a leading linear progression counterpointed by upper or lower thirds or sixths, it follows that the concept of so-called double counterpoint at the tenth or twelfth can have no validity.[25]

For Schenker the significance of music resides in its expression of tonality. Thus a line created by substituting one tonal meaning for another somehow denies the fundamental or natural meaning of the original.

Despite the fact that these counterpoints have an element of the arcane about them, their value lies in their ability to re-express given thematic materials in diverse ways, thereby reinforcing the fundamental musical

---

[24] See Zarlino, *The Art of Counterpoint*, 159.
[25] *Free Composition*, 78.

desideratum of diversity within unity.[26] Nevertheless, with the exception of some limited principles, it is impractical to make generalizations about the tonal meaning of such inversions, precisely because the inversion itself inevitably gives rise to new harmonic and voice-leading structures. Indeed, in the absence of an unambiguous tonal and harmonic basis for these counterpoints, we are forced to consider them more in terms of the older theory of inversion by interval.

The G minor fugue from *WTC II* is one of the most brilliant examples of invertible counterpoint at the octave, tenth and twelfth. Example 3-25 shows how the subject and countersubject express important voices of the matrix in inversion at the octave (paradigms 1 and 2a). The subject and countersubject pair is ideally suited to its treatment. Essentially sequential, and based on the consonant intervals of the sixths, thirds and octaves, each measure elaborates through contrary motion, assuring that parallels will be avoided regardless of the type of inversion employed.

Example 3-25. Bach, Fugue 16 in G minor (*WTC II*), invertible counterpoint at the octave

[26]Schenker was anything but critical of a similar technique in his analysis of Variation 21 of Brahms's Variations and Fugue on a Theme of Handel, Op. 24. Here Brahms reharmonizes the theme in the relative minor, causing a conflict in the tonal meaning of the fundamental line in relation to the original key of B-flat major and the operative key of G minor. While the context is quite different here, the type of reinterpretation involved is similar. See *Der Tonwille* IV, Part 2/3 (April–September, 1924):25–26.

Example 3-26 shows the inversion at the tenth.[27] Here paradigm 1 of the subject ($\hat{5}$-$\hat{4}$-$\hat{3}$) has become paradigm 2 ($\hat{3}$-$\hat{2}$-$\hat{1}$) in the relative major. The countersubject, however, projects the same tonal meaning as in the original form of example 3-25, but in the relative major. The resulting fifths at the beginning of each new bar are broken by the intervening contrary motion.

Example 3-26. Bach, Fugue 16 in G minor (*WTC II*), invertible counterpoint at the tenth

Example 3-27 shows the double counterpoint at the twelfth and its inversion. The subject reverts to its original meaning as paradigm 1 in G minor. The descending motion of the countersubject is reinterpreted as the descending fifth $\hat{2}$-$\hat{1}$-$\hat{7}$-$\hat{6}$-$\hat{5}$. This combination yields the new underlying harmonic meaning V–I rather than I–V–I. The fifths of Example 3-26 become beautifully ornamented 7-6 suspensions. Of course these inversions depend on the other free parts to complete the full voice-leading expression of the harmony.

Example 3-27. Bach, Fugue 16 in G minor (*WTC II*), invertible counterpoint at the twelfth

[27]In the fugue itself alterations are occasionally made at the end of a passage of invertible counterpoint in order to facilitate the linking of sections in the fugue.

INVERTIBLE COUNTERPOINT

In the later parts of the fugue, further combinations arise, based on the principle that a double counterpoint at the octave that uses contrary motion can bear the addition of extra parts in parallel thirds above. This is simply a logical result of the basic principles of invertible counterpoint. In adding a third above, an octave becomes a tenth and a tenth becomes a twelfth. In addition, one can consider that if a counterpoint is capable of inversion at octave or tenth, it can also sustain octave *and* tenth (see example 3-28).[28] Figure 3-2 shows the systematic arrangement of inversion possibilities that governs the form and development of this fugue.

Example 3-28. Bach, Fugue 16 in G minor (*WTC II*), compound invertible counterpoint

---

[28]The technique of adding a line in thirds above or sixth below is common throughout non-imitative music as well. In terms of a contrapuntal fabric, it actually reduces the complexity, since one or more parts relinquish their rhythmic independence. This is quite noticeable as in the final measures of Bach's G minor and B-flat minor fugues (*WTC II*).

Figure 3-2. Bach, Fugue 16 in G minor (*WTC II*), arrangement of subject and countersubject entries

m.	1	5	9	13	20	28	32	36	45	51	59	69
S:		S	CS			CS	S	CS		S	CS+3	S+3
A:		S	CS			S	CS		S+3	S-6	CS	CS
T:	S	CS			S				S	CS	S+3	S+3
B:		S	CS				S		S	CS	S	CS
interval		8va	8va	8va	8va	12th	10th	10th	8va	10th	10th	10th

The Art of Fugue of course includes examples of inversion at the tenth and twelfth. In example 3-29, the subject, with its two primary voices, paradigm 1 and paradigm 3, retains its structural meaning in both forms (compare example 2-14 (a). The countersubject, which centers on D and A, is transposed in the inversion so that it centers on A and E. The conjunct motion observed throughout the countersubject allows for structural reinterpretations as necessary.

Example 3-29. Bach, Contrapunctus 9 (*Art of Fugue*), a, mm. 35–42; b, mm. 89–96

INVERTIBLE COUNTERPOINT

Contrapunctus 10 includes invertible counterpoint at the tenth (see example 3-30). In this case the inversion causes quite radical changes to the structural interpretation. The original form of the countersubject (example 3-30 (a)) leads to a reinterpretation of the essential harmonic significance of the subject, giving it the harmonic character of category 3, paradigm 12a, producing an extended half cadence through a voice exchange on the IV. This form is also found in mm. 75–79 and 103–107. Transposition of the countersubject leads to a completely different structure in B-flat major, found in mm. 85–89 and 115–119 and in slightly altered form in mm. 52–56.

Example 3-30. Bach, Contrapunctus 10 (*Art of Fugue*), a, mm. 44–48, b, mm. 66–70

The analyses of invertible counterpoint presented in this chapter do not consider the compositional context within which invertible counterpoint operates, but merely illustrate the way in which it functions at foreground and high middleground levels of structure. Within broader sections and complete fugues, invertible counterpoint often becomes secondary to the unfolding of larger tonal areas as expressed primarily through the motions of the upper voice and bass, as the complete analyses of chapter 7 illustrate. However, these analyses do illustrate that the distilled voice-leading matrices and paradigmatic structure of examples 3-5 and 3-8 serve as a basis of many and varied invertible counterpoints. These patterns are not the only possible foundations of invertible counterpoint, but they do facilitate invertible counterpoint in the most direct and logical manner, and they do appear with considerable frequency in the literature.

These voice-leading matrices provide a means for reconciling the technique of invertible counterpoint with Schenker's theory by placing invertible counterpoint firmly within the tonal and contrapuntal principles of his theory. Indeed, it is Schenker's middleground that enables us to understand the true structural basis of invertible counterpoint in the tonal era as a counterpoint of linear progressions rather than simply a series of invertible intervals. These analyses demonstrate a method for understanding the working of double, triple, and quadruple counterpoint at the octave through a single, unified tonal perspective that accords with Schenker's structuralist stance. Further, this structural approach clarifies the fundamental distinction between invertible counterpoint at the octave, which is closely tied with concepts of strict counterpoint and structural levels, and invertible counterpoint at the tenth and twelfth, which at best bears a loose connection with such principles.

When seen in the larger context of entire compositions, the passages shown here essentially function as areas of tonal prolongation, often as statements of the local tonal center in the succession of *Stufen* which a given fugue traverses. Therefore, when we begin to consider the tonal structure and voice-leading of entire fugues and other contrapuntal pieces the considerations of invertible counterpoint in fact recede, in favor of a more traditional Schenkerian devotion to the upper voice and bass lines independent of counterpoint. But this shift of focus simply reflects a shift in priorities as we proceed through the levels to the background. Whereas the surface is concerned with developing textures and motives, the deep levels are concerned with the broad sweep of tonal and linear events that project a sense of direction and resolution.

CHAPTER 4

Fugal Exposition

Tonal Structure in Fugal Exposition

Schenker's brief discussion of fugue in *Free Composition* provides a useful focus for understanding the tonal structure of fugal exposition:

> The fifth relation between the first three entries (subject, answer, subject) provided the form with direction and stability.[1]

As his accompanying analysis of Bach's D minor fugue from *WTC I* illustrates, the first three entries provide a I–V–I harmonic basis which establishes the tonality and undergirds the exposition as a subsection of the whole (see example 4-1). We can understand Schenker to mean by *direction* that the three statements give an initial sense of harmonic and voice-leading progression away from and back to the tonic, and by *stability* that they establish an initial tonic-prolonging section that is completed by the third statement. In this view, then, the subject-answer-subject plan encompasses a three-element harmonic structure, I–V–I, expressed in two motions, a departure from and a return to the tonic.[2]

Example 4-1. From Schenker, *Free Composition*, Figure 156, 1 (*WTC I*, Fugue 6 in D-minor)

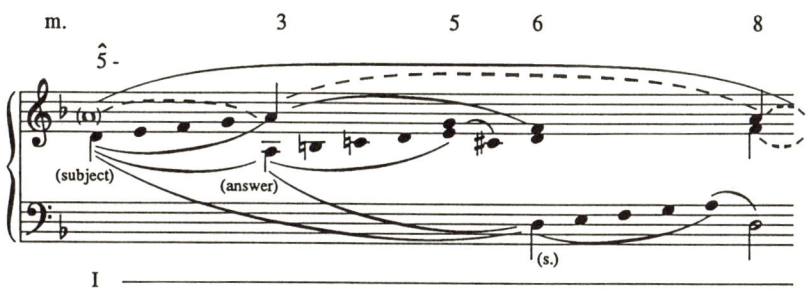

Schenker's discussion, encapsulating as it does the structural issues of fugal exposition in a characteristically aphoristic manner, provides a good point of departure for considering the tonal structure of fugal exposition, but it requires fleshing out to embrace other tonal structures and other schematic arrangements.

In general terms, the nature of fugal exposition is the combination of a formal scheme of imitative entries and a basic tonal pattern centering on I

---

[1] Schenker, *Free Composition*, 143.
[2] In addition, we may infer from Schenker's use of the past tense an implication of historical causality, that the transpositional interval of the fifth motivated to some extent the development of the standard tonal structure of fugal exposition.

and V. Above all, it is the tonal structure of the subject that determines the tonal structure of fugal exposition. Therefore, in general terms the subject and answer categories and paradigms outlined in chapter 2 serve as a basis for the harmonic plan of fugal expositions. Figure 4-1 outlines the basic relationship between subject and answer categories and harmonic structure.

Figure 4-1. Harmonic plans for four-part expositions

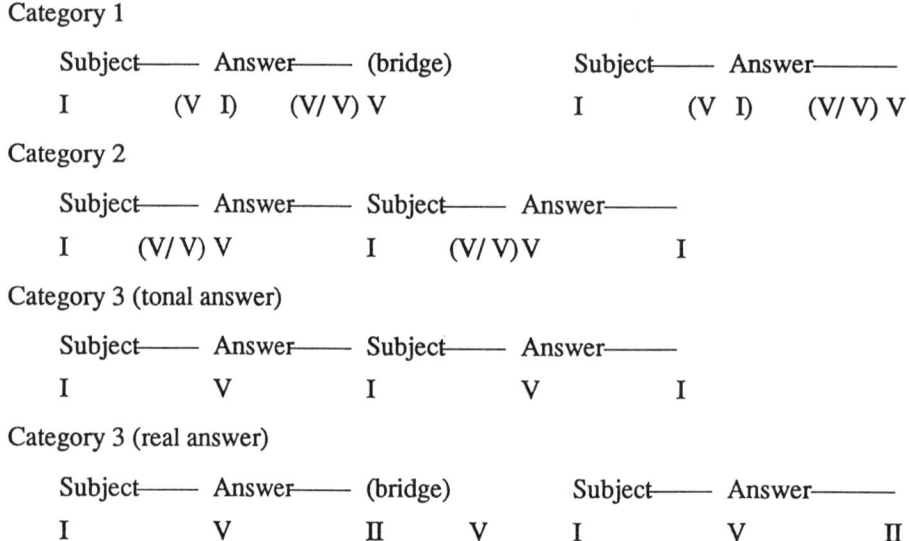

The fundamental tonal fact of any subject is its assertion of I at the outset. Thus, the consistent tonal feature of all four harmonic plans in figure 4-1 is that, following a digression to V at some point within the subject or answer, the beginning of the third entry marks a return to I. Beyond that, divergences mark the correlations between harmonic and motivic forces in the different plans. The plan for category 1 includes a bridge in order to provide for the return to I at the third entry. In category 2 (modulating subjects), the conclusion of the answer itself marks the return to I, thus obviating the need for a bridge.[3] Category 3 may follow the general harmonic plan of either category 1 or category 2, depending on the nature of the answer paradigm, tonal or real, as described in chapter 2. In this broader context, then, Schenker's outline above relates specifically to the tonal patterns of categories 1 and 3 (real answer), where the crucial harmonic activity revolves around the coincidence of the return to I and the beginning of the third entry, but does not apply to the others.

---

[3]A bridge may yet be introduced to accommodate a change of register or a contrasting motivic development, or to prepare a specific tonal problem of the third entry. In Bach's Fugue 7 in E-flat major (*WTC I*), the bridge before the third entry serves two functions: it accommodates the V required to harmonize the first note of the subject in the bass ($\hat{5}$), and it accommodates a repetition and development of the link between the end of the subject and the beginning of the answer in m. 2.

Exposition Schemes

Schenker's recognition of the primacy of the three-statement exposition (subject-answer-subject) is remarkable in light of the prevailing notion that four-part fugue is fundamental. But three-part fugues (and three-statement expositions) in fact predominate in much of the keyboard repertoire, including the *Well-Tempered Clavier*.[4] It is the polyphonic tradition of four singing parts in four distinct ranges, as well as the technique of four-part writing, which were adapted and developed by seventeenth-century composers of the keyboard *ricercare* and *canzona*, particularly Frescobaldi and Froberger, rather than any true contrapuntal necessity, that accounts for the venerable pedagogical tradition of four-part fugue. This is not to dispute the validity of four-part fugue, but to say that from a structural point of view, three entries is all that is really required to fulfill the basic tonal and motivic requirements.

The basis of fugal exposition is the alternation of subject and answer entries through two or more parts. The order of entries can be described as an *exposition scheme*. For any exposition, the number of possible schemes is the factorial of the number of parts: 2 schemes for 2 parts, 6 for 3, 24 for 4, 140 for 5, and so on. Despite the exponentially increasing permutations, only a few of the many possibilities are found with any regularity in actual fugues, since two design principles severely restrict the number:

(1) No subject entry should occur between the ranges of previous subject entries. This rule precludes later entries in the middle parts.

(2) In three parts, the upper parts should alternate subject and answer in order to preserve a close register between the upper parts. In four or more parts subject and answer should alternate reading up or down through the parts.

The three part format thus reflects a trio texture of two high parts against an independent bass. The four and five part formats reflect traditions of vocal writing where each successive part, reading up or down, utilizes a register one half octave higher or lower than the next. Figure 4-2 illustrates the exposition schemes that respect these principles.

It is important to observe that the addition of a fourth or fifth voice does not markedly alter the number of practical exposition schemes available, since the aesthetic considerations embodied in the two basic rules limit the geometric expansion of permutations. Among the four-voice and five voice schemes shown in figure 4-2, those in which there is a gap between entrances in the upper parts (4 (c) and 5 (c) are extremely infrequently to be found. This likely has to do with the desirability of the exposition to project a clear and unbroken registral expansion through the upper parts in those cases that do not begin with the upper part.

---

[4]Three-part fugal textures are also quite common in the Italianate trio-sonata and in the fugal allegro of the French overture.

Figure 4-2. Exposition schemes

Two parts:

2 a.		2 b.	
S	S———	A———	
B	A———	S———	

Three parts:

3 a.		3 b.	3 c.	
S	S———	S—	A———	
A	A———	A———	S———	
B	S—	S—	S—	

Four parts:

4 a.		4 b.	4 c.	4 d.	
S	S———	A-	A-	S—	
A	A———	S—	S———	A———	
T	S—	A———	A———	S———	
B	A-	S———	S—	A-	

Five parts:

5 a.		5 b.	5 c.	5 d.	
S1	S———	S	S	S—	
S2	A———	A-	A-	A———	
A	S—	S—	S———	S———	
T	A-	A———	A———	A-	
B	S	S———	S—	S	

In addition to the basic schemes outlined above, we must recognize the possibility of paired entries in four parts, such that the third and fourth entries represent an imitation of the first and second (see figure 4-3)). The typical example of this is A,S,B,T (exposition scheme 4 (f)). Despite the fact that these schemes break rule (1) outlined above, these plans reflect a traditional vocal format dating back to Palestrina and earlier.[5]

Figure 4-3. Exposition schemes with paired entries

Four parts:

4 e.		4 f.	
S	S—	A———	
A	A-	S———	
T	S———	A-	
B	A———	S—	

---

[5]Palestrina, Kyrie from *Missa Dies sanctificatus* is one among many examples (see Knud Jeppesen, *Counterpoint: The Polyphonic Vocal Style of the Sixteenth Century*, trans. Glen Haydon (New York: Prentice-Hall, 1939), 275). This plan is also reflected in a number of keyboard fugues, such as *WTC II*, Fugue 22 in B-flat minor (example 4-6).

Exposition Patterns for Category 1 Subjects

Combination of the exposition schemes given above with the subject paradigms of chapter 2 gives a specific and limited number of *exposition patterns* that can act as middleground voice-leading structures for expositions, along the lines of Schenker's model in example 4-1. These exposition patterns provide a means of relating subject paradigms to the middleground voice-leading structures at the basis of tonal structure in fugal exposition.

Example 4-2 illustrates the exposition patterns for subject paradigm 1 in each of the possible three-part exposition schemes, and thus represents the basic voice-leading structures implied by paradigm 1 in three parts. The labelling convention employed for exposition patterns has two components. The first number (and letter) represents the subject paradigm and the following number and letter represents the exposition scheme (from figures 4-2 or 4-3). Thus exposition pattern 1-3 (a) illustrates the voice leading implicit in subject paradigm 1 deployed in a three-part exposition of descending entries.

Example 4-2. Three-part exposition patterns for paradigm 1

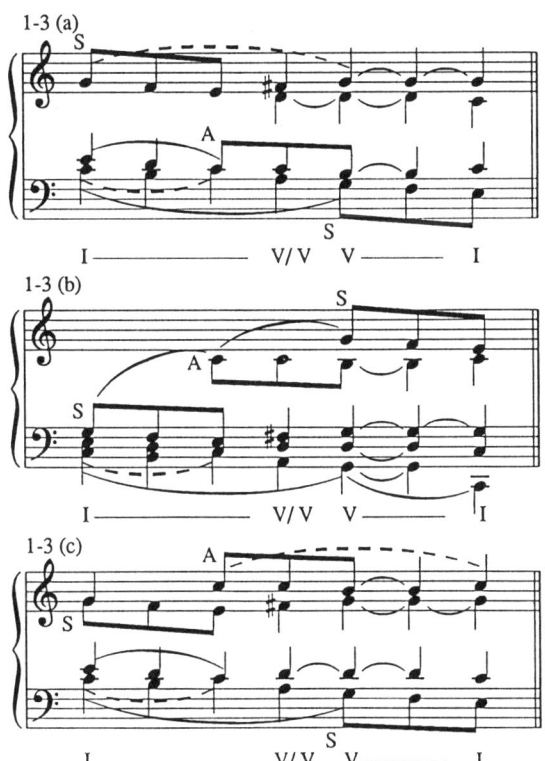

In exposition pattern 1-3 (a) the first statement of the subject is represented by the $\hat{5}$-$\hat{4}$-$\hat{3}$ linear progression and by the implied voices $\hat{3}$-$\hat{2}$-$\hat{1}$ and $\hat{8}$-$\hat{7}$-$\hat{8}$, giving the three voices of the voice-leading matrix. Transformation of paradigm 1 into an answer gives an incomplete neighbor motion $\hat{8}$-$\hat{8}$-$\hat{7}$, where the initial structural note is part of a tonic prolongation and the final note marks a temporary motion to V. The answer, operating in a larger context as the beginning of an inner-voice neighbor motion $\hat{8}$-$\hat{7}$-$\hat{8}$, is a motion to V within a tonic-prolonging exposition, as shown in example 2-2. The co-termini of the subject paradigm, $\hat{5}$ and $\hat{3}$, continue as sharp-$\hat{4}$-$\hat{5}$ and $\hat{3}$-$\hat{2}$, soprano and alto voices in the harmonization of the answer, while the bass—implied or stated by the answer—continues with $\hat{8}$-$\hat{6}$-$\hat{5}$.

While the beginning of the subject implies I, the beginning of the third entry will suggest V instead for paradigm 1 and for other paradigms that begin on $\hat{5}$, in the absence of an initial tonic. Herein lies the wonderful duality of function that makes $\hat{5}$ such a flexible and workable, and commonly seen, initial note for a fugue subject. Thus despite the basic harmonic scheme for category 1 subjects (figure 4-1), no bridge is necessary for simple expositions based on paradigm 1. Instead, the end of the third entry realizes the return to I, giving a satisfying coordinated resolution of both motive and harmony at the end of the exposition. The $\hat{5}$-$\hat{4}$-$\hat{3}$ of the third entry thus fills a linear span over the V–I progression, whereas the $\hat{5}$-$\hat{4}$-$\hat{3}$ of the first entry expands a tonic prolongation. In harmonizing the third statement, the first part continues with $\hat{5}$ as a common tone and also uses $\hat{2}$-$\hat{1}$, the continuation and completion of the previous motion $\hat{3}$-$\hat{2}$. The second part, which began as the answer $\hat{8}$-$\hat{7}$, continues with $\hat{7}$-$\hat{8}$, completing a large neighbor motion. Whereas the first statement implies three voices, the third entry suggests only a single linear progression.

The rising exposition scheme of exposition pattern 1-3 (b) reorganizes the same voices in a different way. It allows an authentic cadence at the end of the third entry. Exposition pattern 1-3 (c) is a much more compact arrangement. Each of these exposition patterns is effective in its own right. This observation is reflected in the fact that all three exposition patterns are frequently found in the literature, in contrast to some other subject paradigms for which examples in the repertoire are seldom or never encountered because of the fundamental voice-leading defects that result. Although the exposition patterns include up to five voices, not all need be present all the time. Some may be implied, in the manner seen in chapters 2 and 3. Thus the tripartite texture that these models represent is based on a four- or five-part polyphony of strict voice leading.

The addition of a fourth part to exposition patterns for category 1 subjects has important effects of the structure of fugue, for the end of the fourth entry (answer) and thus the end of the exposition, is V, not I, creating a disjunction between harmonic and motivic development. A fifth entry or a redundant entry (subject) can rectify this by providing a tonic conclusion to the exposition, but then the composer must beware of excessive length and repetition.

Similar exposition patterns can without difficulty be established for any of the other subject paradigms, and developing exposition patterns along these lines is a useful and instructive process. Construction of exposition patterns can reveal important relationships between subject paradigm and exposition scheme, that is, why certain subject paradigms are found exclusively in certain schemes and not in others. Each pattern sets up its own expectations, limits, and contrapuntal problems. Space considerations prohibit a complete inventory here. Chapter 4 instead illustrates a method for considering issues of voice-leading in fugal exposition and explores the relationship of exposition patterns to the voice-leading of selected fugal expositions in each of the three subject categories. Since category 1 is by far the largest group of subjects, it is the most fertile ground for recognizing recurring patterns of voice-leading in fugal expositions. The following examples illustrate ways in which actual expositions work out the possibilities of the exposition patterns suggested above.

The C major fugue of *WTC II* illustrates exposition pattern 1-3 (c).[6] In example 4-3, the answer paradigm $\hat{8}$ - $\hat{7}$ in the upper-voice is completed as a neighbor motion $\hat{8}$ - $\hat{7}$ - $\hat{8}$ by c^2 at the conclusion of the exposition (m. 13). The counterpoint to the answer begins by filling out the interval e^1-c^1 and then passes to the bass note a in descending stepwise motion ($\hat{8}$ - $\hat{7}$ - $\hat{6}$), after which it leaps to the alto voice sharp- $\hat{4}$ - $\hat{5}$ to form the cadence. The entry of the third part completes a descending fourth, c^1-g, begun by the counterpoint, and continues the descent initiated by the first statement of the subject. The upper part essentially prolongs the leading tone, using upper and lower neighbors to provide consonance with the essential notes of the subject, and resolves to the tonic in the manner of exposition pattern 1-3 (c). The middle part utilizes the notes d^1 and c^1, leading to the cadence motion $\hat{2}$ - $\hat{1}$ at m. 13. With the exception of the retained d^1 in the tenor, the voice leading of exposition pattern 1-3 (c) is entirely preserved in its proper register.

Incidentally, the third statement contains an unusual example of motive overstepping the bounds of strict contrapuntal-harmonic practice: although the c in the lower part at m. 9 is unalterable as part of the subject, it clashes with the prolonged V. A bridge, returning the music to I, would have rectified this problem. But through the changing-note figure in the upper part, Bach gives the structural dissonance a consonant guise on the surface. In mm. 10–13 the upper parts are unrestricted, since there is no countersubject. The soprano line prolongs b^1 through a double-neighbor motion which provides local consonant support for the bass f, which at a deeper level is a passing seventh of V. The middle part, a continuation of the first statement, moves stepwise from the hypothetical alto to the tenor voice (mm. 9–11), cadencing with the active tenor voice notes $\hat{2}$ - $\hat{1}$ rather than the static common tone of the alto. The whole of the exposition is controlled, while working within the framework of pattern 2, by a series of descending tenths, shown in example 4-3. At m. 11 the tenths above the bass

---

[6]The subject and answer are analyzed in example 2-8.

Example 4-3. Bach, Fugue 1 in C Major (*WTC II*), mm. 1–13

switch from the upper to the middle part, and continue to the cadence, at which point the bass regains its main linear progression f-e, and gives parallel sixths instead. The single directional force of this stepwise descent unifies the two complementary harmonic motions of the exposition.

Example 4-4, showing the main structural elements of Bach's C minor fugue exposition (*WTC II*), is also based on exposition pattern 1-3 (c).[7] But in this case the use of a countersubject places specific constraints on the implied voice-leading connections suggested by exposition pattern 1-3 (c) (see example 3-10). At the entry of the answer, the countersubject works out the structural notes of exposition pattern 1-3 (c) through a descending linear progression, the end of which replicates the $\hat{3}$ - $\hat{2}$ - $\hat{1}$ of the voice-leading matrix at the dominant level as $\hat{7}$ - $\hat{6}$ - $\hat{5}$. This progression therefore omits the sharp- $\hat{4}$ of the alto voice seen in the previous example.

Completion of the harmonic motion coincides with fulfillment of the imitative plan at m. 5. A satisfying linear descent from g^1, the beginning of the fugue, to e-flat results in the bass, providing direction and shape to the whole. The end of the third statement is followed immediately by a motion to c, completing the structural bass voice of the exposition.

The bridge serves two functions, neither of which were necessary in the previous example, but both of which are important here. First, the bridge accommodates the necessary raising of the leading tone that establishes the dominant function of V. Second, and just as important, the bridge

---

[7]The subject and answer are analyzed in example 2-5.

FUGAL EXPOSITION   117

Example 4-4. Bach, Fugue 2 in C minor (*WTC II*), mm. 1–5

prepares the register of the upper part for the restatement of the countersubject in m. 4. Since the countersubject to the answer follows the bass voice of exposition pattern 1-3 (c), and since the upper-voice must restate the countersubject at the third entry, a deviation from the hypothetical pattern occurs. The upper voice is not free to express the suggested voice-leading, but must obey the restrictions of the imitation. It thus uses notes of the inner voices of exposition pattern 1-3 (c), notes which are properly continuations of the first part (the middle voice), not the second. Consequently the middle part uses the contrapuntal voice which is properly that of the upper part, i.e. $\hat{7}$ - $\hat{8}$. The theoretical voices are inverted in the two upper parts, resulting in the downward registral shift at m. 4.

The structural role of the bridge can now be understood: it effects the change of register, connecting the end of the answer to the beginning of the countersubject, while at the same time converting the dominant from minor to major. The opening register of the upper voice is restored at the end of the exposition by the upward octave transfer in m. 5. Thus it is fundamentally the countersubject that causes structural modifications to the voice-leading, in terms of the theoretical pattern, and necessitates the bridge. In other cases, such as the F major fugue of *WTC I*, the countersubject follows the alto voice of exposition pattern 1-3 (c), allowing its transposition at the third statement to follow the hypothetical upper voice: sharp- $\hat{4}$ - $\hat{5}$ becomes $\hat{7}$ - $\hat{8}$.

Examples 4-3 and 4-4 are among the simplest examples of the application of exposition patterns in the *WTC*. Each follows very strictly the voice leadings set up through the original subject paradigm and exposition scheme, with modifications as necessitated by surface characteristics of the subject or by the specific contrapuntal requirements of a countersubject.

Example 4-5 illustrates how exposition pattern 1-3 (a) (descending series of entries) contrasts to the above examples. In the exposition of Bach's F-sharp major fugue (*WTC I*) the subject leads directly into the first structural note of the answer (see example 2-26). That is, the g-sharp[1] in m. 2 gives a smooth stepwise connection to the initial note of the answer. Since the subject leads by stepwise motion directly to the beginning of the answer, the countersubject begins with a leap away from the end of the subject. The f-sharp[2] which begins the countersubject connects with the exposed initial tonic f-sharp[2] of the subject. The countersubject itself develops an ascending third motive first seen in the subject (see the brackets in the graph), and this motive is extensively developed throughout the fugue (see chapter 7). Nevertheless, the essential sharp- $\hat{4}$ - $\hat{5}$ structural motion still appears at the end of the countersubject.

Example 4-5. Bach, Fugue 13 in F-sharp Major (*WTC I*), mm. 1–7

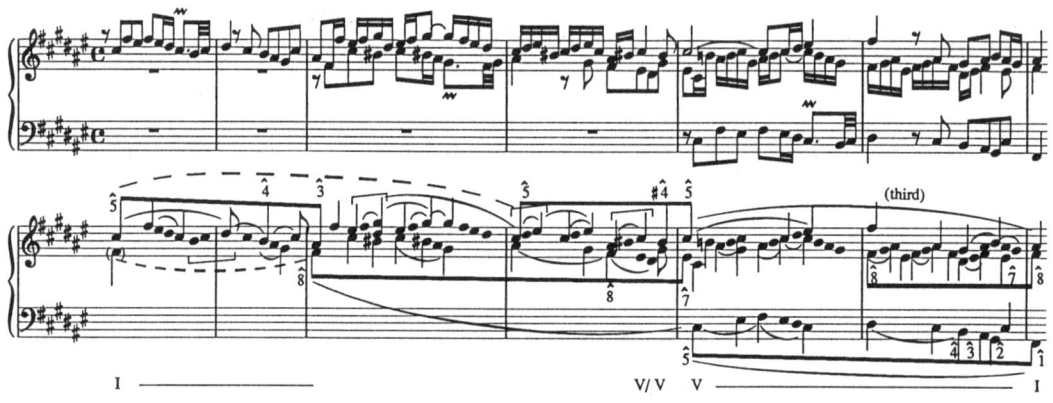

The third entry occurs an octave below the position of exposition pattern 1-3 (a), but discounting this octave separation, the answer leads in a stepwise manner to the beginning of the third entry. Although in this case the third entry could be played an octave higher without crossing parts, the octave separation gives a greater registral space to the exposition and emphasizes the trio-like style of the composition.

In the third entry the subject is altered so that it ends on $\hat{1}$, not $\hat{3}$, giving a root position cadence on I, and providing a formal close to the exposition (see Example 2-26). This alteration can be understood structurally as an exchange of roles between outer voices, so that the soprano takes the third-progression $\hat{5}$ - $\hat{4}$ - $\hat{3}$ which properly belongs to the subject, and the lower part takes a simple bass motion as example 4-5 shows. In this way the upper voice, which according to exposition pattern 1-3 (a) is a prolonged dominant with no directional force, now incorporates a directed linear progression. The upper voice assumes a dynamic role in the overall shape of the exposition, and the problem of upper voice direction in the hypothetical exposition structure is solved. The countersubject, in the middle part at the third entry, is not affected by these alterations, and maintains the $\hat{7}$ - $\hat{8}$ motion of exposition pattern 1-3 (a).

FUGAL EXPOSITION   119

The B-flat minor fugue of *WTC II* demonstrates the effects of a four-part exposition for category 1 subjects, and illustrates exposition scheme 4 (f), in which the fourth entry is in the tenor. From a structural perspective, the first three entries follow the format of exposition pattern 1-3 (c), and the fourth entry can be understood as an additional entry.

Example 4-6. Bach, Fugue 22 in B-flat minor (*WTC II*), mm. 1–21

The characteristic feature of the subject is a long initial ascent (see example 2-12). In fact, the extended ascent of the subject allows a redistribution of tonal events, and it is the resultant disjunction of structure and formal design that animates the exposition: as an element of formal design concludes, a tonal motion begins, while tonal arrivals take place in the midst of formal units. The initial ascent allows the dominant (F minor) to be established half way through the answer, in m. 7. This accommodates the conversion of the dominant from minor-V to major-V^7 in the latter part of the answer, rather than within the bridge. As a result, the bridge acts as a prolongation of V^7, leading to the return to I at the beginning of the third entry, as demanded by the initial tonic of the subject (see example 4-6). As shown in example 3-13, the countersubject echoes the ascent of the subject, after which it provides the $\hat{8}$-$\hat{7}$-$\hat{8}$ voice of the voice-leading matrix. But, as noted in chapter 3, the expected $\hat{7}$-$\hat{8}$ conclusion is supplanted by an *inganno* progression to flat-$\hat{7}$. The conclusion of the answer and countersubject thus represents not I of V but V^7 of I.

The role of the bridge can thus be understood principally as providing a suitable rhythmic means of preparing for the third entry on the downbeat of a new measure. The third entry itself is unremarkable, but the countersubject appears in the alto again, rather than the soprano. This fundamental digression must be seen as growing out of several considerations: if the countersubject were placed in the soprano, either it would be an octave higher, which would overstep the register of the exposition, or if the countersubject were given to the soprano in the lower register, would cause the alto to go too low, and to intrude upon the territory reserved for the fourth entry. Also, if given in the soprano voice an octave higher, the bridge would have to be an ascending one, which would work against Bach's larger plan to utilize a series of descending episodes based on the invertible counterpoint of the first bridge.

The *inganno* ending is repeated at m. 15. The resulting trajectory to IV precludes the introduction of the answer at this time, and instead a short bridge based on the inversion of the previous bridge prepares for the answer in m. 17. As in other fugues with countersubjects, the problem of countersubject range is dealt with here by giving the countersubject twice in the first part, and not at all in the second part during the exposition. Specifically, this allows the leading-tone, a-natural, at the end of the answer to resolve in the proper register to b-flat at the beginning of the third entry, as shown in example 4-6.

Only the fourth and final entry of the exposition ends like the subject, on the minor third of the acting tonal center. It ends with a perfect cadence bridged only on the surface by the 9-8 suspension in the upper voice, and the countersubject finally gives the previously suppressed sharp-$\hat{4}$-$\hat{5}$ motion, providing a fitting conclusion to the exposition. Motivic and formal aspects resolve at this point, but the harmony has moved to V. The play of $\hat{3}$ as third of I and leading-tone to IV (measures 5 and 15), and the corresponding play of $\hat{7}$ as third of V and leading-tone of I (measures 7, 9, and 21) through inflected forms (natural and raised), animates the tonal motion of the exposition in a manner which is impossible in the major key, where both $\hat{3}$ and $\hat{7}$ remain unchanged whether functioning as mediants of I and V or leading-tones of IV and I.[8]

---

[8]The same play operates at the end of the fourth and fifth entries of the B-flat minor fugue in *WTC I*.

Bach's D minor fugue (*WTC II*) illustrates a similar level of complexity, made possible principally by the lengthy melodic ascent which provides the space necessary to allow these structural complexities to occur. In contrast to the transparent texture of the *WTC II* C major fugue, where formal plan and tonal structure coincide beautifully, here formal design and structural design are in opposition. The effect, further intensified by chromaticism, is one of much greater dramatic tension.

Paradigms 2 and 2a ($\hat{3}$-$\hat{2}$-$\hat{1}$ and $\hat{5}$-$\hat{4}$-$\hat{3}$-$\hat{2}$-$\hat{1}$)

Crucial to the structure of expositions based on paradigm 1 is the final note of the subject ($\hat{3}$), which to a large extent determines the tonal structure of the exposition and accommodates a full range of exposition schemes. Also, the disposition of $\hat{1}$ and $\hat{5}$ as structural notes at the beginning of the subject, whether as initiators of linear progressions, or as initial tonics or dominants, contributes strongly to the outlines of the voice-leading patterns. While initiating notes are no different for subject paradigms 2 and 2a than for those previously discussed, the different ending note ($\hat{1}$ rather than $\hat{3}$) yields very different structural patterns. Concluding the subject on $\hat{1}$ also contributes greatly to the stylistic effect of fugal exposition: the series of perfect cadences—actual or elided—which usually occurs, sectionalizes the exposition. Further, each statement of the subject or answer is a complete voice-leading unit, not dependent on subsequent closure. This allows a final subject entry in the soprano as the conclusion of a fugue in a perfect authentic cadence.[9]

Example 4-7 presents the three-part exposition patterns for paradigm 2. The initial tonic is of course necessary in paradigm 2. In its transposition in the answer, the initial tonic assumes its most important structural role, that of linking the end of the subject to the beginning of the answer through the common chord-tone $\hat{5}$. Since $\hat{1}$ and $\hat{5}$ sound together at this point, the answer more naturally enters above the subject, avoiding the perfect fourth that implies an unresolved I–six-four, shown in exposition pattern 2-3 (a). Beyond this basic defect of exposition pattern 2-3 (a), the range of the parts is very compact, and thus limits growth in the exposition. The bridge returns to I through the tritone ($\hat{4}$-$\hat{7}$). Exposition pattern 2-3 (b) rectifies the problems of exposition pattern 2-3 (a), but in its continuation the upper voice traverses a rather wide range and the leading tone does not resolve in its original register. Exposition pattern 2-3 (c) offers a more consistent registral development, and the leading tone of the answer is conveniently resolved by the initial tonic of the third entry. This is the pattern most frequently found in the literature. Indeed, it is the only pattern found for paradigm 2 in the *WTC*.[10] In four parts, only two exposition schemes are possible, B,T,A,S and A,S,B,T, for in any other arrangement an unresolved fourth will occur at the beginning of the answer in the second and fourth entries.

---

[9] See *WTC I* F-sharp minor and *WTC II* F-sharp minor fugues.
[10] Fugues in C-sharp minor and B major (*WTC I*) and in E major (*WTC II*).

Example 4-7. Three-part exposition patterns for paradigm 2

Example 4-8. Bach, Fugue in E Major (*WTC II*), mm. 1–9

The E major fugue from *WTC II* is a good example of an exposition based on exposition pattern 2-3 (c). The subject includes an upper incomplete neighbor, A, which in the answer provides an ascent to the tonic (see example 2-19). As in the B-flat minor fugue (*WTC II*), V is reached in the middle of the answer, allowing an *inganno* cadence. The countersubject structure is based not on $\hat{5}$-sharp-$\hat{4}$-$\hat{5}$, but on $\hat{5}$-$\hat{4}$-$\hat{3}$ (compare the tenor part in mm. 5-6). This permits the third entry to begin without any intervening bridge material. That is, the function of the bridge in exposition pattern 2-3 (c) is concatenated with the end of the answer. The third and fourth entries thus provide an unbroken ascent to e^2 (m. 6), the apex of the fourth entry, an ascent which is elegantly balanced by an even descent of the upper voice to the half cadence in m. 9. Although the fourth entry is again accompanied by the *inganno* form of the countersubject, effecting a return to I at m. 7, the following measures provide for a concluding restatement of the countersubject in its real form in mm. 8–9

Example 4-9 shows the exposition patterns for three-part exposition for paradigm 2a ($\hat{5}$-$\hat{4}$-$\hat{3}$-$\hat{2}$-$\hat{1}$). In exposition pattern 2a-3 (b) the series of entries gradually expands a linear descent, whereas in exposition pattern 2a-3 (a) each succeeding entry increases the upper register by half an octave. In any case, no bridge is required unless the presence of an initial tonic or other strong tonic expression demands that the beginning of the third entry mark a return to I.

A major interest in harmonized settings of subjects and answers based on paradigm 2a is the variety of possible voice-leading details. In paradigms 1 and 2, the three harmonies I–V–I which support the subject are distributed evenly through the three notes of the main linear progression. But in $\hat{5}$-$\hat{4}$-$\hat{3}$-$\hat{2}$-$\hat{1}$ type subjects the same three main chords, which must support five notes, can be distributed in a variety of ways.[11] (In the answer, comparable variety can occur in the placement of the beginning of the secondary dominant.) This variety does not affect the overall exposition structure, but gives many alternatives in surface detail for expositions of paradigm 2a subjects.

Exposition pattern 2a-3 (b) is especially interesting since in its overall plan the upper voice accommodates a descending third, $\hat{5}$-$\hat{4}$-$\hat{3}$ across the entire exposition. The third entry (in the bass) begins as part of the V prolongation, and returns the music to I at its conclusion. The main lines of the upper voices here are the descending third $\hat{5}$-$\hat{4}$-$\hat{3}$ in the soprano, and $\hat{8}$-$\hat{7}$-$\hat{8}$ in the alto, two principle voices of the voice-leading matrix. The three thematic entries provide a continuous stepwise descent. In exposition pattern 2a-3 (c) the first structural note of the answer, c^2, can serve as the beginning of an $\hat{8}$-$\hat{7}$-$\hat{8}$ upper-voice if the upper voices are exchanged at the third entry (shown by small notes). In this case the upper voice retains its higher register but expresses a more static neighbor motion rather than a linear progression.

---

[11]Schenker shows various harmonizations of $\hat{5}$-$\hat{4}$-$\hat{3}$-$\hat{2}$-$\hat{1}$ in *Free Composition*, Fig. 16.

Example 4-9. Three-part exposition patterns for paradigm 2a

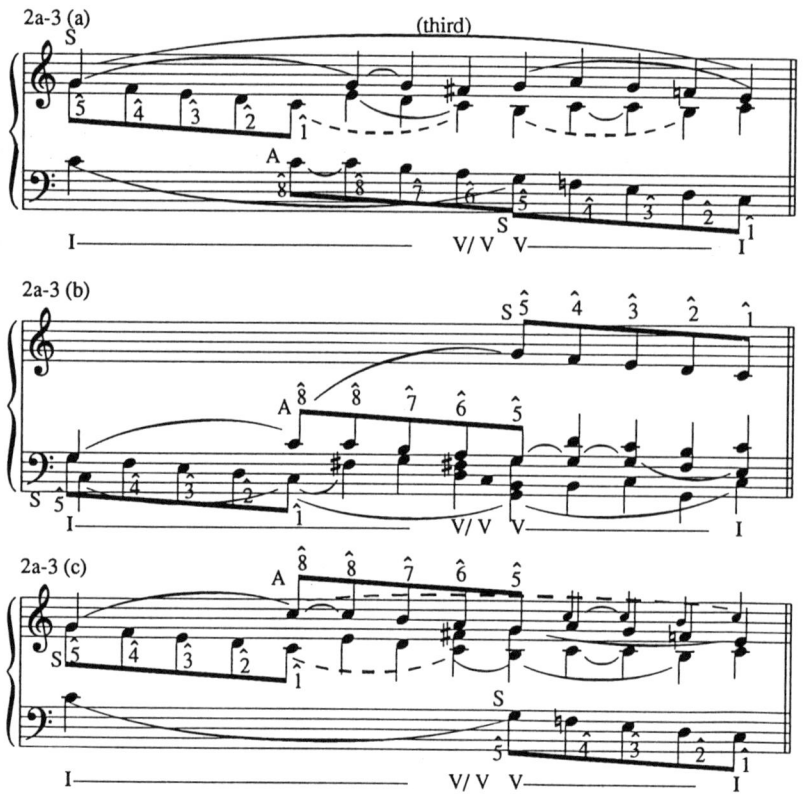

Example 4-10. Bach, Fugue 8 in D-sharp minor (*WTC I*), mm. 1–10

The *WTC I* D-sharp minor fugue is a good example of exposition pattern 2a-3 (b) (see example 4-10). As example 2-23 illustrated, the counterpoint to the answer projects a broad arpeggiation of I before leaping up to the leading tone of V in m. 5. The presence of an emphatic initial tonic makes a bridge necessary before the third entry. The upper voice of the bridge essentially unfolds the dominant in an ascending fashion, balancing the descending progression of the answer. The overall shape of the upper voice in the exposition is a rising arpeggio through the tonic chord, which is completed during the course of the third entry when the upper voice reaches a-sharp^2, the head tone of the entire composition, after which a fifth descent provides for the perfect authentic cadence that concludes the exposition using the notes indicated in exposition pattern 2a-3 (c). This ascent establishes the upper register as the obligatory register for the fundamental line, and the head tone is reasserted at measures 24 and 58, and very powerfully at measure 78, in the concluding augmentation stretto of the fugue (see example 6-5).

Example 4-11 illustrates how exposition pattern 2a-3 (a) compares to the previous pattern.[12] Here the descending order of entries provides a continual stepwise motion downwards and the omission of an initial tonic allows an uninterrupted descent with no bridge. Of course, the fact that the subject itself contains two structural voices in parallel sixths impacts on the unfolding of the voice leading throughout the course of the exposition. The countersubject which accompanies the answer essentially follows the same structure as answer paradigm 1, expanded by an upper neighbor. This is the alto line of exposition pattern 2a-3 (a). The countersubject to the third entry thus follows the outline of subject paradigm 1, as shown in the graph, and the use of a countersubject once again occasions the inversion of the voices of the exposition pattern, as compared to the actual music.

Example 4-11. Bach, Fugue 3 in C-sharp major (*WTC I*), mm. 1–7

Each of the polyphonic lines of the subject has a direct continuation in the succeeding music. The counterpoint to the answer continues the final note of the upper line ($\hat{8}$), while the upper of the answer's two implied-voices continues the opening $\hat{5}$ of the subject in the middle voices. The counterpoint accompanies the answer in parallel tenths.

---

[12]The music is given in example 1-16.

The descending motion of the answer prepares the register for the third entry. The third entry itself functions according to exposition pattern 2a-3 (a), returning the music to I at its conclusion. At the beginning of the third entry the upper voice reestablishes its high register through f-sharp^2, connecting the exposed g-sharp^2 of measure 3 with the counterpoint to the third entry.

The descending order of entries allows the completion of a stepwise octave-descent in the lowest voice, unifying the exposition.[13] The upper voice likewise completes a descending third-progression $\hat{5} - \hat{4} - \hat{3}$, in a similar manner to that of the *WTC I* C minor fugue. Further, as in the *WTC II* C major exposition for example, parallel motion in descending tenths and sixths, shown in example 1-16, gives a consistent foreground motion to this exposition.

Paradigm 5 ($\hat{1} - \hat{2} - \hat{3}$)

Example 4-12 shows the three-part exposition patterns for paradigm 5, another of the most commonly found paradigms. In these patterns the bridge is without question necessary to prepare for the third entry, since its first main note is the tonic. Interestingly, of these three patterns, the rising

Example 4-12. Three-part exposition patterns for paradigm 5

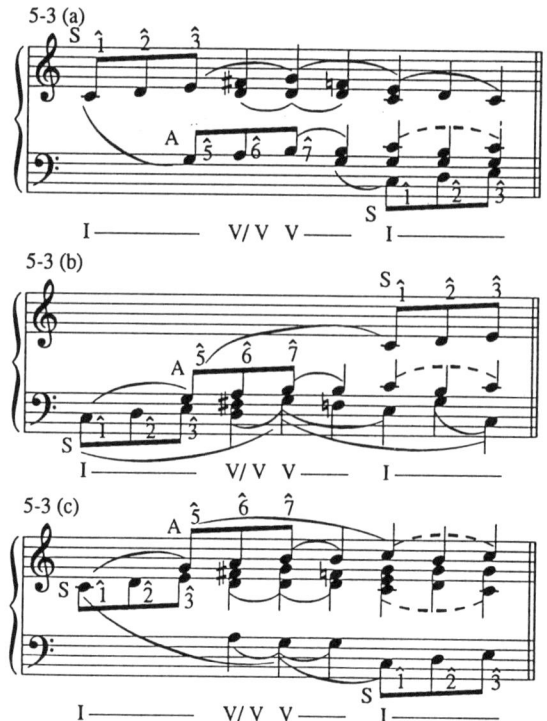

---

[13]Kalib gives a similar analysis of this exposition in "Thirteen Essays," 1:285.

FUGAL EXPOSITION

series of exposition pattern 5-3 (b) does not occur in the *WTC*. It may be the fact that in such a case the conclusion of the answer would lead too directly to the beginning of the third entry.

Example 4-13 illustrates exposition pattern 5-3 (c) with the B-flat major fugue of *WTC II*. Notice that the first part of the answer includes a tonal modification (b-flat^1 rather than c^2 at the end of measure 5), but that this detail involves the arpeggiation rather than the main linear progression. The dominant of the succeeding measure operates within a larger tonic prolongation, as shown in example 4-13, so the third-progression of the answer, which begins in measure 7, originates in a I chord, not a V chord. The answer continues sequentially, and the counterpoint uses primarily the $\hat{3}$-sharp-$\hat{4}$-$\hat{5}$ of the highest inner voice of the exposition pattern, giving a series of parallel thirds. The bridge functions harmonically as in exposition pattern 5-3 (c), but the ingenious exchange of voices shown in example 4-13 gives greater continuity and shape to the exposition. The seventh of V is introduced not in the lower voice as suggested in exposition pattern 5-3 (c), but in the higher voice, by which means the high f^2 of the beginning of the answer is brought into relationship with the rest of the exposition as the beginning of a $\hat{5}$-$\hat{4}$-$\hat{3}$ third-progression in the upper voice. The a^1 which ends the answer continues at the end of the bridge in the lower voice, giving a stepwise preparation for the third entry in the bass.[14] The bridge itself is expanded through stepwise descent as shown in example 4-13.

Example 4-13. Bach, Fugue 21 in B-flat major (*WTC II*), mm. 1–17

---

[14]Thus the structure of the bridge closely resembles that of the *WTC I* C minor fugue. See Schenker, *Das Meisterwerk in der Musik*, 2:67–68.

The third entry follows exposition pattern 5-3 (c)—a rising third-progression prolonging I. However, the voice-exchange in the bridge allows a more interesting upper voice at the third entry than that given in example 4-12. A descending $\hat{3}$-$\hat{2}$-$\hat{1}$ third-progression in the upper voice accompanies the rising third of the bass, giving direction to the upper voice during this tonic prolongation, and, by gesture, preparing for the expected tonic cadence which is elided by suspending the leading-tone in measure 19. (This elided cadence provides for a completion of the bass motion initiated by the rising third of the subject: $\hat{1}$-$\hat{2}$-$\hat{3}$ expands to a full bass progression $\hat{1}$-$\hat{2}$-$\hat{3}$-$\hat{4}$-$\hat{5}$-$\hat{1}$. It articulates without sectionalizing the form and gives a smooth connection to the succeeding part of the fugue.) The descending third-progression links the actual upper-voice note d^2 with the hypothetical upper-voice b-flat[1]; that is, the final cadential motion in the upper voice would have conformed to the hypothetical $\hat{7}$-$\hat{8}$ motion, had the cadential resolution not been elided.

The restatement of the initial tonic as f^2 in the answer gives rise to the extended $\hat{5}$-$\hat{4}$-$\hat{3}$-$\hat{2}$-($\hat{1}$) fifth-progression in the upper voice. Thus the opening initial tonic of the subject acts structurally like the initial tonic in the *WTC I* C minor fugue, which also gives rise to a descending fifth over the course of the exposition.[15]

Exposition Patterns for Category 2 Subjects

The radically different tonal structures of modulating subjects promote radical structural differences in expositions of non-modulating subjects. Whereas non-modulating subjects are generally self-contained units, modulating subjects demand continuation, since their endings occur at the dominant, a transitory point in a larger tonal motion. They and their answers correspond well to the metaphorical labels "question" and "answer," since the second entry completes the tonal segment initiated by the first entry. Schenker's complete tonal motion is expressed through two, not three entries. Therefore, expositions based on modulating subjects normally follow a pattern of subject-answer pairs—even in fugues with an odd number of parts—and more typically generate four-part fugues, whereas expositions based on non-modulating subjects normally follow a pattern of three entries, sometimes expanded by additional entrances.

Example 4-14 illustrates exposition patterns for two of the most commonly found modulating subject-paradigms. Exposition pattern 9-4 (b) illustrates a rising series of entries based on the root-progression subject. The pattern of rising entries effectively accommodates a fluent series of lines in the accompanying parts and each of the accompanying voices fills in the texture. The alternating chordal seventh and leading note resolutions in the accompaniment voices will provide the foundation for two effective countersubjects. In exposition pattern 9-4 (d) the final bass entry facilitates a root motion for the cadence that ends the exposition, while the upper voice nicely rounds off the ascent with a descending third progression. In

---

[15]*Ibid.*, 58–59.

FUGAL EXPOSITION

exposition patterns 8a-4 (b) and 8a-4 (c), the additional content of the subject paradigm requires the voice exchange at the third entry in order to accommodate the third note of the scale in the subject. While the subject paradigm is the same for both exposition patterns, the smooth connection of the rising series creates a much different impression than the more incisive entries of the descending series.

Example 4-14. Exposition patterns for category 2 subjects

The *WTC I* G-sharp minor exposition works out exposition pattern 9-4 (b). Example 2-53 illustrates the way in which the conclusion of the subject suggests an auxiliary cadence to the dominant. But the melodic line which counterpoints this bass is largely implied: after an arpeggiation $\hat{1}$ - $\hat{3}$ - $\hat{5}$, the following sharp- $\hat{4}$ - $\hat{5}$ must be understood as the logical conclusion of the implied upper voice.

Example 4-15. Bach, Fugue 18 in G-sharp minor (*WTC I*), mm. 1–9

The entry of the answer above the first part gives a conclusion to the implied upper voice of the subject, and continues the rising motion which the subject began. Much structural reinterpretation occurs with the answer, since it expresses a very different tonal motion (V–I rather than I–V), since it is a tonal answer, and since it has an accompanying bass which contributes to the tonal expression. The end of the answer coincides with the completion of a tonal unit, I–V–I, but it is the entry of the third part that completes the upper stratum, thereby uniting the second tonal segment of the exposition (entries 3 and 4) with the first.

The third entry continues the upward arpeggiation of the tonic chord, as far as d-sharp², but the fourth entry, in the bass, fails to complete the implied upper voice d-sharp² of the third entry. Why is the fourth entry below, not above? Apparently not only for variety, but more importantly (1) to allow the final statement of the exposition to express its cadential power through the emphatic bass motion $\hat{4}$ - $\hat{5}$ - $\hat{1}$, which is also the "linkage" to the subsequent episode (see example 5-28), and (2) to establish d-sharp² as the head tone, goal of the arpeggiation and highest note of the exposition. It is thus evident that Bach's arrangement, T,A,S,B, is the best one for this particular subject. The direct relationship between motive and structure demonstrated here goes some distance towards accounting for the unity and strength of Bach's fugues.

Also based on a modulating subject, the *WTC I* B minor exposition follows the same tonal plan as the *WTC I* G-sharp exposition—two linked har-

FUGAL EXPOSITION   131

monic motions, I–V–I–V–I—but is much more complex. The intensely chromatic subject has a two-part structure shown in example 2-54. The countersubject proper is a descending scale segment in quarter-notes that begins at the f-sharp^2 (head tone for the entire fugue[16]) in m. 4. The sixteenth-note passage in m. 4 therefore is a link from f-sharp^1 to f-sharp^2.[17]

At the third entry this linking material is reused in inverted form, but again in the alto part, rather than in the tenor, and at the fourth entry the same material is repeated in the tenor part. At each subsequent subject statement throughout the course of the fugue this linking material is reused, both in prime an inverted forms, and perhaps it should be considered a countersubject in its own right, except that it is treated in a free fashion, and it breaks off where the true countersubject begins. Rather, it should be considered the embodiment of the sixteenth-note rhythm that systematically complements the eighths of the subject and the quarters of the countersubject.[18]

Example 4-16. Bach, Fugue 24 in B minor (*WTC I*), mm. 1–16

In terms of tonal structure, the bridge before the third entry is superfluous, since it merely prolongs the tonic through an ascending motion from

---

[16]This interpretation accords with that of Karl-Otto Plum, *Untersuchungen zu Heinrich Schenkers Stimmführungs-analyse* (Regensburg: Gustav Bosse Verlag, 1979), 70.

[17]This figure gives some very free dissonance treatment in m. 4, beat 3—remarkably free even for Bach. Hans Weisse gives an analysis of this passage in "The Music Teacher's Dilemma," *Proceedings of the Music Teachers National Association* (1935), 122–37, reprinted in *Theory and Practice* X/1–2 (July–December, 1985):45–47.

[18]Schenker provides a similar explanation for the linking sixteenth-note passage in the C minor fugue of *WTC I*. See "Das Organische der Fuge," 66.

the inner voice, as shown in example 4-16. But it is necessary for the motivic detail of the piece, since it prepares the register of the upper voices for the countersubject at the third entry. The third entry, as expected, leads the music again to V, but the one-measure bridge to the fourth entry returns the music to I at measure 13. Thus the fourth entry is structurally different from the second entry: a prolongation of I, not a motion to I. Again, variety is not the only factor here. The prolongation of I through measures 13–16 establishes more strongly the terminus for the initial tonic prolongation of the exposition. The upper voice for measures 1–17, a descending fifth, $\hat{5}$ - $\hat{4}$ - $\hat{3}$ - $\hat{2}$ - $\hat{1}$, gives a sense of completion and unity to the exposition. The head tone f-sharp is regained immediately in measure 17, and reaffirmed in measure 19 where Bach anticipates the next thematic entry with the opening notes of the subject in the alto.

The dexterity with which Bach integrates the motivic material into a comprehensive tonal structure in this work is amazing. Although it is a difficult work, with many layers of complexity, including a violent contrast of chromaticism in the thematic areas and diatonic simplicity in the sequences, the overwhelming technique which controls its difficult texture makes it a fitting conclusion to the first book of the *WTC*.

Exposition Patterns for Category 3 Subjects

The tonal structure of exposition patterns based on paradigms of category 3 partakes of elements of category 1 and category 2 exposition patterns. The determining factor of course is the nature of the answer paradigm, tonal (returning to I) or real (ending on II). Example 4-17 illustrates several exposition patterns for category 3 subjects. In every case the real answer requires a bridge which in its basic form uses the auxiliary cadence II–V–I. Exposition pattern 12-3 (a) shows a simple three-part exposition with bridge, whereas exposition pattern 12-4 (b) shows an exposition on the same paradigm with a tonal answer and no bridge. The following patterns illustrate the same issues for a rising subject, paradigm 13. By and large the accompanying parts in example 4-17 nicely complete basic voices of the voice-leading matrix.

Schenker's analysis of the D minor fugue (*WTC I*) shows the structure of an exposition based on a category 3 subject with real answer (see example 4-1). The example is very clear in that it shows how the bridge operates through a third progression $\hat{5}$ - $\hat{4}$ - $\hat{3}$ in the upper voice, while the deeper structure of the upper voice is a prolongation of $\hat{5}$, the head tone for the entire composition. A more detailed analysis would show the local harmonies.[19] Notice that, in contrast to category 1, harmonic prolongations relate with the beginnings rather than with the endings of thematic statements. The dominant prolongation starts at the beginning of the answer, and the return to the tonic occurs at the beginning of the third entry. No

---

[19]Fig. 53-5 in *Free Composition* shows the dominant harmony, but Schenker sees the end of the answer as the upper fifth of V, and not as II, a harmony in its own right. However, this is a matter of attitude rather than substance.

FUGAL EXPOSITION

Example 4-17. Exposition patterns, category 3 subjects

auxiliary cadence to V occurs; instead, the dominant prolongation simply begins at the point where the subject ends and the answer begins.

Example 4-18 illustrates the working out of a category 3 subject with a tonal answer, such that the end of the answer marks a return to I. The fact that the end of the answer in example 4-18 represents an authentic cadence rather than a half cadence means that the countersubject must undergo alterations as well. Whereas the countersubject to the answer outlines a descending third, $\hat{5}$-$\hat{4}$-$\hat{3}$, the countersubject to the third entry becomes $\hat{8}$-$\hat{8}$-$\hat{7}$. Of course, this alteration is of the same order as the comparable alterations necessary for subject paradigm 1 and its answer. This exposition should be compared to that of BWV 949, which appears to be a companion fugue that works out a similar theme in the parallel major key.

Example 4-18. Bach?, Fugue in A minor BWV 947, mm. 1–9

Subject Paradigms and Exposition Patterns

If exposition patterns such as these are taken as structural bases for fugal exposition and are found in simple fugal expositions, departures from them in individual expositions can be largely understood as resulting from two important considerations: (1) idiosyncratic features of specific fugue subjects can dictate special structural modifications that respond to these features, and (2) special contrapuntal procedures, such as the use of countersubjects or inversions, can generate modified exposition patterns that respond to the imitative requirements.

For example, the fact that in the *WTC I* C minor subject (examples 2-1 and 2-2) the initial tonic is above the main linear progression determines the order of entries as M-H-L (exposition pattern 1-3 (c)) in order to avoid crossed parts at the beginning of the answer. In consequence, the answer responds to the initial tonic with g^2 which is then given a voice-leading context as the initiator of an upper-voice fifth-progression spanning the exposition and superseding the hypothetical $\hat{8}$-$\hat{7}$-$\hat{8}$ neighbor motion of exposition pattern 1-3 (c).[20] Again, the two-voice polyphony of the *WTC I* C-sharp major subject dictates the descending order of subject statements in the exposition (see example 4-11). Since the main structural voice in the subject uses the lower notes, the descending order of entries allows this main progression to appear continuously in the lowest sounding-part, exerting a structural influence over the entire exposition as a descending conjunct motion.

---

[20]"Das Organische der Fuge," 66–68, substantiates these points.

The *WTC II* B major subject works the opposite way (example 2-34). The presence of the $\hat{5}$-$\hat{6}$-$\hat{7}$-$\hat{8}$ linear-progression in the uppermost notes of the subject suggests the rising order of entries and yields the ascending arpeggiation as a primary structural element. Thus the nature of the subject impacts on the exposition pattern, and contrapuntal devices, especially invertible countersubject, impact on the way that the voice leading is realized. Even the most abstruse and convoluted expositions will often be found to bear some direct relation to basic exposition patterns, albeit through a greater number and complexity of structural levels and transformations. It is consistent to view all these cases as variants and more sophisticated expressions of elementary exposition patterns which represent the purely voice-leading aspect of the design and which provide a means for understanding structural similarities in expositions that in other respects seem quite different.

It should be clear at this stage that there are extremely important and fundamental relationships to be seen between subject paradigms and exposition patterns. The most frequently occurring and most flexible subject paradigms, such as paradigm 1, are found frequently in a wide range of exposition patterns. Other patterns, or patterns with special constraints, are encountered only in a greatly reduced number of exposition patterns. Only an exhaustive tabulation would reveal the full extent of such relationships. One wonders the extent to which such corelations were for composers such as Bach the results of trial and error, or part of an instinctive or indeed conscious knowledge of principles akin to those presented here.

The extent to which repetitive patterning in fugue expositions pervades the literature is illustrated by example 4-19, which aligns the expositions and succeeding episodes of the first fugue in each book of the *WTC*. The composite structural analysis (c) shows how the voice-leading backgrounds of the two are nearly identical. This is all the more remarkable, given that one fugue utilizes paradigm 5 in four parts and the other uses paradigm 1 in three parts. The most crucial structural notes occur in equivalent places and registers in both expositions, and a great many surface details are similar or identical as well. These relationships are made possible by the facts that the *WTC I* subject has a latent potential to be understood as paradigm 1, and that the third entry in this fugue is an answer, not a subject, allowing the final entry to perform the concluding function of the return to I. No doubt the internal structures of the episodes differ, as each is based on a different working of the initial subject matter, the first being in stretto, the second in canon, yet they both expand I in a rising fashion and lead to cadences in the dominant which are based on identical voice-leading in identical registers.[21] One is tempted to speculate that as

---

[21]Johann Nepomuk David, *Das wohltemperierte Clavier, Versuch einer Synopsis* (Göttingen: Vandenhoeck and Ruprecht, 1962), 17, notes some aspects of similarity between these two fugues, such as the identical range of subjects and the identical a–f-sharp^1 interval in the counterpoint to the answer. He compares the structure of the subject and counterpoint of the two fugues, and also draws attention to the similarity in the cadences to the dominant, but he does not discuss the deeper relationship which is based on similarity of voice-leading structure.

Bach began composing the C major fugue of *WTC II* he turned to the opening of *WTC I* for inspiration.

Example 4-19. a, Bach, Fugue 1 in C major (*WTC I*), mm. 1–10; b, Fugue 1 in C major (*WTC II*), mm. 1–22; c, comparative structural analysis

FUGAL EXPOSITION

CHAPTER 5

Sequence and Episode

Chapter 5 deals with two interrelated topics, sequence and episode. The terms themselves are often confused and sometimes equated in the literature. For the purposes of structural analysis, it is important to distinguish them here. In the context of tonal music, sequence involves transposed repetition of musical elements. Sequences are based on patterns of voice-leading, thus they are a technique of strict counterpoint. Sequence is not limited to any specific portions of fugue; indeed, subjects themselves can contain sequential elements (see examples 2-12, 2-32, 2-54, 2-69 and 3-25). Episode is a connecting or contrasting passage between subject statements in fugue, thus episode is a component of form and structure. Ultimately, episode is any portion of a fugue where neither subject nor any of its substantive transformations (i.e., tonally altered forms or transpositions) is present.[1] On the other hand, this is not to deny that episodes can employ, and often exploit at great length, motivic elements of subject or countersubject. Despite their different significations, sequence and episode are intimately linked in that episodes are commonly but not always based on a sequential structure, and sequences are most conspicuous in fugues when they are used as the structural basis of episodes. Indeed sequence is the typical means by which episodes project a sense of unity and directed motion.

A Schenkerian perspective on *sequences* in fugue naturally focuses at the foreground level on the concept of voice-leading as a framework that gives them tonal logic and permits effective development of surface motivic activity. Strictly speaking, issues of prolongation and progression, and of structural levels and harmonic function, have no relevance to the study of pure sequences, just as questions of prolongation and structural levels are not a part of Schenker's consideration of strict counterpoint. On the other hand, consideration of *episodes* from a Schenkerian perspective views the manner in which episodes serve prolonging and progressional functions, and how they relate to the deeper levels of structure in larger spans. Accordingly, chapter 5 focuses on the underlying patterning of sequences and examines how they function within the complete episodes as patterns of prolongation and progression. At the same time, issues of invertible counterpoint and imitation explored in chapter 3 are further developed. Chapter 7 provides insights into the function of episodes in the larger context of tonal structure and formal design.

Schenker does not deal directly with sequential progressions either in *Counterpoint* or in *Free Composition*, despite his obvious interest in the parallels which are inevitably implicit in sequences, as evinced in his edition of

---

[1]In the terminology of fugal analysis, however, *bridge* uniquely describes an episode within an exposition.

of Brahms manuscript *Oktaven u. Quinten u. A.*,[2] despite his claim to be the first to solve the problem of parallel octaves and fifths, and despite his point that it is the relationship between strict and free counterpoint, i.e., between the foreground and middleground that provides the *locus* for that solution.[3] Clearly a basic reason for avoiding the topic of sequences within his work on strict counterpoint is the larger avoidance of repetitive patterning, and thus of motivic development, within that work. One of the difficulties that sequences presented for Schenker and his theory of tonal structure is that for the duration of a sequence a given pattern of voice-leading takes precedence over any harmonic considerations. Thus a typical sequence is not so much tonal in itself, but represents a passage between two points of a tonal system.

The Voice-leading Structure of Sequences

Sequences are formed by the transposed repetition of tonal elements—chords, motives, and combinations thereof. By their nature, sequences project an effect of directed motion, an effect that can be attributed to their structure. When an element or *proposition* is followed by its transposed repetition at a given interval, a directed tonal motion or *digression* is established. A further transposed repetition at the same interval and in the same direction provides *confirmation* of that directed motion. This three-step pattern, proposition-digression-confirmation, completes the formal outline of a sequence. Any further sequential repetition is redundant since it adds nothing of significance to the already established pattern.[4]

In that the basic condition of any sequence is transposition, up or down, the most abstract conception of sequence is the systematic alteration of pitch over time, and this concept forms the basis for the classification outlined here. The primary distinction is between descent and ascent, giving two large categories, descending sequences and ascending sequences. Within this broad division are three subdivisions, characterized by interval of transposition: step, third, and fifth. Thus, in terms of interval of transposition, there are six distinct sequence patterns: those that descend (1) by step, (2) by third, (3) by fifth, and those that ascend (4) by step, (5) by third, and (6) by fifth (see example 5-1).

Example 5-1. Basic sequence patterns

---

[2] Johannes Brahms, "Brahms's Study, Octaven u. Quinten u. A., with Schenker's Commentary Translated", trans. by Paul Mast, *The Music Forum* V (1980): 1–196.

[3] *Free Composition*, 56–57.

[4] Adumbrations or extensions of a sequential progression must be considered in their larger context; the analyses in chapter 7 illustrate.

SEQUENCE AND EPISODE

Some explanation is necessary as to why the intervals of the step, third and fifth are admitted but the fourth, sixth and seventh are excluded. First, it seems natural to consider ascent or descent by step as the most fundamental means of creating the directed motion needed for a sequence to assert itself. After all, stepwise motion is the basis of Schenker's notion of melodic progression, conceptualized as the linear progression (*Zug*). Ascent or descent by third is a similar but more emphatic directed motion in which the series of thirds often reflect the harmonic structure of a single triad at deeper levels. However, the fourth is omitted for the following reason: in a series of descending fourths reduced within an octave span, alternate members of the series exhibit a rising stepwise relation, and in an ascending series of fourths reduced to an octave span the alternate members exhibit a falling relationship (see example 5-2). Thus, although one may conceptualize an ascending sequence in fourths, the effect on the listener is that of a falling sequence of fifths. For this reason, descending and ascending fifths are admitted as sequence patterns 3 and 6. Like the fourth, the sixth and seventh are dismissed as inversions of the third and second. The effect of series' of descending sixths or sevenths within the ambitus of an octave is ascent; the effect of a series of ascending sixths or sevenths is a descent. Thus each direction, ascent and descent, contains three possibilities, motion by second, third and fifth. As the discussion proceeds, it will become clear that these three sequential intervals have inherent structural relationships that link them closely to one another.[5]

Example 5-2. a, ascending fifths; b, descending fifths

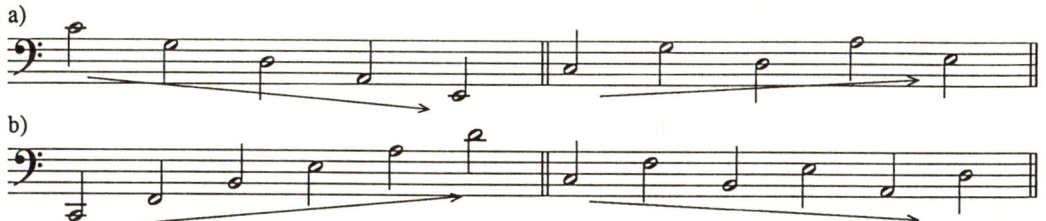

Whichever pattern forms the basis of a sequence, the fundamental voice-leading problem is the amelioration of the parallel fifths implied by the transposed repetition. Example 5-3 illustrates this problem, and anyone familiar with structural analysis has no doubt encountered similar situations. Example 5-3 is Schenker's analysis of a simple sequence descending by step. Schenker marks the parallel fifths with brackets above the staff, and illustrates the manner in which the parallels are broken up by 5-6 motion, which creates intervening chords on the weak beats. This is a good illustration too of Schenker's attitude that the harmonic progression through the

---

[5]Recent works inspired or influenced by Schenker have considered the voice-leading basis of sequences (Edward Aldwell and Carl Schachter, *Harmony and Voice Leading* (New York: Harcourt Brace Jovanovich, 1989), 246–66, 410–17, and 585; Allen Forte and Steven Gilbert, *Introduction to Schenkerian Analysis* (New York: Norton, 1982), 83–100, and Gauldin, *A Practical Approach to Eighteenth-Century Counterpoint*, 15–18), but none to my knowledge includes a complete and systematic presentation such as is given here.

circle of fifths that so frequently occurs in sequences is in fact the result of contrapuntal concerns rather than a reflection of the harmonic function which the descending fifth implies.

Example 5-3. Schenker, *Free Composition*, Fig. 54-10

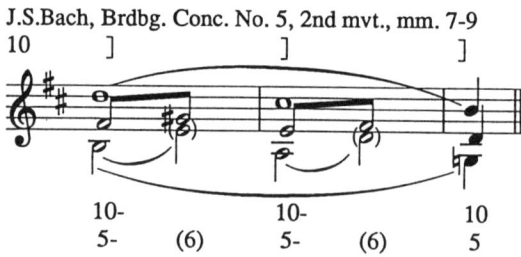

Example 5-3 also provides a useful point of comparison with the voice-leading complex of invertible counterpoint. If we consider example 5-3 in terms of B minor, the upper voice represents paradigm 2 ($\hat{3}$-$\hat{2}$-$\hat{1}$), the middle voice is paradigm 1 ($\hat{5}$-$\hat{4}$-$\hat{3}$), and the lower voice substitutes $\hat{8}$-$\hat{7}$-$\hat{6}$ for what would have been paradigm 3 ($\hat{8}$-sharp-$\hat{7}$-$\hat{8}$) (compare example 3-5). That is, the raised leading tone and its upward resolution is replaced by a descending resolution closely related to the *inganno* device seen previously. In all other respects the voice-leading is the same.

In the D minor Fugue of *WTC II*, Bach provides an explicit comparison of the voice-leading complex with this sequence pattern. Example 5-4 shows a triple counterpoint that simply prolongs I as the themes are tossed from voice to voice. The principal theme in sixteenths represents paradigm 1 ($\hat{5}$-$\hat{4}$-$\hat{3}$), and the counterpoints contain paradigms 2 and 3 ($\hat{3}$-$\hat{2}$-$\hat{1}$ and $\hat{8}$-$\hat{7}$-$\hat{8}$), completing the voice-leading complex. In addition to supporting a descending octave transfer in the upper voice (f^2-f^1), this brief passage which simply prolongs I has the principal function of repeating motivic ideas of the first important sequence of the composition, shown in example 5-5. But in example 5-5 the same contrapuntal structure is realized as a sequence by descending fifths rather than a tonic prolongation. The $\hat{7}$ of paradigm 3 is converted into a chordal seventh and suspended into the following leg of the sequence, where it resolves through the $\hat{3}$-$\hat{2}$-$\hat{1}$ of the other voice; that is it becomes paradigm 2 of the next harmony. The final leg of the sequence breaks the chain of sevenths as the leading tone e^2 replaces the chordal seventh e-flat^2 in the upper voice. Beyond the detail of the sequence, example 5-5 provides a good illustration of the kind of broad tonal meaning that a sequential episode can imply. As the graph shows, while the chord-by-chord analysis (in parentheses) gives a directed motion, at a deeper level the sequence and following cadence simply create a lengthy prolongation of V that resolves to I in m. 10. Such an occurrence, in which a foreground *progression* expands a middleground *prolongation,* is by no means uncommon in sequential episodes.

SEQUENCE AND EPISODE   143

Example 5-4. Bach, Fugue 6 in D minor (*WTC II*), mm. 12–14

Example 5-5. Bach, Fugue 6 in D minor (*WTC II*), mm. 7–10

Sequence Pattern 1: Descent by Step

Descent by step is the most commonly encountered form of sequence; it can be considered in abstract terms as a replica of a descending scale segment, which Schenker considers the most basic melodic structure, as seen in the fundamental line. Example 5-6 1(a) shows however that if simple triads are treated sequentially in a stepwise manner parallel fifths and octaves result. The schemes that follow, 1(b) through 1(n), illustrate several means of eliminating the parallels, at least at the surface level. The parallels will nevertheless remain at the upper-middleground level to be removed again at the deeper middleground levels.[6]

---

[6] Schenker emphasizes this point in *Free Composition*, 56–57.

Example 5-6. Sequence pattern 1

Although four chords or four stages appear in example 5-6 1(a), only the first three form the sequential progression itself, and would be elaborated in a repetitive manner. The final chord represents a state of resolution that concludes the sequence. Put another way, each leg of the sequence has a beginning and ending. Thus four points are needed to connect three statements. That the beginning and ending points therefore represent a fourth relationship is often structurally significant at deeper levels.

In sequence pattern 1(a) the parallels are removed by altering the sequence from root position in four parts to first inversion in three. This resulting *fauxbourdon* texture is often enlivened in actual music by the addition of 7-6 suspensions—or more rarely 5-6 anticipations (1(c) and 1(d)).

Pattern 1(e) provides two alternate forms of each chord, thus replacing the parallel motion with contrary motion. In pattern 1(f), lower-third chords appear on the weak beats, creating subsidiary contrapuntal harmonies that break up the parallels. More commonly the harmonies that are introduced in this manner form fifth-relationships with the primary chords. Sequence patterns 1(g) through 1(n) show the various forms that this can take, using both triads and seventh chords in a variety of inversions: 1(g) shows the simplest root progression that yields contrary motion at every step; 1(h) inverts the intermediary chords, giving canonic effects between the outer and inner pairs of voices that are often used as the basis of canonic sequences; 1(i) introduces sevenths for the inserted chords, elaborating the triadic pattern of 1(g); 1(j) inverts the seventh chords to give more step-wise motion; 1(k) gives root position seventh chords to the first inversion arrangement found at 1(b) and 1(d); 1(l) inverts the seventh chords, again giving additional stepwise motion. 1(m) provides sevenths for all the chords in root position and 1(n) inverts the alternate chords, giving complete stepwise motion in all four parts, and complete canonic imitation as well. That is, each of the four voices is simply a descending scale-segment in whole notes.

It may be argued that these progressions are based on the cycle of fifths, rather than on stepwise motion. It is true that, in the abstract, sequences by step and by fifth approach one another at this point, but in actual music the motivic repetition and the general perception of the sequence, as understood by the realization of a basic linear progression, is fundamentally a descent by step. Ultimately the sequence is characterized melodically rather than harmonically. Sequences which are genuinely based on descent by fifth rather than by step are characterized by a more extensive element of repetition, and by repetition of that element at each fifth (see below). Example 5-3 shows Schenker's thinking on this point. Schenker shows the interpolated dominant sevenths as a harmonic means of achieving the 5-6 exchange that is necessary to remove the direct succession of parallel fifths—a contrapuntal rather than a harmonic phenomenon.

An important feature of example 5-6 that connects with Schenker's viewpoint is that sequences are based not on concepts of functional harmony but on concepts of figured bass, the dominant ideology of the seventeenth and eighteenth centuries. Thus Schenker's voice-leading approach complements the older tradition. Bach himself makes this clear in his own figured-bass exercises (see example 1-12). It is important to note that when Bach took a concept such as the descending sequence by step as the basis of a composition, however, he felt compelled to raise it from the level of exercise to art by investing it with a much greater degree of tonal functionality on the one hand, and of structural levels on the other hand. I refer here to the *WTC I*, Prelude 1 in C major (example 1-13), which includes modulation and secondary VII chords rather than simply the diatonic basis of the exercises. Nevertheless, as the examples from the literature show, a greater or lesser degree of functionality is often projected in sequences at the foreground level. Secondary dominants can easily be created through chromaticisation of the diatonic patterns in example 5-6, and extended functional progressions (IV–VII–III–VI–II–V–I) can be extrapolated from the circle of fifths in patterns 1(g) through 1(n).

The following examples illustrate the basic sequential patterns in actual music, and consider the functioning of sequences within the larger concerns of voice-leading and structure.

Example 5-7 illustrates a simple two-part sequence that is typical for a bridge in an exposition, leading from V back to I in preparation for the third entry and in the case of minor converting minor-V to a dominant seventh. The tonal structure of this episode is thus a prolongation of V, guided by the descending fourth f^1-c^1 in the lower voice. A guiding voice (leader) such as this is usually clearly discernible in sequential progressions. The motivic content of the sequence grows naturally out of the immediately preceding material, in this case the end of the answer and of the countersubject. The deceptive resolution leads to a descending series of secondary dominants, the chromaticised form of sequence pattern 1 (n). It is important to note here that had the final two sonorities of m. 10 not been altered—i.e., if the sequence continued as it had been established—the point of resolution would have been III, not I. This shows that while a *sequence* may have a certain goal in its directed motion, the *episode* that contains it may in fact realize a quite different goal, in this case a prolongation of V and resolution to I. Thus the intervallic pattern that a sequence projects by no means determines the tonal significance of an episode.

Example 5-7. Bach, Fugue 22 in B-flat minor (*WTC II*), mm. 7–11

Example 5-8 shows another episode in the same fugue, this time in four parts. The passage contains two sequences. In the first a stepwise chordal motion is broken up by interposed fifth-related chords that act as dominants. Only two statements of this sequence occur (mm. 21–25), but the sequence that follows (mm. 25–27) continues the directed motion. Here, however, an acceleration of motion drives towards the resolution to I. Thus this episode does not prolong V, but rather proceeds from V to III, and from III to I. The end of the episode marks the entry of a subject statement in the tenor. While either sequence might be considered too brief by itself, the combination of two, the second an adumbration of the first,

proposition, digression, confirmation and further digression, and finally confirmation of the further digression.

Example 5-8. Bach, Fugue 22 in B-flat minor (*WTC II*), mm. 21–27

Example 5-9 illustrates a similar two-stage episode descending by step, with first inversion secondary dominants interposing between the primary chords. The analysis shows how two repetitions encompass a descending third progression, VI–IV, the first sequence of the episode. The second part of the episode is also a descending sequence by step, IV–II, but here a canonic surface appears. The canon, based on alternating sixths and thirds, takes advantage of the fact that the interposed chords are related by fifth to the surrounding ones. This second sequence, which again has only two statements, not three, leads from IV to II over a second four-measure span, giving a balanced structure. The final two measures of the episode provide the cadential progression II–VII–I that completes the episode and leads to the entry of the subject in the bass. From the aspect of structure, although the sequences are by step, the cumulative effect is of descending thirds, VI–IV–II, at a deeper level, as in example 5-8. The motivic structure is entirely derived from the subject. As for the previous example, the fact that each of the two sequences has only two statements may be justified by the circumstance that two related sequences follow in succession. Comparison of these two examples of sequences suggests that Bach was very much aware of the effect of repetition in the forward progress and development of his contrapuntal music.

Example 5-9. Bach, Fugue 1 in C major (*WTC II*), mm. 29–39

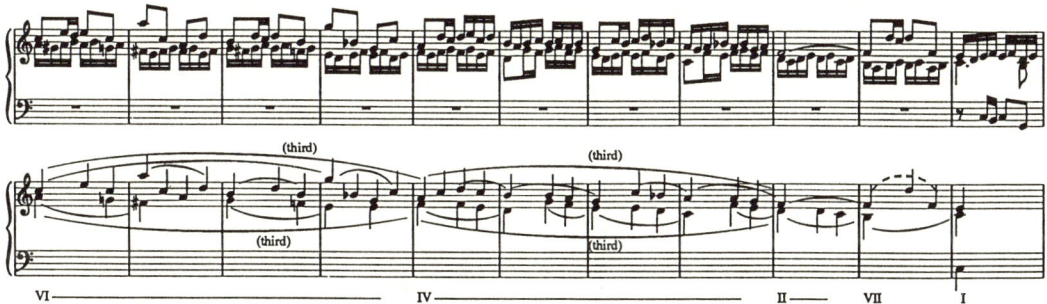

Example 5-10 illustrates another use of canon in descending sequences by step. Again, as in the C-major example above, the canonic structure is based on an alternation of roots and thirds in chords related by fifth (sequence pattern 1 (h)). Although only two full statements of the sequence appear here, any further repetition would sound redundant since between the two voices we hear a total of four statements of the melodic pattern—each leg of the sequence includes two statements, one in each part. Further, as with all episodes, the tonal context is crucial. Here the episode effects the modulation from I to III through a descent from the dominant, V–IV–III, that requires by its nature only two full repetitions, V–IV and IV–III.

Example 5-10. Bach, Fugue 22 in B-flat minor (*WTC II*), mm. 31–33

Example 5-11 shows the use of a triple invertible counterpoint in a sequential progression. Particularly attractive here is the rhythmic independence of each theme—sixteenths, eighths, and tied quarters. Note that the invertible counterpoint is not simply at the octave, but includes counterpoint at the tenth in the sixteenth notes. Example 5-11(a) is based on sequence pattern 1 (f). When the sixteenths are put in the bass (example 5-11 (b)), they are transposed in such a way as to create sevenths on the strong beats (sequence pattern 1 (i)), and to avoid weak six-fours at its lowest notes (F, E-flat and D-flat roots would be C–B-flat–A-flat fifths). At (c) the inversion produces sequence pattern 1 (l). This is a good example of invertible counterpoint at the tenth, developed not so much as an imitative technique, but more as a means of inverting a counterpoint that is not amenable to inversion at the octave.

Example 5-11. Bach, Fugue 17 in A-flat major (*WTC II*), a, mm. 11–13; b, mm. 14–16; c, mm. 19–21

SEQUENCE AND EPISODE   149

The closest possible imitation occurs when all parts repeat the same motives in a quadruple canon. This is seen in example 5-12. By its definition, a quadruple canon is completely invertible, since the only theme is already present in the bass. Sequence pattern 1 (n) is the obvious basis of such canonic passages in a descent by step.

Example 5-12. Bach, Fugue 14 in F-sharp minor (*WTC I*), mm. 35–37

Sequence Pattern 2: Descent by Third

Example 5-13 illustrates the basic sequence forms available for a descending motion by thirds. With the normal threefold repetition, the underlying harmonic motion is a descending seventh, typically I–II or IV–V. In 2(b) passing chords remove the parallels of the underlying progression. In 2(c) an arpeggiation serves the same purpose; 2(d) gives inverted forms of the passing chords, resulting in a stepwise motion in parallel tenths in the outer voices; 2(e) is a more elaborate form still, that adds an inverted auxiliary cadence to each stage of the sequence.

Example 5-13. Sequence pattern 2

Example 5-14 shows a simple sequence descending by thirds. Here it is secondary dominants that provide the essential counter-force to the parallel motion and at the same time provide stepwise melodic connections that fill the thirds, according to example 5-13 (e). Chromatic motion enhances the sonorities and provides a motivic link to the chromatic subject. Although the sequence represents a progression at the foreground level (V–III–I), at a deeper level it acts as a prolongation of V which serves the dual function of a register transfer and a change of chord quality from minor to major. At a deep middleground level this episode would be understood as V–I–V–sharp-3, supporting a neighbor note motion in the upper voice, e^2-f^1-e^1.

Example 5-14. Bach, Fugue 6 in D minor (*WTC II*), mm. 15–17

In example 5-15, another simple descent by thirds (sequence pattern 2 (b)), a greater degree of harmonic activity occupies each span of the sequence. Once again the sequence acts as a progression in the foreground (I–VI–IV) but as a prolongation of G-sharp minor in the middleground through I–IV–VII–I (see the dotted slurs). The descending fifth which occupies the upper voice of the sequence forms a sixth in the G-sharp minor prolongation.

Example 5-15. Bach, Fugue 23 in B major (*WTC II*), mm. 63–68

Canons are also possible in sequences that progress by thirds. The episodes of *WTC I*, Fugue 12 in F minor make a study of canonic sequence, just as the subject statements are a study in invertible counterpoint (see example 3-21). In example 5-16 (a) the canon is only hinted at (see upper and lower voices, but already the potential for a canon at the fifth is suggested in the middle voice of m. 10. The lower two voices of (d) realize the canon at the fifth in another descending sequence by thirds. Example 5-16(e) repeats the music of mm. 10–13 one tone lower and with the addition of a free part in the soprano while (b) utilizes the same motive (taken from countersubject 1) in inversion as the motivic basis for an ascending sequence that is canonic at the octave. Example 5-16(c) descends by step in canon at the octave.

Example 5-16. Bach, Fugue 12 in F minor (*WTC I*), a, mm. 10–13; b, mm. 16–19; c, mm. 22–25; d, mm. 30–33; e, mm. 43-47

Sequence Pattern 3: Descent by Fifth

Example 5-17 shows the basic repertoire of forms that sequences by descending fifth exhibit. Again, sequence pattern 3(a) is the simple form, using parallel motion. 3(b) introduces contrary motion, but here already we can see how the cycle of fifths begins to resemble the descending sequence by step. It is the treatment of the motives that determines whether it is the step or the fifth that is the basis of such a progression. If the motive is replicated at each stage in the circle of fifths, we receive the impression that each of the stages is an independent leg on the journey through the sequence, whereas if the motivic structure alternates, it creates an association between alternate pairs of chords, emphasizing the stepwise relationship

SEQUENCE AND EPISODE

that they exhibit. The examples below clarify this point. Sequence pattern 3(c) shows how the employment of a fifth progression in the bass in each measure provides a motivic basis for hearing the progression as fundamentally a cycle of fifths rather than a stepwise motion. Patterns (d) and (e), which show elaborations through the seventh and through inversion, also have cognates among the sequences by descending step (example 5-6, (m) and (n)). Example 5-17 (d) shows the full five-voice texture that the use of sevenths admits. The following series of progressions illustrates the use of secondary dominants and inversions in further ways. Patterns 3(e), 3(f) and 3(g) all exhibit an underlying canonic pattern in the upper voices as they exchange root and third at each stage. Pattern(h) shows the fully chromatic form of the cycle of dominant seventh harmonies, which again permits canonic motion in the paris of upper voices. Pattern (i) illustrates an inverted form that allows canonic motion in all the parts.

Example 5-17. Sequence pattern 3

Bach's Fugue in F-sharp major is one of the most tightly knit fugues in *WTC II*. Example 5-18 shows one of the sequences that descend by fifth. Comparison of this with those that descend by step above should clarify the distinction. Here the entire motivic pattern, most conveniently followed by tracing the rising series of half notes (an augmentation of the pattern found in the subject itself), repeats fifth by fifth, not step by step, in accordance with sequence pattern 3(g).

Example 5-18. Bach, Fugue 13 in F-sharp major (*WTC II*), mm. 12–20

This example is also a good study of the lattitude of which a sequence is capable, for no measure or part of a measure is a direct transposition of any other measure or part. Thus, the surface has a certain freedom, while the sequence exists beneath the foreground in the abstract progression that the music represents. In this case triadic inversion plays its part in developing the complex texture. The chromaticism that is added here, in particular the b^1 in m. 14 and the e^1 in m. 16, also refer to the flattened seventh in the subject. Here, as in other cases, the episode is not so much an occasion for contrasting material, as for reworking old material. Looking at the overall structure of the episode, it represents simply a prolongation of I that supports a rising third-progression in the upper voice.

The freedom enjoyed by the upper voices has a further purpose, in that the entire sequence is repeated with the upper two parts inverted, beginning at m. 44. This is instructive on another count, for the transposed repetition of the sequence forms a transition between VI and IV. Whereas mm. 12–20 are at the deep level a *prolongation* of I, the repetition at mm. 44–52 is a *progression*, VI–IV. This observation has nothing to do with the sequence proper, but simply with the way that the episode containing the sequence is connected to the material that precedes it. While mm. 12–14 represent a descent of a third, mm. 44–46 are a descent of a fifth, thus accounting for the ultimate third-descent of the latter sequence.

Example 5-5 shows another descending sequence by fifth, this time incorporating a triple canon. It should be clear from the analysis that it is the consonant support of the third eighth in the lower voice that is crucial in facilitating the canon at the unison with the upper voice. Interestingly, the same fugue contains another example of the same type of sequence, canonic descending fifths, in mm. 19–21, although in this case the upper two voices share the imitation of the lower voice at the octave (see example 5-19).

Example 5-19. Bach, Fugue 6 in D minor (*WTC II*), mm. 19–21

IV   CS   VII   CS   III   CS   VI   V^7

Sequence Pattern 4: Ascent by Step

Example 5-20 illustrates the basic patterns of sequences ascending by step. The parallels inherent in the simple form of sequence pattern 4(a) are most commonly removed by the contrapuntal 5-6 motion of 4(b), the importance of which Schenker stressed on several occasions.[7] 4(c) extends this type of motion to a series of sevenths, which has the interesting characteristic that the sevenths act as suspensions rather than as harmonic factors, and thus they resolve in an ascending manner. Again, this pattern forms canonic possibilities among the pairs of voices. 4(d) shows a simple reaching-over pattern that avoids the direct parallel motion without introducing any new pitch content. Patterns 4(e) and 4(f) show the introduction of secondary dominants as chromatic intensifications of the underlying 5-6 motion of 4(b) in root and inverted forms. The *fauxbourdon* pattern of example 4(g) requires no comment; 4(h) shows the use of interpolated back-relating dominants that break up the parallels, and at this stage the ascent by step begins to intersect with the ascent by fifth (see below).

Example 5-21 (a) illustrates a simple sequence ascending by step (IV–V–VI–VII). The episode as a whole functions as a prolongation of I through the harmonic cycle I–IV–V–I. There are several remarkable aspects to the passage. The first is that since the sequence is based motivically on the head of the subject (in the bass), and since the conclusion of the subject follows the end of the sequence, the cumulative effect is of a wonderful expansion of the subject itself. Second, the upper voice for these measures outlines the basic structure of the subject, $\hat{5}$ - $\hat{6}$ - $\hat{4}$ - $\hat{3}$, in a greatly expanded form. Taken as a whole, this episode is an inspired reworking of the basic tonal and motivic materials of the composition. Following the sequence of mm. 89–93 is a second, more compact sequence that retraces the same tonal ground (example 5-21 (b)). But here we can see in the upper voice this time a rising fourth, c^2-f^1, again taken from the subject, which is immediately followed by the rapid descent of the fundamental line that con-

---

[7] See *Free Composition*, 58–59.

Example 5-20. Sequence pattern 4

cludes the composition. This is not just a matter of technique, however, for the formal placement must be understood as a summing up and uniting of subject and episode in a single gesture as a conclusion to the fugue. We have here a beautiful example of how an episode can successfully fulfill the function of a conclusion to a fugue, where one would normally expect a final tonic statement of the subject. It is patently obvious that the two episodes are based on the same underlying tonal structure, so that the second acts as a reinforcement and confirmation of the first at the conclusion of the piece.

Example 5-21. Bach, Fugue 11 in F major (*WTC II*), a, mm. 89–95; b, mm. 95–99

SEQUENCE AND EPISODE 157

The following two examples are taken from the C major fugue of *WTC II*. In example 5-22 the underlying progression of the sequence is I–VI. VI is the pivot that becomes II of V, leading to the cadence on V at the end of the episode in m. 22. This sequence is based on a chromaticized form of sequence pattern 4 (b), but is also closely related to sequence pattern 4 (e). In this example the head of the subject combines with itself in canon. The free part in the bass is derived from the second half of the subject.[8] The guiding voice (leader) is the upper voice, which traverses the fourth, g^2–c^3. In example 5-23, a later repetition of the same sequence, the guiding voice is the bass, which traverses the same fourth, G–c, supporting the tenths in the upper voice and effecting a return from V to I.

Example 5-22. Bach, Fugue 1 in C major (*WTC II*), mm. 13–18

---

[8]Combination of the first and second halves of the subject is a basic objective of the piece (see chapter 7).

Example 5-23. Bach, Fugue 1 in C major (*WTC II*), mm. 55–62

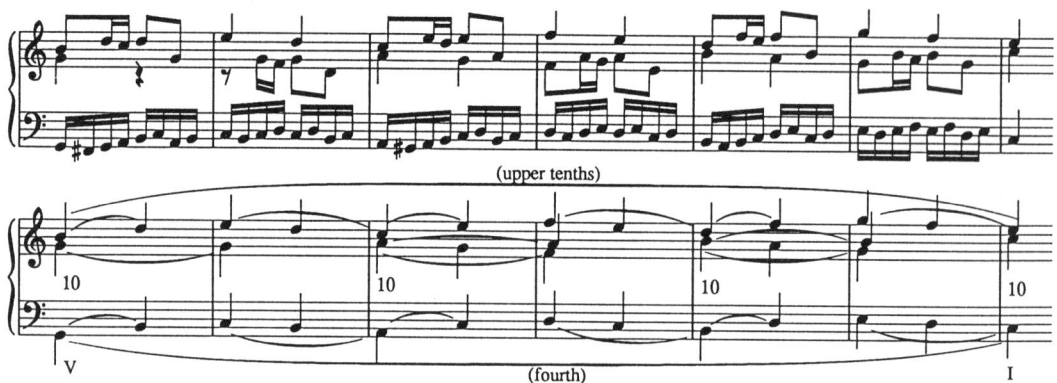

Example 5-24 illustrates another canon by step in the upper voice of the Fugue in B-flat minor (*WTC II*). The bass uses a coupling of two registers throughout the passage. The chromatic rising motion expands a chromatic voice exchange that prolongs VII and converts it into a leading-tone chord, returning the music to I. The additional statement of the motive in the upper voice at m. 66 gives further intensity to the passage, since the upper voice taken alone signifies an acceleration of motion as the apex of the episode approaches, coinciding with the tritone leap e-flat–A in the bass.

Example 5-24. Bach, Fugue 22 in B-flat minor (*WTC II*), mm. 62–67

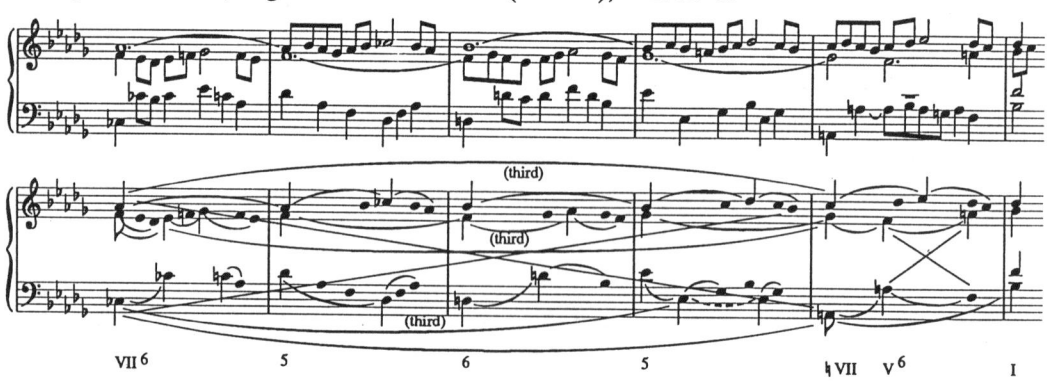

Example 5-25 illustrates a fully canonic arrangement based on sequence pattern 4 (c). The paired relationship of the four canonic parts causes the sequence to unfold in a duple rhythm, producing a hemiola against the prevailing triple rhythm of the fugue (compare example 5-10 from the same fugue). Thus, imitative counterpoint may have a formative influence not only on tonal structure, but even on meter and rhythm.

The B-flat major fugue of *WTC II* contains a brilliant series of sequences that demonstrate triple counterpoint at several intervals (see example 5-26). The three voices are beautifully distinguished by rhythmic pattern and direction of motion. If we consider the voice in dotted half notes (A) as the structural basis (which, by the way, is a replica of paradigm 5, the rising third of the subject itself—see example 4-13), we can consider the first sequence as the prime form (example 5-26 (a)): the crucial intervals are the fifth and

SEQUENCE AND EPISODE   159

Example 5-25. Bach, Fugue 22 in B-flat minor (*WTC II*), mm. 77–80

Example 5-26. Bach, Fugue 21 in B-flat major (*WTC II*), a, mm. 33–36; b, mm. 41–44; c, mm. 48–51; d, mm. 64–67; e, mm. 79–86

octave of the eighth-note voice (B) and the third (tenth) that resolves the suspension and fifth of the third voice (C). The combination of these structural notes is a simple root position triad. At (d) a simple inversion at the octave occurs in the upper parts only.

Placing either of the upper voices in the bass with octave inversion yields fourths. At (e) B and C retain the same relationship with each other as at (a) and (d) while A is inverted at the tenth (in relation to (d)). In this formation A must remain in the bass to avoid fourths. In (c), B and C are inverted at the twelfth, allowing B to appear in the bass. At (b), B is inverted at the 10th and C at the 9th, which is most unusual. Let us examine the features that facilitate this remarkable collection of inversions: A, simply a single note must always be a consonance—root, third, or fifth of the underlying harmony—and it occupies all three roles in the series of inversions that Bach uses. B has the special nature that any of its notes can be considered chord tones and any non-chord tones, as it is simply a descending scale ornamented with "sigh" motives. C normally acts as a suspension resolving down by step, followed by a motion to the third above, but can also be understood as a decorated suspension that resolves upwards at the third beat, and it is this form that is invoked to realize the inversion at the ninth in mm. 42–43.[9] In the design of this fugue, the prevalence of sequences clearly has to do with the exploitation of the inversion permutations which this set of motives possesses.

Sequence Pattern 5: Ascent by Third

Example 5-27 illustrates the basic voice-leading involved in ascending sequences by third. In sequence pattern 5(b) interposed harmonies give contrary motion and a reaching-over effect in the upper part. In 5(c) the thirds are filled with passing notes that provide the foundation of new harmonies (with the same upper voice as (b)). Pattern 5(d) introduces secondary functions.

Example 5-27. Sequence pattern 5

Example 5-28 shows a very simple sequence ascending by thirds. The bass repeats the final segment of the subject (see example 2-53), accompanied in simple block-chords by the right hand.[10] Progressing through only two legs (but growing out of the previous iteration at the end of the exposition—see example 4-15.), this sequence provides a simple modulation to the dominant, where the next entry occurs. The design of the fugue is quite interesting at this part, after which Bach introduces a mirroring descending

---

[9]Tovey notes the usefulness of this suspension figure in *A Companion to 'The Art of Fugue,'* 46.

[10]This passage recalls the continuo style described in chapter 1.

SEQUENCE AND EPISODE 161

Example 5-28. Bach, Fugue 18 in G-sharp minor (*WTC I*), mm. 9–11

sequence by thirds (mm. 12–15) that again evolves out of the end of the subject. Thus the sequences participate not only in motivic and tonal events but also in explicit design considerations.

A similar sequence is found in *WTC II*, Fugue 23 in B major (example 5-29), but here three full statements lead the music from VI to V. The next passage, a free episode (mm. 71–74) prepares for the return to I and a fresh subject statement in the bass by lowering the register of the upper voices. Both upper voices use a reaching-over pattern, and could have been written as a strict canon, but Bach has given decorated resolutions to the suspensions in the middle voice instead of simple note repetitions. It may be noted in passing that this is the only passage in the fugue in which sixteenth notes occur. Everywhere else, eighth-note motion predominates. If the sixteenth notes in this passage were rewritten to form a continuous eight-note motion, then the decorated suspensions would not work, although the canon mentioned above would work. But the suspension figure is retained in order to reinforce earlier statements, particularly those in mm. 51–53, and m. 59.

Example 5-29. Bach, Fugue 23 in B major (*WTC II*), mm. 68–71

Interestingly, like the *WTC I* G-sharp minor sequence discussed above, this one also has a twin that descends by third, which occurs immediately prior to this sequence (see example 5-15). Thus the two sequences by thirds are again complementary. Particularly here, the retrograde of the main bass tones, d-sharp^1–b–g-sharp with g-sharp–b–d-sharp^1 is readily apparent to the ear. Bach's use of sequences by third here may also relate to the fact that the entire subject is created out of the interval of the third and its inversion, the sixth (see example 2-34).

Example 5-30 illustrates the use of canon in an ascent by thirds. The canon is in the upper two voices. This example has the same basic tonal structure as the previous one: VI moves to V, to be resolved back to I. The bass, while not in canon, uses similar material. The bass could have joined the canon, moving in parallel tenths with the upper voice, but that would have simplified the texture by reducing the independence of the bass part. This is not the first time that we have seen Bach avoid the use of a canon that could easily be achieved. Imitation is only one of the facets of the contrapuntal art. In an effective composition, imitation must be integrated with other considerations, including texture and tonal structure.

Example 5-30. Bach, Fugue 11 in F major (*WTC II*), mm. 38–44

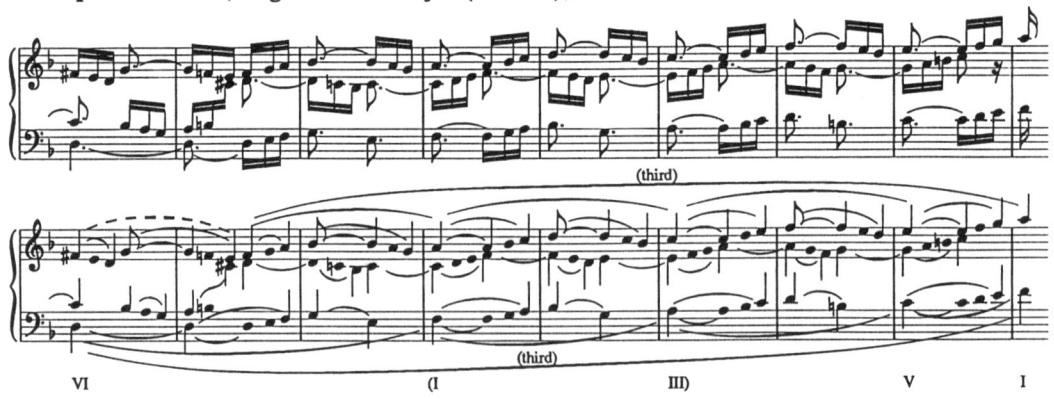

Sequence Pattern 6: Ascent by Fifth

The ascent by fifth of sequence pattern 6(a) is shown in example 5-31. The pattern at 6(b) may be compared with pattern 4(h) (example 5-20), and again, it is the foreground activity and the context of the sequence that ultimately determines whether at deeper levels the progression is by step or by fifth. Pattern 6(c) introduces secondary dominants and 6(d) introduces secondary sevenths; 6(e) shows an alternation of root position and first inversion that has interesting possibilities for canonic effects between the outer parts; 6(f) adds secondary dominants to the progression of 6(e) and maintains the canonic pattern of the outer voices.

Example 5-32, a sequence by ascending fifths, happens to be the music that immediately follows example 5-30. Here the bass is the guiding voice, prolonging each of the steps, f^1–c^1–g–d in turn, through a descending octave. Thus we have the unusual situation of a sequence built of ascending

SEQUENCE AND EPISODE

Example 5-31. Sequence pattern 6

Example 5-32. Bach, Fugue 11 in F major (*WTC II*), mm. 45–52

fifths that in fact descends, due to the introduction of a descending octave transfer at each step of the progression.

The brief sequence in example 5-33 illustrates a triple invertible canon applied to a sequence descending by fifths. At each step a secondary dominant strengthens the motion to the next fifth, but because the motives are tossed from part to part no leg of the sequence is a direct transposition of another (compare example 5-18). Taken as a whole, the episode is a compact and effective progression from the relative major to the tonic, III–I. Although the triple invertible canon of example 5-32 is perfect in itself, it has none of the potential for development or variation embodied in the triple invertible counterpoint of example 5-26, which in six forms exploits only half of its possibilities.

Example 5-33. Bach, Fugue 20 in A minor (*WTC II*), mm. 11–12

Like subjects and answers, sequences arise out of a limited number of recognizable voice-leading patterns inherent in the boundaries of the tonal system itself. The tonal meaning of a sequence within an episode, and for that matter of an episode within a fugue, is determined ulimately by its larger context. Such contexts will become apparent later, since many of the episodes discussed in chapter 5 are contained in the three complete fugal analyses of chapter 7.

CHAPTER 6

Stretto and Other Devices

> When he listened to a rich and many-voiced fugue, he could soon say, after the first entries of the subject, what contrapuntal devices it would be possible to apply, and which of them the composer by rights ought to apply, and on such occasions, when I was standing next to him, and he had voiced his surmises to me, he would joyfully nudge me when his expectations were fulfilled.[1]

To what extent is C. P. E. Bach's reportage of his father's talents exaggerated, and to what extent is it an accurate record? There is no reason to doubt the substance of this passage, given the absolutely extraordinary genius that J. S. Bach possessed as a composer. But what mechanism might have allowed Bach to recognize the inherent possibilities of a given subject, whether in the music of others as this quotation reports, or indeed as he developed his own compositions, for surely Bach would have recognized inherent possibilities in his own themes as well. Earlier chapters have already demonstrated the prevalence of repetitive patterns of structure at foreground and middleground levels in a variety of aspects of fugue. Chapter 6 considers these questions and suggests some answers by exploring the types of structural patterning frequently encountered in typical contrapuntal devices.

Stretto, broadly speaking the compositional idea of counterpointing a motive with itself, serves as a conceptual basis for understanding other complex imitative techniques such as inversion, augmentation, and diminution. While essentially the same contrapuntal technique as canon, stretto is integrated into a larger contrapuntal fabric. A true canon, by contrast, continues unbroken to the conclusion of a piece and establishes its own formal design. The underlying structural patterns of stretti can be grouped conveniently in relation to patterns most of which have been established in earlier chapters: prolonged harmony, linear progressions, the voice-leading complex, and sequences. In each case a clear structural basis provides an essential tonal context for the counterpoint. As the examples will suggest, it is perhaps the recognition of similar underlying patterns that allowed Bach's imagination to speedily assess and realize the imitative potential of any given theme.

Prolonged Harmony

The use of a single prolonged harmony as the basis for stretto or canon has a compelling logic since problems of harmonic progression and parallel motion are largely eliminated. This type of stretto is most appropriate for imitation at the unison or octave rather than other intervals because each part must project the same harmony. However, with tonal alterations it is also possible for a stretto at the fifth or fourth to project a

---

[1] C. P. E. Bach, letter to Forkel (c. 1774), trans. in David and Mendel, *The Bach Reader*, 277.

single harmony. Since only a single harmony is utilized, the problem of faulty harmonic progression is eliminated. The situation never arises in which the leading part moves to a new chord while the following part remains on the original harmony.

As its title suggests, Bach's *Canon in Einklange*[2] (example 6-1) is a model of this type of imitation. The theme links the notes of the triad through passing tones, ascending and descending. It expresses complete consonance and gives up to eight parts. For the purpose of discussing the technique of stretto, it is convenient to distinguish two variables, the *distance* between entries in beats, and the *interval* between entries in pitch. Although Bach presents this music as a four-part canon in unison at the distance of two beats set against its inversion in four parts beginning one beat later, Marpurg points out that the third and fourth measures in fact reveal an eight-part canon at the unison at the distance of one beat.[3] Since the tonal structure is so limited, its potential for musical expression is severely restricted. Within the context of longer works such imitation leads to passages of overt tonal prolongation which in their barrenness ultimately impede the sense of tonally directed motion that vitalizes musical structure.

Example 6-1. Bach, *Canon in Einklange* BWV 1072

Example 6-2 shows how the prolongation of a single harmony can serve as the basis of a simple canon at the octave. Bach is careful to employ contrary motion and contrasting rhythm in order to establish the independence of the parts. Such canons effectively establish a tonic prolongation in the operative key, but demand tonal motion in the succeeding music.

[2]BWV 1072, found in Marpurg's *Abhandlung von der Fuge*, 2 vols. (Berlin, 1754), Vol. 2, Table 37, Fig. 1. According to Marpurg, Bach called it *Trias Harmonica*, the harmonic triad.
[3]*Ibid.*, 2:97.

STRETTO AND OTHER DEVICES

In this case Bach provides this movement in the canonic sequence by descending thirds that follows.

Example 6-2. Bach, Invention 8 in F major BWV 779, mm. 1–3

Bach's *Canon triplex a 6 vocibus* illustrates how prolongation of a single triad can be expanded to encompass a greater variety of thematic material in a freer manner. Each of the three themes in example 6-3 (a) develops linear progressions within the tonic triad. The leading theme (middle part) is none other than paradigm 2 with the initial ascent and upper neighbor pattern so familiar from example 2-20. The upper part alternates ascent to the tonic and descent to $\hat{3}$, while the lower voice expands an arpeggiation of the tonic chord with passing notes. Although all tones that are not part of the tonic triad can be understood in a purely contrapuntal manner as passing or neighboring tones, the combination of passing tones and the progression c–d–G in the bass begin to project a simple harmonic motion as well (I–II–V–I). Example 6-3 (b) is the melodic inversion of example 6-3 (a) at the distance of one measure. Each of the voices is now in mirror inversion around the note B, such that G and D, root and fifth, interchange. Since all notes that are not part of I act in a contrapuntal manner, the possibility of inversion itself is a given. Bach's canon is realized by the combination of (a) and (b) simultaneously. The only obstacle that Bach had to overcome here was the avoidance of forbidden motion. This is accomplished through allowing the doubled leading-tone of m. 2 to resolve in contrary motion. Again, despite its harmonic progression, the fully worked canon is ultimately static and cannot sustain a lengthy development.

Example 6-3. Bach *Canon triplex a 6 vocibus* BWV 1076

In example 6-4 a three-part stretto based on a single arpeggiated harmony is used within an actual composition. Mm. 52–53 contain a three-part stretto that prolongs G-sharp minor, and the following measures contain an inversion of the same, prolonging F-sharp major. It is important to understand that it is the ability of this particular subject to prolong a single harmony through its first two measures (see example 2-23) that accommodates this particular type of stretto, a prolongational type *per arsin e thesin*.[4] Further, the balanced formation of the subject facilitates its inversion and consequently its application to stretto in inversion. The cadential part of the subject, which no longer prolongs the tonic harmony, cannot be utilized in this way. Consequently each of these stretti dispenses with the conclusion of the subject.

Example 6-4. Bach, Fugue 8 in D-sharp minor (*WTC I*), mm. 52–56

Prolonged harmony is the obvious locus for such procedures as augmentation and diminution stretti as well. It should be evident that a subject will most easily combine with itself in augmentation if it prolongs a single harmony, since the problem of harmonic progression is thereby eliminated. The final portion of the same fugue is a superb example of this technique (see example 6-5). While the upper part sounds a broad augmentation of the subject, the lower part presents the subject in its original form. In each case, alteration of the first note from D-sharp to E-sharp accommodates the prevailing dominant harmony. The middle part gives the subject in a partially augmented form. The lower part includes the entire subject, varied in rhythm, so as to maintain the eighth-note movement, and in register, to facilitate keyboard performance. As the graph illustrates, the combination of bass and treble in this instance produces a double counterpoint based on the voice-leading matrix, with $\hat{3}$ - $\hat{2}$ - $\hat{1}$ in the bass and $\hat{5}$ - $\hat{4}$ - $\hat{3}$ in the treble. The added c-double-sharp[1] in mm. 79 completes the harmony as it effects

---

[4]By alternating weak and strong beats—i.e., at the distance of one quarter note.

STRETTO AND OTHER DEVICES

the change of register in the bass. While the structural origin of this stretto is prolongation of harmony, the combination of lines yields a harmonic progression at the point where the cadential part of the subject is introduced.

Example 6-5. Bach, Fugue 8 in D-sharp minor (*WTC I*), mm. 77–82

An additional subject statement in the middle part at m. 80 at the subdominant level is a fortuitous extra entry facilitated by the fact that the bass is here at liberty to provide a convincing tonal context for the upper parts. For example, the fourth d^1-g^2 in m. 81 is rendered consonant by b supplied by the free counterpoint of the bass.

Bach pursues a systematic and impressive stretto design throughout the final third of this fugue. The augmented subject appears once in each part; first in the bass, then in the middle part, and finally, following an answer statement in the middle voice and a two-measure episode that prepares the return to I, in the crowning statement in the upper part, after which the conclusion of the fugue quickly follows. Each of the augmentation statements provides the basis for a set of stretti involving all three parts.

The opening portion of the C minor subject of *WTC II* has much the same structure as the previous example (see example 2-5). Example 6-6 shows how Bach utilizes the arpeggiated character as the foundation of a similar augmentation stretto. In m. 14 the upper parts simply prolong a neighboring six-four. In the next measure the bass is accommodated as a free inversion of the subject, leading to a harmonic resolution to I in m. 16.

Example 6-6. Bach, Fugue 2 in C minor (*WTC II*), mm. 14–16

In example 6-7 Bach realizes the *Canon in Einklange* within a broad harmonic progression.[5] As in example 6-1, Bach develops eight independent parts through this prolongational imitation of ascending and descending fifths between root and fifth of the prevailing harmony. Each part reverts to free counterpoint after presenting its ascending or descending fifth, thus providing a necessary variety to the texture. The bass of Choir II sustains the roots of an underlying harmony that changes every two bars in a sequence by descending thirds (sequence pattern 2). Bach uses 5-6 technique in the stepwise root progressions of mm. 4-5 and 8-9 in order to avoid parallels. At a deeper level, the entire twelve-measure passage represents an expository prolongation of I.

Example 6-7. Bach, Sanctus in D major BWV 241, mm. 1–12

[5]Example 6-7 omits the orchestral doublings and the text in order to illustrate the structural basis of the imitative texture.

STRETTO AND OTHER DEVICES

Harmonic prolongation also provides the basis for an extremely rare stretto technique in which the subject is divided into separate components, and a separate stretto is constructed out of each. In example 6-8, the first stretto works up through three entries beginning in the bass, followed by an additional statement of the opening of the subject in the bass. The second stretto works from the treble back down through the alto and bass, leading to the conclusion of the composition. This arrangement forms an impressive arch structure which Bach reserves for the conclusion of the work. Apart from the anacrusis of the first statement, the entire stretto represents simply a tonic prolongation through arpeggiation and passing motions. Again, the nature of the subject, an arpeggiation of I, permits the stretto at the octave and also facilitates the free stretto treatment utilized by Bach.[6]

Example 6-8. Bach, Toccata in G major BWV 916-3, mm. 93–97

Example 6-9, from Contrapunctus 5, shows the basis of an *inversus* stretto of the outer parts in the same formation, prolonging as it does a single harmony with neighbor motions that produce a contrapuntal V chord. The inner parts simply reinforce the harmonic implications of the outer parts throughout this passage.

Contrapunctus 6 shows a similar technique, including not only *rectus et inversus* but also diminution of the theme. The breadth of register, in which each of the three parts uses a separate octave at the outset is necessary to avoid part crossing in this stretto.[7]

---

[6]Handel too uses this design with great effect, in the fugue from Suite 8 in F Minor, mm. 95–104. Schenker himself remarks on this passage, in "Brahms: Variations and Fugue on a theme of Handel, Op. 24," *Der Tonwille* IV, Part 2/3 (April–September, 1924), 34.

[7]Contrapunctus 7 adds to the scheme of Contrapunctus 6 augmentation of the theme as well, but never combines diminution, original value, and augmentation simultaneously.

Example 6-9. Bach, Contrapunctus 5 (*Art of Fugue*), mm. 33–34

Example 6-10. Bach, Contrapunctus 6 (*Art of Fugue*), mm. 1–4

The cluster of examples shown here all share features in common: arpeggiation of the tonic chord as a structural basis, which allows the techniques of stretto, inversion, and augmentation to be successfully applied. Common structural features lead to similar imitative techniques. These examples thus do point to a knowledge of the potential for imitative development of fugal themes as described by C.P.E. Bach.

Linear Progression

Many of the examples shown here have included passing notes that convert a simple triadic gesture into a stepwise scale segment, yet in each case the underlying premise has been the prolongation of a single harmony through root, third and fifth of that harmony. But the scale itself, considered apart from harmonic prolongation, has its own distinct but related possibilities outside the bounds of imitation at the octave or prolongation of

STRETTO AND OTHER DEVICES

a single harmony. In particular the scale forms a natural basis for stretto passages in parallel thirds or sixths. Example 6-11 illustrates some possibilities for this idea. It is the province of the larger context to establish the tonal meaning of a passage based on such structures. The most common scalar segment is the ascending fifth progression $\hat{1}$ - $\hat{5}$, which can be seen as directly expanding the possibilities of the prolonged harmony form as seen in the *Canon in Einklange*. A great strength of these patterns is that the same scalar design allows imitation not only at the octave but also at the fifth; indeed a stretto at any interval can be contrived through this form, the governing factor being the distance between entries. In example 6-11, (a) through (c) illustrate rising patterns, (d) through (f) show descending patterns, and (g) through (i) are combinations. The patterns are by no means limited to only two parts. In parallel motion three can be combined briefly in six-three formations. Contrary motion allows the simultaneous combination of four or more parts.

Example 6-11. Scalar stretti

Imitation through the scale and through prolonged harmony were both employed in the pre-tonal era, and examples of both are legion.[8] Examples 6-12 and 6-13 from Palestrina's *Exultate Deo* are representative. Examples such as these, though predating the tonal era, bespeak a strong orientation towards triadic harmony. Indeed, it is worth considering that the imitative procedures of patterns such as these may have played a significant role in the gradual development of the tonal system, for these patterns naturally tend to establish prolongations of triadic harmony and such prolongations tend to establish tonal centers.

---

[8]"The ear comprehends their relationship best when the voices are close together in time, and for this reason composers strive to keep them so, if possible, in fugal writing. But constant practice of this close imitation has resulted in such a common idiom that a fugal pattern cannot be found that has not been used thousands of times by various composers." Zarlino, *The Art of Counterpoint*, 127. It was in fact the development of surface ornamentation in the instrumental style that gave a new lease on life to imitative counterpoint in the Baroque era.

Example 6-12. Palestrina, *Exultate Deo*, mm. 42–45

Example 6-13. Palestrina, *Exultate Deo*, mm. 49–53

Handel composed numerous stretti based on scale segments. Examples 6-14 and 6-15 are taken from the final movement of the *Messiah*. Example 6-14 is based on ascending fifth progressions and example 6-15 is based on descending fifths. (The motive itself is the initial ascent from the opening of the subject, see example 2-35.) The important difference to be recognized between this pattern and the *"Canon in Einklange"* is that here imitation at the fifth naturally leads to a sequential progression rather than a prolongation. It is a linear rather than harmonic technique. Example 6-14 is based on a rising sequence from I to III, followed by a more rapid movement from III to V. At any given point the parts are in parallel thirds or sixths with each other, and paired in contrary motion. Example 6-15 reverses the process through a series of overlapped descending fifth-progressions.

STRETTO AND OTHER DEVICES

Example 6-14. Handel, "Worthy is the Lamb" (*Messiah*), mm. 116–120

Example 6-15. Handel, "Worthy is the Lamb" (*Messiah*), mm. 143–146

Example 6-16 illustrates the same type of imitation used as the basis of an instrumental composition, Handel's *Fuga* from the Suite in F-sharp minor. Again a stretto at the fifth (each set of three statements is a fifth higher) develops naturally into a sequential pattern (compare example 5-17 (c). This passage is virtually identical to the central section of the ritornello in the second movement of Handel's Organ Concerto, Opus 4, No. 1. The only important distinction is the change of mode from minor to major.

Example 6-16. Handel, Suite VI in F-sharp minor, *Fuga*, mm. 57–62

That Handel developed such patterns consciously is tangibly demonstrated by his surviving composition studies. Alfred Mann's excellent edition of the composition lessons from the autograph collection in the Fitzwilliam Museum gives us a window into Handel's workshop.[9] Pages 53-54 show the schematic basis of Handel's scalar stretti in both ascending and descending forms. On page 55 we find the pattern of the rising tetrachord (see below). Page 51 shows the equivalent of Bach's stretti based on chordal prolongation. Handel's subject, however, is the well known chorale "*Aus tiefer Noth*," used several times by Bach as well, not to mention many others composers. The subject has the same structure as the *WTC I* D-sharp minor subject (example 2-23) with an added $\hat{5}$ at the beginning, and of course is especially adapted to both augmentation and inversion stretti. Thus, Handel too, like Bach, developed a systematic concept of close imitation on the basis of simple underlying scalar and harmonic elements.

Bach's Contrapunctus 5 includes virtually the same stretto patterns as Handel's, in both ascending and descending forms (examples 6-17 and 6-18). In example 6-17 the ascending fifths form a rising sequence through the circle of fifths in a four part stretto. The dotted rhythm allows the stretto to operate *per arsin et thesin* without forming accented dissonance. Example 6-18 is an inversion of example 6-17, with slight alterations of detail. It is no mere coincidence that the twin giants of Baroque composition developed virtually identical stretto schemes. Rather, it reflects their respect for and understanding of the potential and limitations of the tonal system within which they worked.[10]

---

[9] Handel, *Aufzeichnungen zur Kompositionslehre,* (Kassel: Bärenreiter, 1978). See also Alfred Mann, *Theory and Practice*, (New York: Norton, 1987), 17–19.

[10] The canonic sequences of example 5-16 also follow this pattern.

Example 6-17. Bach, Contrapunctus 5 (*Art of Fugue*), mm. 53–56

Example 6-18. Bach, Contrapunctus 5 (*Art of Fugue*), mm. 65–68

While the norm for scalar stretti is imitation at the octave or fifth, imitation at the fourth or seventh is also possible, if the second entry follows at a distance of one note rather than two. The stretti of the B-flat minor fugue of *WTC II* are all based on this possibility. Although the foundation of these stretti is simply the rising scale-segments of the subject's initial ascent (see example 2-12), the expressive leap of m. 2 gives an inverted interval as the stretto proceeds. Examples 6-19 through 6-22 illustrate the tonal structure of the various stretti: *rectus, inversus, rectus et inversus*. The graphs are intended here primarily to illustrate the contrapuntal relationship among the stretto parts and their implications for tonal structure. The free parts reinforce the implied tonal structure. Examples 6-19 and 6-20 essentially embody prolongations of the operative tonality, including relatively strong cadences that coincide with the ends of the stretti. However, the *rectus et inversus* forms in example 6-21 lead to less tonally unified passages that rely much more upon their context to establish deeper tonal meanings. The four-part stretto of example 6-22 reverts to a simpler harmonic and voice-leading structure that prolongs I and supports the ultimate descent of the fundamental line. The VI that begins the excerpt is a tonal means of binding this stretto to the previous music and avoiding a perfect authentic cadence (PAC) at the point where the soprano restates the subject in its original form. As the examples show, the underlying tonal meaning of such passages cannot be determined completely on a theoretical basis. Rather, the unique context of a given scalar stretto invests the passage with a distinct harmonic significance. Chapter 7 illustrates the context of these stretto passages within the deeper structure of the entire fugue.

Example 6-19. Bach, Fugue 22 in B-flat minor (*WTC II*), a, mm. 27–31; b, mm. 33–37

Example 6-20. Bach, Fugue 22 in B-flat minor (*WTC II*), a, mm. 67–71; b, mm. 73–77

STRETTO AND OTHER DEVICES

179

Example 6-21. Bach, Fugue 22 in B-flat minor (*WTC II*), a, mm. 80–84; b, mm. 89–93

Example 6-22. Bach, Fugue 22 in B-flat minor (*WTC II*), mm. 96–101

In the D minor fugue of *WTC II*, Bach incorporates a chromatic motion within a scalar descent. While the ascent projects parallel thirds by following a stretto at the fifth at a distance of two eighths, the following descent develops a series of descending sixths, as the leading part reverses in advance of the following part. The bass enters with the contrasing theme of the episodes at a point which allows a contrary motion to develop against the descent of the upper parts. The parenthetical A is a good illustration of the manner in which a fugal bass implies its structural role rather than explicitly stating it. The A clarifies the harmony and provides a contrapuntal origin for the following B-natural, but is omitted for the sake of the motivic design.

Example 6-23. Bach, Fugue 6 in D minor (*WTC II*), mm. 14–15

Purcell seems to have had a special interest in developing contrapuntal devices as points of imitation. The first movement of his Trio Sonata VI includes a twofold augmentation at the fifth and octave. While this stretto is based on an ascending scale segment, the structural technique is totally different. The theme itself appears in the bass in quarters (see example 6-24). As a bass, this theme represents paradigm 4 (compare example 2-31), but as a melody could well be thought of as paradigm 2. In this type of fugue it is most convenient to have the quickest iteration of the subject in the bass, so that after only two measures it is freed to support and clarify the tonal meaning of the stretto that continues in the upper parts. The first violin begins simultaneously at the octave in a double augmentation, such that its first three notes, c^2–d^2–e^2, span the underlying harmonic progression I–V–I of the bass. In this manner, the first three notes of the subject function as

STRETTO AND OTHER DEVICES 181

paradigm 5 in counterpoint against paradigm 4. The second violin enters at the fifth after two beats, in an augmentation of the theme. This middle part is unquestionably of less structural significance. It projects the underlying harmony with less clarity, although the the fourth note of the subject comes into play here as the resolution of the leading tone. Its ending must be varied to accord with the continuing double augmentation of the first violin.

Example 6-24. Purcell, Trio Sonata VI in C major, i, mm. 1–6

Although the subject of the third movement of Bach's Second Trio Sonata possesses many leaps and a variety of rhythms, it resolves structurally to a full descending octave, reflecting once again the fundamental importance of the descending scale in Bach's technique from the homophonic prelude right through to the fugal stretto. The second entry, following at two bars and at the unison, produces a series of parallel thirds in combination with the first entry. For the bulk of the stretto the bass is at liberty to support the counterpoint of the upper parts. At m. 94 the bass begins the subject. The basis of this passage then is a simple prolongation of tonic harmony through the scale, not conceptually different than the simple scalar descents exhibited in chapter 1. However, while the scalar passages form a framework, the additional notes of the theme project a broad third progression in the upper voice that resolves in m. 94.[11]

---

[11] The fugue of Bach's Toccata and Fugue in D minor BWV 538 *(Dorian)* illustrates the potential for an entire octave ascent and descent to develop a lengthy stretto. The ascent establishes a chain of sixths and the descent develops the inversion, a chain of tenths.

Example 6-25. Bach, Sonata II in C minor for organ BWV 526, iii, mm. 86–96

Tetrachordal Stretto

Perhaps in order to allow more unified imitative themes to be used in stretto formations, many composers developed stretto structures that utilize the ascending fourth as a basis of imitation, but which then continue with a descending motion, such that the imitative subject is endowed with an essential $\hat{3}$ - $\hat{2}$ - $\hat{1}$ background structure, embellished by initial ascent and upper neighbor, giving some form of $\hat{1}$ - $\hat{2}$ - $\hat{3}$ - $\hat{4}$ - $\hat{3}$ - $\hat{2}$ - $\hat{1}$ (paradigm 2) as the basic pattern. This pattern may be conceived historically as a representation of the lower tetrachord, since the response completes the stretto idea by utilizing the upper tetrachord. Just as in the "regular" relationship between subject and answer for $\hat{3}$ - $\hat{2}$ - $\hat{1}$, in stretto too the upper neighbor of the subject becomes a point of tonal focus, $\hat{1}$, when transposed to the answer.

An early example of this can be found in Sancta Maria's *Arte de tañer Fantasia*, a remarkably progressive work in terms of its approach to the incipient concept of four-part harmony that was to develop in the following century.[12] In example 6-26 the endings of the second and third entries are altered for the sake of the harmony, but the final entry reverts to a complete statement of the original subject.

---

[12]Tomas de Sancta Maria, *Arte de tañer Fantasia*, 2 vols. (Valladolid, 1565).

STRETTO AND OTHER DEVICES   183

Example 6-26. Sancta Maria, *Arte de tañer Fantasia*, 2:79, mm. 1–10

A similar pattern occurs at the opening of Orlando Gibbons's Voluntary of Four Parts, although the ascent includes in this case a leap, giving $\hat{1}$ - $\hat{2}$ - $\hat{4}$ - $\hat{3}$ - $\hat{2}$ - $\hat{1}$ as a basic pattern (see example 6-27).

Example 6-27. Gibbons, A Voluntary of Four Parts, mm. 1–4

Purcell uses a similar pattern for a similar stretto development in his Second Trio Sonata (example 6-28).

Example 6-28. Purcell, Trio Sonata II in B-flat major, v, mm. 4–8

The subject of Bach's E major fugue (*WTC II*) again takes the same form (see example 2-19), and again serves as a basis of similar stretto structures (see example 6-29).[13]

---

[13]Froberger's Fantasy 12 in E Phrygian is apparently a model for Bach's fugue, prefiguring not only the subject but also the stretto techniques and diminutions.

Example 6-29. Bach, Fugue 9 in E major (*WTC II*), mm. 9–12

Example 2-20 illustrated the popularity of this simple subject form of paradigm 2 among a wide range of composers. Each of these cases develops similar stretto patterns to those illustrated here. One may add to this list the second theme of Handel's *Halleluia* (*Messiah*) mm. 12–14, despite the fact that he does not utilize its stretto potential in this movement. Mozart, in his Finale of Symphony 41 (*Jupiter*), continues this tradition right through the height of the classical style.

Perhaps the most beautifully worked example of tetrachordal stretto is the first chorus from Bach's Cantata BWV 29, "*Wir danken dir.*" Bach's satisfaction with his work here is attested to by his reuse of the same music twice more in the *B Minor Mass*, in the middle of the *Gloria* and at the end of the *Agnus Dei*. Example 6-30 shows how the opening stretto creates a wonderfully paced ascent through four voices.

Example 6-30. Bach, Cantata BWV 29-2, mm. 1–8

STRETTO AND OTHER DEVICES 185

The implication of these examples, an implication which begs further study, is that certain basic contrapuntal structures were reused over and over by generation after generation of composers, perhaps bequeathed from teacher to pupil in an oral or improvisatorial tradition of which we can glimpse only scattered traces. The question, which would be extremely difficult to answer, but perhaps could be speculated upon, is to what extent these composers considered the process of composition to be the art of reworking existing patterns, and to what extent composers re-invented similar patterns generation after generation. We should not consider any sense of plagiarism in connection with such similarities, for it is the tonal system itself that coaxes them into being as the imitative plans that are successful in projecting a sense of tonality and accommodating a cogent imitative texture.

Voice-leading Complex

Example 6-31, from the opening of the second movement of Bach's *Second Brandenburg Concerto*, illustrates how the voice-leading complex can serve as the basis for a fully developed canonic passage of music. Each succeeding phrase introduces another of the basic contrapuntal voices of the voice-leading complex—first $\hat{5} - \hat{4} - \hat{3}$, then $\hat{3} - \hat{2} - \hat{1}$, and finally $\hat{8} - \hat{7} - \hat{8}$—while the independent continuo fills out the harmony and supplies a consistent bass progression. (The structure exhibited here is virtually identical to that shown in example 5-4.) This structural basis ensures complete compatibility among the voices as a canonic texture unfolds at the opening of this slow movement. Much of the remainder of the piece consists of rearrangements and transpositions of this basic pattern.

Example 6-31. Bach, Brandenburg Concerto 2 in F major BWV 1047, ii, mm. 1–7

Example 6-32 illustrates how the combination of subject and answer in stretto can complete the matrix pattern. Here the subject is essentially $\hat{8}$-$\hat{7}$-$\hat{8}$, and the answer $\hat{5}$-sharp-$\hat{4}$-$\hat{5}$. But in combination the answer is divided into two parts. The first, $\hat{5}$-$\hat{4}$-$\hat{3}$, combines with the $\hat{8}$-$\hat{7}$-$\hat{8}$ of the subject. The following sharp-$\hat{4}$-$\hat{5}$ then completes the motion to the dominant at a deeper level. This pattern repeats for the next two entries, completing a stretto exposition that condenses the regular tonal structure of an exposition, ending on V. In mm. 11–18 the same passage is repeated in the subdominant. Thus in the larger view, mm. 1–18 is a large scale prolongation of I as I–V, IV–I.

Example 6-32. Bach, Cantata BWV 19-1, mm. 1–5

The fugal subject of Bach's Sonata 3 in C major for unaccompanied violin BWV 1005 is based on paradigm 1 but includes an upper neighbor plus lower thirds for each of the main notes. The answer follows the patterns of paradigm 1, but with tonal chromatic alteration is capable of retaining the tonic harmony. As example 6-33 illustrates, this allows the answer to be reinterpreted as a prolongation within the tonic that expands the two voices $\hat{3}$-$\hat{2}$-$\hat{1}$ and $\hat{8}$-$\hat{7}$-$\hat{8}$. The combination of subject and answer in this manner yields the voice-leading matrix.

Example 6-33. Bach, Sonata 3 in C major for unaccompanied violin BWV 1005, *Fuga,* mm. 92–96

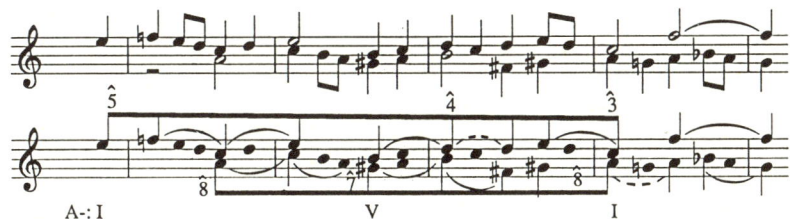

Sequential Stretto

Chapter 5 has already demonstrated that certain sequence patterns are ready-built to contain stretto or canonic passages, since they have an integral repetition structure.[14] The purpose of the following examples is to show the incorporation of full subject statements or other important thematic materials within such patterns. Example 6-34 illustrates how a subject that is itself sequential in nature, combines with itself in a complementary rhythm and direction to form a simple stretto in two parts. As with episodes based on sequential progressions, this passage forms a simple prolongation of V, resolving to I. A similar sequential stretto recurs at mm. 21–26 (example 6-35). While the stretto may be considered as encompassing all four parts, in fact the first two entries in the middle voices take no part in the development of the sequential passage of mm. 24–25.

Example 6-34. Krebs, Fugue in C major BWV 553, mm. 13–16

Example 6-35. Krebs, Fugue in C major BWV 553, mm. 21–26

---

[14]Examples 5-5, 5-9, 5-10, 5-12, 5-16, 5-19, 5-22, 5-23, 5-24, 5-25, 5-30, and 5-33 all include canonic textures.

The six-part *Ricercare* from *A Musical Offering* includes a brilliant example of four-part canon in sequence. This is a fascinating example, because here Bach takes the tetrachordal structure illustrated earlier as the basis of a sequence by descending fifths. The other three parts represent a melodic continuation of the first idea in a canonic manner, using the same technique as in example 5-18, but in four parts. While the motivic material of this sequence is not the main subject of the *ricercare* itself, it is included here because it is clearly based on the familiar tetrachordal structure that grows out of paradigm 2.

Example 6-36. *Ricercare a 6 (A Musical Offering)*, mm. 98–104

In light of the survey of stretto patterns presented in chapter 6, we can easily perceive the general means by which Bach could display such all-encompassing knowledge of the imitative possibilities inherent in a given fugue subject. As with other aspects of imitative counterpoint treated earlier, stretto, thematic inversion, augmentation, and diminution all operate by and large according to a limited number of simple underlying structural patterns. And just as in other parts of fugue, it is these underlying patterns of structure that provide a basis for tonal coherence in the dense web of motivic activity that such passages display. It is not difficult to understand how Bach was able to comprehend so quickly and precisely the imitative possibilities implied by a given subject, and how they might be worked out properly and effectively within a fully developed fugue.

CHAPTER 7

Complete Fugue

> He who is not acquainted with Bach's fugues cannot even form an idea of what a true fugue is and ought to be. In fugues of the ordinary kind, there is nothing but a certain very insignificant and sloppy routine (*Schlendrian*). They take a theme, give it a companion, transpose both gradually into the keys related to the original one, and make the other parts accompany them in all these transpositions with a kind of thorough-bass chords. This is a fugue; but of what kind? It is very natural that a person acquainted with only such fugues can have no great opinion of the whole species. How much art does it, then, require to make oneself master of such commonplace?
>
> Bach's fugue is of quite another kind. It fulfills all the conditions which we are otherwise accustomed to demand only of more free species of composition. A highly characteristic theme; an uninterrupted principal melody, wholly derived from it and equally characteristic from the beginning to the end; not mere accompaniment in the other parts, but in each of them an independent melody, according with the others, also from the beginning to the end; freedom, lightness, and fluency in the progress of the whole; inexhaustible variety of modulation combined with perfect purity; the exclusion of every arbitrary note not necessarily belonging to the whole; unity and diversity in the style, rhythm, and meters; and, lastly, diffused through the whole, so that it sometimes appears to the performer or hearer as if every single note were animated — these are the properties of Bach's fugue, properties which necessarily excite admiration and astonishment in every judge who knows how much power of mind is required for the production of such works.[1]

Despite his efforts to enumerate objectively and in a technical manner the strengths of Bach's fugal art, touching on many points of his genius as a contrapuntist, Forkel's account is largely subjective and impressionistic. Note in particular Forkel's reference to thoroughbass fugue (partimento) as a lower form of composition, and his sensitivity to Bach's efforts to unify the upper voice through an "uninterrupted principal melody," which might be interpreted in our day as a perception of linear coherence beneath the surface of the music. Although one is tempted to consider this as a foreshadowing of Schenker's concept of fundamental line, it is likelier that Forkel refers only in a general sense to the especially convincing melodic continuity evident in Bach's fugues.

Schenker's description of Bach's fugal technique, given below, is also quite general, yet it accounts concisely for the variety, consistency and quality of Bach's fugal art in a more objective and theoretical manner:

> Despite the fact that each one exhibits a different design, the fugues of J. S. Bach are genuine fugues in the strictest sense; they are always determined by

---

[1] Forkel, "On J. S. Bach's Life," trans. in David and Mendel, *The Bach Reader*, 324–25.

> the subject, by its dimensions and harmonic content, and are controlled by a fundamental structure. . . . Without improvisational gift, that is, without the ability to connect the composition to the middleground and background, no good fugue can ever be written.[2]

Each author in his own way affirms that Bach's rigorous and thorough technique controls all levels of a fugue and unites motivic and formal aspects of each composition in a unique masterwork.

Schenker seems to have had a special regard for the unique qualities of fugal form, since he devoted a separate section to it near the end of his chapter on form in *Free Composition*. From this we can understand that in Schenker's world fugue is not a genre within the simple binary or ternary forms, but is its own complex form.

> Growing out of imitation, the fugue became the first unified form of larger dimensions. The fifth-relation between the first three entries (subject, answer, subject) provided the form with direction and stability. Once it had gained some power, this principle penetrated the other parts of the fugue and helped to make it possible for the fugue to come under the control of the fundamental structure, of the fundamental line and bass arpeggiation. Just this relationship to middleground and background enabled the master composers to treat the entrances and imitative content of the foreground in very free fashion.[3]

A key point in a Schenkerian view is that form develops essentially out of tonal structure and voice-leading rather than a scheme of keys and imitative techniques.

> The textbooks and analyses always describe the organization of a fugue in terms of an exposition, restatement, episodes, as well as all imaginable maneuvers such as contrary motion, retrograde, augmentation, stretto, etc.— but they do not speak about that which is most important: of that utterly secret connection which alone makes a fugue an organic whole, a work of art as such.[4]

The preceding chapters have considered the structure of the subject and answer, invertible counterpoint, exposition, episode, and special contrapuntal techniques, and have demonstrated the means by which the imitative materials of fugue develop effective middleground tonal progressions and prolongations over relatively brief spans. It remains for chapter 7 to consider the technical means by which the unity among sections and through structural levels suggested above is achieved in actual fugues. Chapter 7 examines three fugues as complete compositions in order to consider the interaction of several factors, including the relationship between

---

[2]Schenker, *Free Composition*, 143–44.
[3]*Ibid.*, 143.
[4]Schenker, "The Organic Aspect of the Fugue," trans. in Kalib, "Thirteen Essays," 2:283. See also *Free Composition*, 143. In Schachter's view, "a study of the enormous literature on fugue will show how infrequently the fugal theorists have been able to reassemble into some kind of connected whole the *disjecta membra* produced by their analyses," "Bach's Fugue in B-flat Major," 239–40.

the structural patterns illustrated in previous chapters and the deeper structural levels, the relationship between design and tonal structure in fugue, and the relationship between subject and overall structure. The C major fugue of *WTC II* is representative of *simple fugue,* that is, fugue with no countersubject and no special contrapuntal artifice; the F-sharp major fugue of *WTC I* is a good example of extensive use of invertible counterpoint, both in countersubjects and in sequences; the B-flat minor fugue of *WTC II* deals exhaustively with stretto and motivic inversion.

William Rothstein's clarifications of Felix Salzer's distinctions between design and structure will be found especially useful in connection with fugal form.[5] *Outer form* (design), in the context of fugue, describes the layout and presentation of thematic elements. *Inner form* (structure), is "the tonal dynamic of a work," as revealed through structural levels and voice-leading relationships. Indeed it is to a great extent the unique relationships between design and tonal structure that characterize the wealth of formal possibilities that fugue exhibits as a genre.

Bach, Fugue 1 in C Major (*WTC II*)

The opening fugue in the first volume of the *WTC* is a striking composition. It is a statement of intent, symbolizing the scope and intensity of the entire set in its use of twenty-four statements of the subject, the number of major and minor keys in the volume. Indeed, it is a miniature *tour de force* of stretto writing. In such a composition, where the subject occurs so often within a brief span, stretto is in fact a necessary device. Like those seen in chapter 6, the simple scalar ascent which opens the subject provides the contrapuntal basis for the many and varied stretti that follow.

In comparison to the powerful contrapuntal technique of the opening fugue in *WTC I*, the first fugue in *WTC II* seems almost apologetic. Simple, understated, and in only three parts, it boasts no outstanding technical features such as stretto, inversion, or countersubject. Perhaps Bach's intent was to begin *WTC II* in an elementary manner and to reserve more complex techniques for later fugues, as he did in other pedagogical works both earlier and later, the Fifteen Inventions and the *Art of Fugue,* for example.[6] But although the *WTC II* Fugue in C Major is unpretentious it actually contains the remarkable contrapuntal effect that the beginning and the ending of the subject can combine in counterpoint with each other. It is the development of this possibility that gives a convincing motivic unity throughout the course of the composition.

Example 7-1 shows the main structural elements of this fugue. The exposition, mm. 1–13, prolongs the tonic harmony with inflection to the dominant at the end of the answer, supporting an initial arpeggiation through I that culminates in the head tone g^2 at m. 13, while the bass

---

[5]William Rothstein, *Phrase Rhythm in Tonal Music* (New York: Schirmer, 1989), 104.

[6]Elwood Derr, "The Two-part Inventions: Bach's Composers Vademecum," *Music Theory Spectrum* III (1981):26–48, illustrates the systematic pedagogical ordering of the original version of the inventions.

gradually extends its range downwards to e. (example 4-3 gives a detailed analysis of the exposition.) Measures 13–20 provide an ascending sequence that places the head of the subject in canon with itself in the upper parts, counterpointed by the sixteenth-note pattern of the end of the subject in the bass, and concluding with a PAC in V at m. 22 (see example 5-22). The junction of the end of the exposition and the beginning of the sequence is forged effortlessly, by treating the upper part that presents the head tone as if it were a fourth subject entry and at the same time extending the established pattern of sixteenths in the bass. Following this rather conventional opening, it is the overlap of a subject entry in the middle part at m. 21 with the ensuing cadence that causes the music to alter its trajectory from V towards II. Here a design element initiates a structural event. As example 7-2 shows, V in m. 22 is thus understood at a deeper level as a back-relating dominant. Measures 22–29 provide a motion to II as a contrasting minor key, supporting two entries, alto and soprano, and introducing $\hat{4}$ in the fundamental line over the supertonic at m. 26. The extensive sequence that follows unfolds II over a large span and carries $\hat{4}$ through a full octave descent by m. 37 (see example 5-9). Although this entire passage prolongs II it also provides at m. 29 the modulation that returns the music to the tonic key.[7]

Measure 39 marks the midpoint of the composition both in terms of proportion and of fundamental-line descent. Here $\hat{4}$ resolves to $\hat{3}$ in the lower register as the music returns to I, marked by a restatement of the subject in the bass. The primary structural function of mm. 42–60 is to reassert the obligatory register of the fundamental line. This is accomplished through a combination of ascending sequences and subject statements that unfold e^1–c^2 of I (mm. 39–47), followed by b^1– f^{21} of V^7 (mm. 50–60), as shown in example 7-2. (The details of mm. 55–62, a recomposition of the first sequence, are shown in example 5-23.)

At m. 61, $\hat{3}$ appears for the first time in the obligatory register, supported by another return to I. The predictable descent of the upper voice over the following measures promises a concluding cadence in the near future, and $\hat{2}$ appears already in m. 64, well in advance of the final cadence. In fact, the early "Kellner" version of the piece concluded with a simple cadence at what would be m. 68, and did not include mm. 69–83.[8] Bach's decision to substitute a deceptive cadence at this point and thus to dramatically recast the proportions and balance of the composition provide insights into his concepts of structure and design. The added measures do not alter the background structure but merely prolong the motion to the final cadence. They allow the lower voice to extend to C, while the upper voice unfolds d^2–b and e^1–c^2, reflecting the couplings and unfoldings of the earlier part. These couplings improve the registral balance of the composition

---

[7]Schachter discusses how a single prolongation such as this can support a change of key in "Analysis by Key: Another Look at Modulation," *Music Analysis* VI/3 (1987):289–318. See especially pp. 292–95.

[8]See *Bach Werke*, Vol. 36 (Leipzig: Bach-Gesellschaft, 1890):224–25.

Example 7-1. Bach, Fugue 1 in C major (*WTC II*), foreground

and provide for a concluding series of subject entries after the long episode of mm. 55–68. The added entries of the subject in a simplified form (see example 2-8 (b)) contain the most explicit demonstration in the fugue of how the first and second halves of the subject counterpoint against each other (mm. 69–74). The structural effect of this extension is not unlike that of the C major prelude of *WTC I*, which is also based on large-scale coupling of registers in the upper voice, and which also underwent a dramatic revision of the ending that balanced the composition through an ascending unfolding to the obligatory register.[9]

[9]See example 1-13.

Example 7-2. Bach, Fugue 1 in C major (*WTC II*), middleground and background

The earlier, "Kellner" version of the fugue was in common time. Bach apparently substituted two-four when the ending was expanded, and it is clear that these two modifications are related, for up to m. 68 the odd measures carry a metric accent through regular grouping into pairs of measures, 1–2, 3–4, and so on. However, from m. 70 to the end it is the even measures that carry the metric stress. Two-four is a simple notational expedient that accommodates this metric shift.

The balanced couplings of g^1–g^2, f^2–f^1, and e^1–e^2 in the first half of the composition do not in themselves require that either octave be considered the obligatory register, although the prominence of the upper one naturally gives it a better claim. However, the end of the composition leads undoubtedly to c^2 by omitting an explicit tonic arrival at c^1. Nevertheless, the final subject entrance implies a descent to the lower tonic in the inner voice at the end, as example 7-2 shows. Thus both registers have a sense of completeness about them.

The register of the bass is equally carefully controlled. Beginning on c^1, the exposition expands a descending 6th, to e. At the modulation to II in m. 23, d is reached, and c appears at m. 39 where I is reasserted at the midpoint of the composition. The bass reaches G several times in the next thirty measures, and resolves finally to C at m. 76. Thus the bass unfolds through two octaves during its course, in a manner not dissimilar to that in *WTC I* Prelude in C major.

As noted above, two main harmonic motions, mm. 1–39 and 39–76, subdivide the piece into two almost perfectly equal halves.[10] The notes of the fundamental line are distributed in two corresponding progressions, $\hat{5}$-$\hat{4}$-$\hat{3}$ and $\hat{3}$-$\hat{2}$-$\hat{1}$, and the prolongations of each span are carried out through complementary octave couplings in the episodes. Thus, in addition to their conventional design function, the extended sequences of the fugue which realize the octave couplings play the important structural role of facilitating the tonal motion. Design and structure retain a close association throughout this fugue. The two components work in concert in the establishment of broad tonal motions, and the final extension improves both design and structural aspects as it balances the proportions.

While the prominent neighbor note of the subject finds no expression in the composing-out of the fundamental line, as frequently occurs in fugues as well as other genres,[11] it does appear in enlarged form in the bass motion of mm. 65–76. Indeed, it is conceivable that a hidden purpose of the revised ending was to introduce a deep level reference to the subject in the bass through the deceptive cadence, thereby uniting the structural levels of the composition in a motivic and tonal sense.

Bach, Fugue 13 in F-sharp Major (*WTC I*)

The F-sharp major fugue of *WTC I*, also a three-voice fugue, is based upon a very different organization and voice-leading structure. The subject presents two special characteristics, arpeggiation to the upper tonic and an incomplete upper neighbor, that play important roles in the structure of this fugue (see example 2-26). While in the *WTC I* C minor fugue the answer form of the arpeggiation to the tonic provides the head tone for the fundamental line (see example 2-2), the tessitura of the key of F-sharp prevents a similar realization here. The higher key of this fugue prohibits the answer from entering above the subject and prevents the establishment of the fundamental line in the higher register (i.e., c-sharp^3 to f-sharp^2). Instead, the answer must enter below the subject, and it is the $\hat{5}$ of the subject itself, the first note of the piece, that acts as the head tone of the fundamental line. Therefore in this fugue the register of f-sharp^2 which the tonic arpeggiation exposes must act in the manner of a cover tone or as an inner voice placed above the fundamental line (see example 7-3). In addition, the design factors of an invertible countersubject as well as a second countersubject (introduced in m. 12)—factors not present in the *WTC II* C major fugue—contribute to the complexity of the composition by determining the register and voice-leading to a great extent.

---

[10] In the "Kellner" version the proportion would be closer to 2:1.

[11] See Christopher Wintle, "'Skin and Bones': The C Minor Prelude from Bach's *Well-Tempered Clavier, Book 2*," *Music Analysis* V/1 (1986):85–96.

Example 7-3. Bach, Fugue 13 in F-sharp major (*WTC I*), foreground

Example 7-4. Bach, Fugue 13 in F-sharp major (*WTC I*), middleground and background

The plan of this fugue hinges on strategically placed statements of the subject and two countersubjects interspersed with extensive episodes. Bach achieves a remarkable unity of character through unity of motivic detail among the various themes and between subject and episode. In particular, the teasing interval of the third shown in example 4-5, which is introduced in a sequential manner in countersubject 1, also provides the seed for the episodes, while the repeated-note pattern of the episodes spawns the rhythmic figure of countersubject 2. Whereas the subject spans a descending octave, countersubject 2 spans an ascending octave. The contrapuntal structure that results from combining the subject and two countersubjects is a strong harmonic prolongation which conditions the tonal motion of the composition and prevents the free use of subject entries seen in the *WTC II* C major fugue.

Unlike the *WTC II* C major fugue, the soprano maintains a consistent register throughout. The trio-like texture avoids any extensive passage for less than three voices, again quite different from the C major fugue of *WTC II*. One can understand the paucity of subject statements in this fugue by recognizing the unity of themes and the unity of motivic material between subject and episode.

Example 4-5 illustrated the manner in which the three entries of the exposition developed a downward sweep in the bass, culminating in the cadence at m. 7. This is summarized in example 7-3. The episode of mm. 7–12 arrives at a PAC in V at m. 12 and extends the bass to its deepest note, C-sharp. An immediate return to I coincides with another subject statement in the original register, this time accompanied by countersubject 1 in the alto and countersubject 2 in the bass. Here we can see that Bach's intent was to begin a new point of imitation in the original tonality. Had a second countersubject not been introduced into the piece, these measures would have served no purpose. By omitting the second countersubject, the music could have proceeded directly from m. 11 to m. 17, omitting mm. 12–16. Instead, this music expresses a supplementary exposition of a new idea. Thus the motivic design causes a tonal repetition that is not necessary to the progress of the voice-leading.

The following music, touching on D-sharp minor, leads through a subject entry in the alto to a second PAC on V at m. 17. The descending fourth of the subject, f-sharp^2–c–sharp^2, finds a broader expression in the descending fourth-progression in the upper voice of mm. 12–17, bringing the covering f-sharp^2 into contact with the fundamental line. A second episode, derived from the first, leads on to a prolongation of V/VI, expressed through the subject and countersubject 2. This resolves on a PAC on VI at m. 23 as a contrasting minor key area, which supports the upper neighbor of the fundamental line in the background. A third episode leads the music back to the tonic through IV (m. 29), where a further subject and countersubject 2 are given. The concluding measures contain a final subject statement in I in the original register, with countersubject 1 in the bass. This subject statement in fact carries $\hat{4}$ and $\hat{3}$ of the fundamental line, while the concluding $\hat{2}$-$\hat{1}$ is implied in the inner voices of the final tonic prolongation. While the obligatory register requires a resolution of the fundamental line to f-sharp^1, the reassertion of the upper octave echoes and resolves the original register of the subject at the opening, and in fact produces an augmentation of the first four notes of the subject at the very end.

Like the C major fugue of *WTC II*, this piece contains two main harmonic motions. The first (mm. 1–12) is a simple modulation to the dominant. The second is more involved. Its intricate web of voice-leading expresses direct motivic references to the subject at very deep levels, in the fundamental line of the upper voice and also in the lower voice, as shown by the bracket in example 7-4.[12] Further, the alteration of the end of the third entry of the subject, noted in example 2-26, receives an additional justification through repetition, in the motivic expansion in the bass, and at the same time provides the basis by which the complete bass motion of the enlargement finds a motivic meaning in the composition. The upper voice presents an upper neighbor $\hat{6}$ over a large span (see m. 23), understood structurally in exactly the same way it is understood in the subject itself, as an incomplete upper neighbor which moves to $\hat{4}$ through a passing $\hat{5}$ ($\hat{5}$-$\hat{6}$-($\hat{5}$)-$\hat{4}$-$\hat{3}$) (see example 7-4). Motive and structure—form and content—become one, in Schenkerian terms an organic whole.

The music of m. 7 plays an important dual role in the composition. It establishes the motive of the episodes as it regains the upper register of the upper voice in preparation for the descending sequence. But in m. 33 the same music reasserts the cover tone f-sharp^2 as it expresses a hidden repetition of the head of the subject.

Incidental to the underlying voice-leading structure of this fugue, but not to Bach's compositional process, is the recomposition of measures 11.5–17 at the subdominant level, and in inversion, as measures 28–33.5.[13] By this means the modulation from I to V in the first part becomes a modulation from IV to I in the second part. Obviously such treatment is more suited to, and more common in, fugues with one or more countersubjects, where repetition is more abundant, since it is groups of themes that require literal or transposed repetition. Bach uses a similar manner of subdominant repetition leading back to I in other fugues, such as *WTC I*, Fugue 10 in E Minor, and in other pieces as well, such as *WTC I*, Prelude 9 in E major and Invention 8 in F major.

Bach's use of register is completely different in this fugue as compared with the previous one. In the C major fugue, register provides the essential

---

[12]Although the variant reading of A-sharp as the last bass note in measure 32 (found in the Hoffmeister copy) gives a more exact reference to the motivic expansion of the subject in the bass, it spoils the surface detail, which in this case is a descending series of thirds, d-sharp–B–G-sharp, exploited throughout the piece.

[13]As in the *WTC II* C major fugue, a metric shift occurs here, as can be seen by comparing these passages. In this case Bach chose not to resort to two-four, perhaps because the presence of a second metric shifts rectifies the situation by the end of the fugue, precisely through the repeated music of m. 7.

COMPLETE FUGUE 199

drama, but here the sustained register in the upper voice prolongs the fabric while the bass provides a dramatic profile through a wide range that reinforces the main points of tonal motion and resolution (see example 7-4).

Bach, Fugue 22 in B-flat Minor (*WTC II*)

The B-flat minor fugue of *WTC II* is an extraordinary example of stretto *per arsin et thesin, rectus et inversus*.[14] Figure 7-1 shows the remarkably regular plan of entries and stretti.

Figure 7-1. Subject entries in Bach, Fugue 22 in B- flat minor (*WTC II*)[15]

M.	1			27	33	42		67	73	80	89	96
S:		A			S		S^i		S^{i9}	S^i		S
A:	S	cs	cs	S^7		S^i			S^i		S^i	$S^{3/6}$
T:			A	S	S^i			S^i			S	S^{i3}
B:		S	cs	S^7			S^i		S^{i9}		S	S^i

An exposition of four entries is followed by two stretti at the seventh, the second an inversion of the first. M. 42 begins a second exposition of four entries of the *inversus* subject, followed by two *inversus* stretti. Thus up to m. 73 the plan of entries is perfectly balanced. Beginning at m. 80, the final three stretti illustrate the possibilities of *rectus et inversus*, in two parts, in inversion, and finally in all four parts at once as a concluding peroration. The entire fugue, then, consists of three sets of eight entries each, *rectus*, then *inversus*, and finally *rectus et inversus*. Further, each part states the subject or answer twice in each of the three sections.[16]

In a stretto fugue such as this, the requirement to provide a large number of subject entries reduces the need for any lengthy episodic material, except in so far as it provides temporary relief or assists in tonal motion. Whereas in the F-sharp major fugue the episodes furnish a special means of developing motives and provide a tonal foil to the static prolongations of the double and triple counterpoints of the subject and its countersubjects, lengthy episodes here would simply obstruct the cumulative effect of stretto combinations that is the object of this fugue. Indeed, lengthy episodes of varied materials would hinder the developing intensity that the accumulation of entries provides. Likewise, in this fugue the countersubject is merely a means for integrating the exposition, which otherwise would require a large amount of free counterpoint. That the countersubject never reap-

---

[14]Examples 6-19 through 6-22 illustrate the stretti of this fugue.

[15]Superscript "i" indicates inversion of the subject or countersubject. Superscript numbers indicate stretto interval.

[16]This type of formal plan may be equated with the Hegelian concept of thesis, antithesis, synthesis.

pears in its original form after the exposition is in fact a necessity, since the object of this fugue is the exploration of stretto and inversion possibilities.[17]

Despite its compelling logic, a rigid plan of entries such as this is fraught with the danger of over systematic repetition and development. As Schenker cautions:

> Only this type of fugal writing [where the motives are subject to the fundamental structure and to voice-leading] belongs to the realm of art; in contrast to it stands the fugal composition which follows a rigid plan of entries. Often it is just such mechanically assembled fugues which the unschooled ear finds easiest to assimilate, since they indulge in orgies of readily recognizable repetition, with their entrances almost rattling in the ear.[18]

In this context, Bach's challenge is to create a coherent and satisfying musical utterance *in spite of* the rigid plan of entries.

The exposition (analyzed in detail in example 4-6) reaches and maintains f^2 as $\hat{5}$ of the fundamental line. Following the end of the exposition in m. 21, a brief sequence touches on the relative major at m. 25 (see example 5-7), but only as a step on the way from V back to I at m. 27, where the stretti begin. The stretti at mm. 27 and 33 form a pair, the second an inversion of the first. The scalar basis of the stretti allows these sections to prolong single harmonies, I for the first stretto and III for the next, connected by a brief episode (see example 6-19).

A somewhat longer episode based on the bass continuing the final motive of the theme—a species of linkage technique—returns the music again to I at m. 42, and it is here that the inversion of the subject begins. The coincidence of the return to I and the beginning of a new thematic idea here is similar to the procedure found in the previous fugue. A series of four entries marks a balance with the opening exposition, and elevates this section to the status of a second exposition, albeit only in design, for Bach provides a wealth of tonal variety here, avoiding the monotony that a true second exposition in B-flat minor might entail (see example 7-5). The sequence of keys IV–V–VI–VII develops a great deal of harmonic tension in comparison with the first exposition, as it carries the music into the wonderfully dark region of A-flat minor as a point of furthest harmonic remove at m. 62. A-flat minor is chromatically inflected back to B-flat minor at m. 67 with great intensity through an extended voice exchange operating over the length of the canonic sequence in mm. 62–67 (see example 5-24). At the same time the return to I marks the conclusion of a broad fifth-descent in the upper voice, giving m. 67 a strong tonal articulation (see example 7-6). Measures 67 and 73 present stretti of the inverted subject at the ninth and at the seventh within a tonic-dominant prolongation that reasserts the head tone, forming a balance with the earlier pair of subject stretti (see example 6-20). The strong return to I at m. 67 after an extensive tonal digression

---

[17]Fragments of the countersubject appear in *inversus* form in the *inversus* exposition, beginning at m. 42.

[18]Schenker, *Free Composition*, 143.

COMPLETE FUGUE   201

divides the tonal structure of the fugue at this point into two groups of twelve entries. Thus while the outer form is three groups of eight entries, the inner form supports two groups of twelve entries. What might be termed a hemiola at the deepest level is one of the most important means by which Bach avoids the sterility inherent in his rigid plan of entries and provides an overarching tonal momentum.

Example 7-5. Bach, Fugue 22 in B-flat minor (*WTC II*), foreground

Example 7-6. Bach, Fugue 22 in B-flat minor (*WTC II*), middleground and background

A rising sequence of four voices in canon at m. 77 (example 5-25) prepares for the impressive series of combinations which comprise the final portion of the piece. *Rectus et inversus per arsin et thesin* at m. 80 is balanced by the inversion at m. 89 and completed by *rectus et inversus per arsin et thesin* in four parts at m. 96, which forms the ultimate combination and conclusion, since in its use of all four parts simultaneously it negates the requirement of a paired opposite as utilized in all previous stretti (see examples 6-21 and 6-22). While the stretto of m. 80 is prepared by the preceding episode, it is by no means a point of tonal or structural focus, but merely a dividing dominant within a tonic prolongation, as shown in example 7-6.

There is speculation that this fugue is in a sense a recomposition of the less successful A minor fugue of *WTC I*. For one, it is likely that this fugue was actually composed in A minor and then transposed, a practice known to have occurred in other cases when Bach desired a composition in a remote key.[19] Second, the expansive initial ascent of the theme and the progressive series of combinations and inversions has parallels with the A minor fugue. But what sets the B-flat minor fugue apart is the masterful skill with which the design is carried out in connection with an ingenious tonal scheme that effectively supports the numerous subject entries. In particular, the developmental character of the *inversus* exposition is crucial to the success of the work, because it allows concurrently for an exposition of motivic material and a development of tonal material. By contrast, the A minor fugue of WTC I loses its forward momentum as it presents many more stretti, many of which are incomplete. Less tedious but more systematic and tonally unified, the B-flat minor fugue achieves what was mere intention in the A minor fugue and at the same time points the way towards Bach's orderly and artistic masterpiece, the *Art of Fugue*, which must have occupied a large portion of the time that Bach devoted to fugal composition once *WTC II* had been completed in 1742.

Form and Tonal Structure

Traditional theories of formal design often place fugue within the ternary forms on the basis of a three-part tonal structure, i.e. a beginning tonic section, a digression to related keys, and a return to the tonic. Yet this tonal structure describes just about any baroque form, whether binary or ternary dance, through-composed prelude, concerto, or *da capo* aria. The simple fact of departure from the tonic and subsequent return does not of itself define a ternary form, for according to this sense every tonally unified composition is ternary. Considering the design aspect, a ternary form is often deduced from the return of the subject at its original pitch or in an octave transposition near the conclusion, in confirmation of the opening subject entries of the exposition. Each of the fugues analyzed in this chapter possesses this characteristic. However, this argument is no more convincing than the previous one. Of the two basic options for thematic material, sub-

---

[19]The A-flat major fugue of *WTC II*, for example, exists in the more common key of F major as BWV 901.

ject or episode, it only makes logical and rhetorical sense to conclude with the former, which is after all the primary motive of the piece. While a perception of form in fugue no doubt arises from the interplay of motivic and tonal factors such as these, certain apparent formal events, tonal or motivic, may just as likely be resultants of other factors, including purely rhetorical ones.[20] In the end, the form of any given fugue is a unique result of the process of exposition, transformation, contrast and combination, expressed through a tonal plan that supports the ideas in an effective manner.

Schenker connects harmonic and modulatory patterns and upper voice characteristics (such as upper neighbor) intimately with notions of form. This is the basis of his understanding of binary and ternary forms, and, especially in connection with interruption, undergirds his theory of sonata form as well. But although fugue too has such characteristics of harmonic motion and upper voice structure, it does not regularly conform to standard formal categories.

> In most cases the older masters organize longer movements according to the arpeggiation I–V–I, with an extended prolongation of V. This, however, does not give rise to a three-part form; much rather the effect is of illusory keys spread out around a neighboring note of V.[21]

With few exceptions the tonal structure of fugues is one part at the deeper levels. That is it supports a single background melodic descent over a single underlying harmonic progression. Interruption plays no part in typical fugal structure; nor does ternary form with contrasting middle section.[22] However, as the analyses indicate, fugue often exhibits structural returns to I in a manner not characteristic of other forms. When a tonic appears at the beginning of a sonata development or at the beginning of the second part of a binary form, it normally acts as a middleground passing-chord within a larger motion to a secondary key such as the subdominant. Thus it acts in a contrapuntal not a structural role. However, the repetitions of I that fugue frequently exhibits articulate important points of design, and at deep levels often act as reiterations of an underlying tonic prolongation.[23] This feature of fugue no doubt stems from its historical origins in the *ricercare* and motet, both of which were organized in their simplest forms as series of fugatos or "points" of imitation, each constituting a more or less discrete tonal segment within the tonic key or mode or within a closely related tonal area.[24] In a tonal sense, such restatements of the tonic seem to work against

---

[20] Gregory Butler discusses the extensive history of the application of rhetorical concepts to fugue in "Fugue and Rhetoric," *Journal of Music Theory* XXIV (1980):49–109. In "Rhetoric and Fugue: An Analytical Application," Daniel Harrison works out rhetorical implications in a complete fugal analysis.

[21] Schenker, *Free Composition*, 145.

[22] The fugue of Bach's Prelude and Fugue in E minor for organ BWV 548 (the *Wedge*) is a rare example of a true ternary form in fugue.

[23] This ancient principle accords with Bach's practice, in the C major fugue at m. 39, in the F-sharp fugue at m. 12, and in the B-flat minor fugue at mm. 42 and 67.

[24] Czackzes bases his fugal analyses on this approach, and essentially sees each *WTC* fugue as a series of expositions. See *Analyse des WTC*.

the development of a broad harmonic and voice-leading structure. Wallace Berry's analysis of Bach's D-sharp minor fugue (*WTC I*) in terms of cadential arrival points disregards this prolongational aspect and minimizes the structural importance of such returns to I.[25] Berry infers instead that V is prolonged from m. 43 to the final cadence, as part of an overarching I–III–IV–V–I progression, since no cadence to I occurs before the end of the piece. However, there is at least one structural return to the tonic, at m. 52, where the stretto must be heard as a deep level prolongation of I. In this view, at least some of the motions to V that Berry links into a prolongation of V must be considered only temporary digressions from deeper tonic prolongations.

In the diverse modulatory plans of fugues, modulations to related keys are considered from a Schenkerian viewpoint as principally contrapuntal or neighboring motions at a middleground level, but not necessarily leading to a resulting formal categorization as binary or ternary as they sometimes do in other genres. Yet, as the analyses illustrate, fugues seem to project certain characteristic structural aspects, the most important of which is the substantive return to I within the body of the composition as a means of articulating design elements.

The analyses of complete fugues also make clear what is implicit in earlier chapters, that as perception of structure moves toward the background, the outer voices increasingly take on the aspect and function of structural upper voice and bass arpeggiation as conceptualized by Schenker for tonality in general. The highest sounding part is *de facto* the "melody" in Schenkerian terms, regardless of which part may be stating the subject or any other important motive at any given time. Likewise, the lowest sounding part is the functional bass. In Schachter's words,

> In principle the analysis of a fugue should present no problems essentially different from those encountered in other types of music. Fugal procedures, after all, grow out of the contrapuntal and harmonic elements fundamental to tonality. And two fugues by the same composer may well differ by at least as much as two rondos, two sonata movements, or two nocturnes.[26]

Jonas frames this point in more technical terms that emphasize the voice-leading aspect:

> It is idle to speak of polyphony versus homophony. The contrapuntal basis of a Bach fugue is no different from that of a Mozart sonata or a Schubert song. The conduct of the voices is always governed by that contrapuntal basis and by the triad for which those voices speak.[27]

A more recent (non-Schenkerian) formulation provides further insight:

---

[25] Wallace Berry, "J. S. Bach's Fugue in D-sharp Minor (*WTC I*, No. 8): A Naive Approach to Linear Analysis," *In Theory Only* II/10 (January, 1977):4-7.

[26] Schachter, "Bach's Fugue in B-flat Major," 238.

[27] Oswald Jonas, *Introduction to the Theory of Heinrich Schenker*, trans. and ed. by John Rothgeb (New York: Longman, 1982), 83.

> In all contrapuntal settings, the *bicinium* remains the governing force. Textures for more voices spell out what the inherent polarity of two voices already contains; for neither the character of up and down nor that of consonance and dissonance can be drastically changed. It can only be further clarified and intensified.[28]

At least in terms of the bass, this view is not dissimilar to that developed by Rameau in the eighteenth century, which recognized a distinction between fundamental bass and actual bass. Whereas in the simplest context the two are identical, in more complex textures such as fugue they diverge to a considerable extent at the surface level. Indeed, the outer voices in fugue generally traverse more obscure voice-leading paths than are customarily found in other genres. The polyphonic treatment of the materials that makes this diversity possible without ultimate disruption of tonal or voice-leading coherence in fact demands such liberty, since the outer, structural parts are also to some extent co-equal among the other parts as a bearers of motivic material.

In the final analysis it is the coherence and conviction of the voice-leading connections that validates a fugue as an artistic work in Schenkerian terms. Thus, when we consider the tonal structure and voice-leading of entire fugues and other contrapuntal pieces, the considerations of imitative counterpoint presented in the previous chapters in fact recede in favor of a more traditional Schenkerian focus on the upper voice and bass lines independent of surface counterpoint. This is most clearly perceived in the recognition of similar structural processes at work in the *WTC I* Prelude in C major and the *WTC II* Fugue in C major, as noted above. But this shift of focus simply reflects a shift in perspective as we proceed through the levels to the background. Whereas the surface and foreground concerns itself with developing textures and motives—and invertible counterpoint, imitative sequence, and stretto are highly developed forms of motivic and textural design—the deep levels deal with the broad sweep of tonal and linear events that project a sense of direction and resolution.

The Fundamental Line

Discovering or recognizing the path of the fundamental line in a fugue often constitutes a major difficulty for the analyst. The very nature of fugal style includes copious voice-exchanges, voice crossings, register shifts, subsidiary motions to and from inner voices, superposition of inner voices above the main voice, rests in both outer voices, and the unique demands which the various imitative techniques place on the voice leading. Further, the through-composed form of many fugues gives little in the way of definite structural indicators for the analyst.

---

[28]Ernst Levy and Siegmund Levarie, *Musical Morphology: A Discourse and a Dictionary* (Kent, Ohio: Kent State University Press, 1983), 126.

Individual movements within older forms such as the suite or the concerto frequently offer more difficulties to the understanding than, for example, a sonata movement by Beethoven. The principles of voice-leading and especially those of linear progressions are, of course, the same in both; but in older music the foreground diminutions, which conform more closely to strict counterpoint, render insight more difficult. Also, despite the unparalleled mastery of their voice-leading, the linear progressions themselves are not as sweeping or determinative of form as those in the works of the later masters. This, too, is related to the continuous strictness of the diminutions.[29]

The more intricate, involved, and longer fugues of Bach demand a much greater application of analytical ingenuity, for the problems of structural coherence multiply. In the words of William Benjamin,

> the problems of trying to account for harmonic coherence in contrapuntal music . . . become even more intractable when broader spans of music are under consideration [i.e., broader than segments of a few measures] . . . and positively unmanageable with respect to intensely imitative music, in which the notion of a single structural upper voice becomes a veritable fiction.[30]

The problems do proliferate, but not to the point where they become *absolutely* unmanageable. If the ear can intuitively appreciate the intricate beauties of a complex fugue, then surely the intellect can untangle that art into meaningful elements and relationships. To the extent that a fugue consists of a logically unified expression, including a coherent upper voice design, it should yield its formal secrets to the powers of a comprehensive analytical procedure.

Despite the structural problems engendered by the complex motivic and textural processes of fugue, it is possible to make some generalizations regarding the fundamental line in fugue. It seems more natural to consider $\hat{5}$ as the likely head tone in fugue, since there is very often a great emphasis on $\hat{5}$ and $\hat{1}$ resulting from transposition of the subject to form the answer, and the general motivic structuring around the tonic and dominant notes. $\hat{5}$-line fugues are indeed much more commonly found but are by no means exclusive. Schachter provides a convincing analysis of the *WTC I* B-flat major fugue from $\hat{3}$, but, as he points out, the $\hat{3}$ is firmly established through the nature of the subject itself, a rise from $\hat{1}$ to $\hat{3}$ (paradigm 5), stated in the first and highest part in the exposition.[31] Nevertheless, in most instances $\hat{5}$ is the more likely head tone for the further reason that it occupies a prominent place in many of the fundamental subject paradigms and in their corresponding answers. The more natural, hence more likely (but by no means necessary) choice of head tone for fugues based on the various subject types are suggested in the following table.

---

[29]Schenker, *Free Composition*, 145.
[30]William E. Benjamin, "Models of Underlying Tonal Structure: How Can They Be Abstract, How Should They Be Abstract?" *Music Theory Spectrum* IV (1982):40.
[31]"Bach's Fugue in B-flat Major," 241.

Figure 7-2. Common subject paradigms and suggested head tones

Subject Paradigm		Suggested Head Tone
1:	$\hat{5}$ - $\hat{4}$ - $\hat{3}$	$\hat{5}$
2:	$\hat{1}$ - $\hat{2}$ - $\hat{3}$	$\hat{3}$
2a:	$\hat{5}$ - $\hat{4}$ - $\hat{3}$ - $\hat{2}$ - $\hat{1}$	$\hat{5}$
2c:	$\hat{1}$ - $\hat{2}$ - $\hat{1}$	$\hat{5}$
3:	$\hat{3}$ - $\hat{2}$ - $\hat{1}$	$\hat{3}$ or $\hat{5}$
3a:	$\hat{5}$ - $\hat{6}$ - $\hat{7}$ - $\hat{8}$	$\hat{5}$
5:	$\hat{1}$ - $\hat{2}$ - $\hat{3}$	$\hat{5}$
7:	$\hat{8}$ - $\hat{7}$ - $\hat{6}$ - $\hat{5}$	$\hat{5}$
8a:	$\hat{1}$ - $\hat{2}$ - $\hat{3}$ - #$\hat{4}$ - $\hat{5}$	$\hat{5}$
12a:	$\hat{5}$ - $\hat{6}$ - $\hat{5}$	$\hat{5}$
13:	$\hat{1}$ - $\hat{2}$ - $\hat{3}$ - $\hat{4}$ - $\hat{5}$	$\hat{5}$

Although paradigms 1 and 2a suggest $\hat{5}$ as head tone, $\hat{3}$ is not at all out of the question even here, especially in the many cases where the transposition of the upper neighbor $\hat{6}$ in the subject gives a prominent $\hat{3}$ in the answer, and where the answer is in the highest part. John Rothgeb's analysis of the exposition of Bach's *Sinfonia 8* in F major suggests this form.[32] Paradigm 2 suggests in itself $\hat{3}$ as the head tone, but the necessary initial tonic gives a prominent $\hat{5}$ in the answer form. Paradigm 13 suggests $\hat{5}$ as head tone, and this theory finds support in Schenker's analysis of the D minor fugue of *WTC I*.[33] Likewise, paradigm 3a does not suggest $\hat{3}$ in either its subject or answer form. The neighbor-note paradigms (2c and 12a) suggest $\hat{5}$ as head tone, whether in the subject itself or in the answer, since these forms center on $\hat{1}$ and $\hat{5}$. It cannot be overstated, however, that these guidelines, based only on general theoretical considerations, must not be taken as "rules." Their are no *a priori* restrictions as to which background structure a fugue must follow, and any of the fundamental line forms is possible with any subject type. The first statement of the subject or answer, indeed the entire exposition, need not necessarily establish the head tone in its firmest expression. In Salzer's analysis of Bach's D major fugue (*WTC I*), the head tone is reached through initial ascent only at measure 7, after the four subject entries of the exposition are complete.[34] One might also consider the theoretical possibility of the overall structure of a fugue based on an expansive arpeggiation and rising through the tonic triad for the greater part of its length.[35]

---

[32]John Rothgeb, "Thematic Content: a Schenkerian View," *Aspects of Schenkerian Analysis*, ed. David Beach (New Haven: Yale University Press, 1983), Example 8, p. 48.

[33]Schenker, *Free Composition*, Fig. 156.1.

[34]Salzer, *Structural Hearing*, 2 vols. (New York: Dover, 1962), Vol. 2, Example 474a (pp. 240–41).

[35]Although not fugal analyses, Schenker's Figures 40.2, 40.7, and 40.8 in *Free Composition* illustrate this structure.

Beyond the important question of the head tone in fugue lies the distribution of the notes of the fundamental line over the course of the work. It can be stated as a premise that, except in the case of an extensive initial arpeggiation, the head tone, $\hat{5}$ or $\hat{3}$, will appear within the initial tonic prolongation of the exposition, and the cadential $\hat{2}$ and $\hat{1}$ near the end, in the context of the principal PAC in I. What is at issue then is the distribution of the inner elements, the upper neighbor if there is one, and in the case of a $\hat{5}$-line, $\hat{4}$ and $\hat{3}$ of the fundamental line. In the above analysis of the C major fugue, the main elements of the fundamental line are disposed across the two principal harmonic movements as $\hat{5}$-$\hat{4}$-$\hat{3}$ and $\hat{3}$-$\hat{2}$-$\hat{1}$, forming the structural basis of a balanced form. In *Free Composition*, Schenker shows a similar background plan in the *WTC I* D minor fugue: $\hat{5}$-$\hat{4}$-$\hat{3}$-$\hat{2}$-$\hat{1}$ forms two broad third-progressions over two harmonic progressions.[36] In this case, however, Schenker indicates that the second harmonic progression, mm. 28–43, is in some sense subordinate to the first. The F-sharp major fugue analyzed above reserves the fundamental-line descent for the concluding measures, and occupies the bulk of the piece with prolongation of the head tone in connection with I and V, and motion to the upper neighbor $\hat{6}$ in connection with the related harmonies (VI and IV) that form the tonal digression. In the B-flat minor fugue the head tone is prolonged throughout, until the final subject statement initiates the structural descent.

It is certainly much more typical for the $\hat{4}$-$\hat{3}$ descent of the fundamental line to occur later rather than earlier, since repetitions of the subject or answer in the tonic in the upper voice will naturally support a retention of the head tone at these points. The D minor fugue of *WTC I* and the C major fugue of *WTC II* must therefore be considered exceptional. In the D minor fugue, it is the *inversus* presentation of the subject in m. 27 that effects the descent to $\hat{3}$, while in the C major fugue the coupling of registers facilitates the presentation of the subject in the lower register of the upper part at m. 76 without reasserting $\hat{5}$ as the background upper voice.[37]

Motion to the upper neighbor, as demonstrated in the F-sharp major fugue, is perhaps the most compelling of all the deep structural patterns in fugue, for it fulfills the ideal of union of motive and structure as the fundamental line traverses the path of the subject itself, $\hat{5}$-$\hat{6}$-$\hat{5}$-$\hat{4}$-$\hat{3}$(-$\hat{2}$-$\hat{1}$). Jonas's brief analysis of the *WTC I* F major fugue illustrates the same structure, as does Kalib's analysis of the G minor fugue of *WTC I*.[38]

---

[36]Fig. 156.1.

[37]Kalib deals with a similar problem in the G minor fugue of *WTC I*. But without any coupling such as in the C major fugue, the logical background analysis, as Kalib shows, is the retention of $\hat{5}$ through the first large harmonic progression. See "Thirteen Essays," Vol. 1, Fig. 224.

[38]Jonas, *Introduction*, Fig. 144, p. 94. Kalib, "Thirteen Essays," Vol. 1, Fig. 214, p. 290. The F minor fugue of *WTC II* is another superb example.

Epilogue

A recurring thread throughout this study is repetitive patterning as understood through voice-leading. Evidently such patterning retains validity through very deep levels of structure indeed—remarkably so considering the extreme diversity of design possibilities that fugue can project. Patterning is strongly evident at foreground and higher middleground levels, but recedes in prominence from there to the background, where the fundamental structure once again provides a regularly recurring formal basis. This structural condition admirably reflects the special formal freedom of fugue as a genre.

Through its systematic procedures of voice leading patterns, fugue was able to support the most complex involved, and original masterworks of the Baroque era. Only the advent of the revolutionary tonal and motivic plan of sonata form, with its expansive breadth of formal outline, has been able to sustain greater possibilities of creative freedom and develop challenging new models of structure within the western tonal system.

One might consider that the approach presented here, dealing as it does extensively in repetitive patterning, is anti-Schenkerian. After all, it recognizes similarities rather than unique differences among fugues. But the recognition of repetitive patterning such as this is simply an extension of the formalism implicit in Schenker's theory of fundamental structure as it is elaborated through transformations at higher levels. A clear and systematic process of recognition of structural similarities within the genre of fugue in fact provides the best basis upon which to identify and assess the unique qualities that individuate fugues and give each creative work its characteristic shape and expression.

Appendix

Bach, Fugue 1 in C Major (WTC II)

211

Bach, Fugue 13 in F-sharp Major (WTC I)

APPENDIX

Bach, Fugue 22 in B-flat Minor (WTC II)

APPENDIX

Bibliography

Aldwell, Edward, and Schachter, Carl. *Harmony and Voice Leading*. 2nd. edition. New York: Harcourt, Brace, Jovanovich, 1989.

Arnold, Franck Thomas. *The Art of Accompaniment from a Thorough-Bass*. 2 vols. London: Oxford University Press, 1931.

Bach, Carl Philip Emmanuel. "Einfall, einen doppelten Contrapunct in der Octave von sechs Tacten zu machen, ohne die Regeln davon zu wissen." in Friedrich Wilhelm Marpurg, *Historisch-kritisch Beyträge zur Aufnahme der Musik*, Vol. 3 (1757):167–74.

_____. *Essay on the True Art of Playing Keyboard Instruments*. Berlin, 1753. Translated by William Mitchell. New York: Cassel, 1949.

Bach, Johann Sebastian. *Bach Werke*. [*Johann Sebastian Bachs Werke*]. 46 vols. Leipzig: Bach Gesellschaft, 1851–1926.

_____. *Clavier-Buchlein von Wilhelm Friedemann Bach*. Edited in facsimile with a preface by Ralph Kirkpatrick. New Haven: Yale University Press, 1959.

_____. *Das Wohltemperierte Clavier* [I]. Facsimile edition of the autograph Mus. ms. Bach P.415 in the Deutsche Staatsbibliothek, Berlin, edited, with prefaces, by Hans Pischner and Karl-Heinz Köhler. Leipzig: Deutscher Verlag für Musik, 1962.

_____. *Das Wohltemperierte Clavier II*. Facsimile edition of the autograph manuscript British Library Add. MS 35021, edited with an introduction by Don Franklin and Stephen Daw. London: The British Library, 1980.

_____.(attr.) *Praeludia et fugen del Signor Johann Sebastian Bach* [the Langloz manuscript]. Berlin, Staatsbibliothek Preussischer Kulturbesitz, Musikabteilung, Mus. Mn. P 296.

_____. *Vorschriften und Grundsätze zum vierstimmigen Spielen des General-Bass . . . 1738*. Translated as *Rules and Instructions for Playing Thorough-bass or Accompaniment in Four Parts . . . .* in David and Mendel, *The Bach Reader*, 392–98.

Benjamin, William E. "Models of Underlying Tonal Structure: How Can They Be Abstract, How Should They Be Abstract?" *Music Theory Spectrum* IV (1982): 28–50.

_____. "Pitch-class Counterpoint in Tonal Music." *Music Theory: Special Topics*, edited by Richmond Browne. New York: Academic Press, 1981, 1–32.

Berry, Wallace. "J.S. Bach's Fugue in D-sharp Minor (*WTC I*, No. 8): A Naive Approach to Linear Analysis." *In Theory Only* II/10 (January, 1977):4–7.

Brahms, Johannes. "Brahms's Study, *Octaven u. Quinten u. A.*, with Schenker's Commentary Translated." Translated by Paul Mast. In *The Music Forum,* Vol. 5. Edited by Felix Salzer and Carl Schachter. New York: Columbia University Press, 1980, 1–196.

Brandt-Buys, Hans. *Het Wohltemperierte Klavier van Johann Sebastian Bach.* Arnheim: L. Slaterus, 1955.

Van Bruyck, Carl. *Technische und äesthetische Analysen des Wohltemperirten Claviers nebst einer allgemeinen, Sebastian Bach und die sogenannte contrapunktische Kunst betreffenden Einleitung.* Leipzig: Breitkopf & Härtel, 1867.

Buelow, George J. *Thorough-Bass Accompaniment According to Johann David Heinichen.* Revised edition. Ann Arbor: UMI Research Press, 1986.

Butler, Gregory. "Fugue and Rhetoric." *Journal of Music Theory* XXIV/1 (spring, 1980):49–109.

Cherubini, Luigi. *Cours de contrepoint et de fugue* (actually by Halévy). 2 vols. Paris, c. 1837. Translated by J. A. Hamilton, New York: Cocks and Co., 1841.

Czackzes, L. *Analyse des WTC: Form und Aufbau der Fuge bei Bach.* 2 vols. Wien and München: Österreichischen Bundesverlag, 1965.

Dahlhaus, Carl. *Studies in the Origin of Harmonic Tonality.* Translated by Robert O. Gjerdingen. Princeton: Princeton University Press, 1990.

David, Hans T. and Mendel, Arthur. *The Bach Reader.* Revised edition. New York: Norton, 1966.

David, Johann Nepomuk. *Das wohltemperierte Clavier: Der Versuch einer Synopsis.* Göttingen: Vandenhoeck and Ruprecht, 1962.

Derr, Elwood. "The Two-Part Inventions: Bach's Composers' Vademecum." *Music Theory Spectrum* III (1981), 26–48.

Forkel, Johann Nicholaus. *On Johann Sebastian Bach's Life, Genius, and Works.* Leipzig, 1802. Translated by Augustus Frederic Christopher Kollmann in David and Mendel, *The Bach Reader,* 293–256.

Forte, Allen and Gilbert, Steven. *Introduction to Schenkerian Analysis.* New York: Norton, 1982.

Fux, Johann Joseph. *Gradus ad Parnassum.* Vienna, 1725.

Gasparini, Francesco. *L'armonico practico al cimbalo.* Venice, 1708.

Gauldin, Robert. *A Practical Approach to Eighteenth Century Counterpoint.* Englewood Cliffs, New Jersey: Prentice-Hall, 1988.

Gedalge, Andre. *Treatise on Fugue.* Paris, 1900. Translated by A. Levin. Mattapan, Mass: Gamut Music Co., 1964.

Gjerdingen, Robert O.. *A Classic Turn of Phrase: Music and the Pshychology of Convention.* Philadelphia: University of Pennsylvania Press, 1988.

Handel, George Frederick. *Aufzeichnungen zur Kompositionslehre* (*Composition Lessons*). Published as *Hallische Händel-Ausgabe, Supplement*, Band I. Edited by Alfred Mann. Kassel: Bärenreiter, 1978.

Harrison, Daniel. "Rhetoric and Fugue: An Analytical Application" *Music Theory Spectrum* XII/1 (Spring 1990):1–42.

_____. "Some Group Properties of Triple Counterpoint and their Influence on Compositions by J.S. Bach." *Journal of Music Theory* XXXII/1 (spring 1988):23–49.

Heinichen, Johann David. *Der General-Bass in der Composition*. Dresden, 1728.

Helm, Eugene. "Six Random Measures of C.P.E. Bach." *Journal of Music Theory* X (1966):139–51.

Higgs, James. *Fugue*. London: Novello [1878].

Hill, Robert. "Die Herkunft von Bach's 'Thema Legrensianum'." *Bach Jahrbuch* LXXII (1986):105–7.

Iliffe, Frederick. *The Forty-Eight Preludes and Fugues of Johann Sebastian Bach Analysed for the use of Students*. London: Novello [1897].

Jeppesen, Knud. *Counterpoint: the Polyphonic Vocal Style of the Sixteenth Century*. Translated by Glen Haydon. New York: Prentice- Hall, 1939.

Jonas, Oswald. *Introduction to the Theory of Heinrich Schenker*. Translated and edited by John Rothgeb. New York: Longman, 1982.

Kalib, Sylvan. "Thirteen Essays from the Three Yearbooks *Das Meisterwerk in der Musik* by Heinrich Schenker: An Annotated Translation." 3 vols. Ph.D. diss., Northwestern University, 1973.

Keller, Hermann. *The Well-Tempered Clavier by Johann Sebastian Bach*. Translated by Leigh Gerdine. New York: Norton, 1976.

Kirkendale, Warren. *Fugue and Fugato in Rococo and Classical Chamber Music*. Durham, North Carolina: Duke University Press, 1979.

Kirnberger, Johann Philipp. *The Art of Strict Musical Composition*. 4 vols. Translated (Vol. I and part I of Vol. II only) by David Beach and Jurgen Thym. New Haven: Yale University Press, 1982.

_____. *Gedanken uber die verschiedenen Lehrarten in der Komposition als Vorbereitung zur Fugenkenntniss*. Berlin, 1782.

_____. *The True Principles for the Practice of Harmony*. Translated by David Beach and Jurgen Thym. *Journal of Music Theory*, XXIII/2 (fall 1979):163–225. (This treatise is possibly the work of Kirnberger's student J.A.P. Schulz. See this translation, 164, and Joel Lester, *Compositional Theory in the Eighteenth Century*, 240.)

Kittel, Johann Christian. *Der angehende praktische Organist*. 3 vols. Erfurt, 1801–1809.

Knorr, Iwan. *Die Fugen des Wohltemperierte Clavier in bildischen Darstellung*. 2nd. edition. Leipzig: Breitkopf & Härtel, 1926.

Knorr, Iwan Otto. *Lehrbuch der Fugen Komposition.* Leipzig: Breitkopf & Härtel, 1911.

Ledbetter, David. *Continuo Playing According to Handel.* Oxford: Oxford University Press, 1990.

Lester, Joel. *Between Modes and Keys: German Theory 1592–1802.* Stuyvesant, New York: Pendragon Press, 1989.

_____. *Compositional Theory in the Eighteenth Century.* Cambridge, Massachusetts: Harvard University Press, 1992.

Levy, Ernst, and Levarie, Siegmund. *Muiscal Morphology: a Discourse and a Dictionary.* Kent, Ohio: Kent State University Press, 1983.

Mann, Alfred. "Bach and Handel as Teachers of Through Bass." in *Bach, Handel, Scarlatti Tercentenary Essays.* Edited by Peter Williams. Cambridge: Cambridge University Press, 1985, 245–57.

_____. *The Study of Fugue.* New Brunswick, New Jersey: Rutgers University Press, 1958.

_____. *Theory and Practice.* New York: Norton, 1987.

Marchant, Arthur W. *Five Hundred Fugue Subjects and Answers: Selected, Arranged and Edited.* 2nd. edition. London: Novello, 1892.

Marpurg, Friedrich Wilhelm. *Abhandlung von der Fuge.* 2 Vols. Berlin, 1753–1754. Partial translation in Alfred Mann, *The Study of Fugue*, 139–220.

Marshall, Robert. *The Compositional Process of J.S. Bach.* 2 vols. Princeton: Princeton University Press, 1972.

Martin, Bernhard. *Untersuchungen zur Struktur der "Kunst der Fuge" J.S. Bachs.* Ph.D. diss., University of Cologne. Regensburg: Heinrich Schiele, 1940.

Mattheson, Johann. *Kleine General-bass Schule.* Hamburg, 1735.

_____. *Der Vollkommene Cappelmeister.* Hamburg, 1739.

McCreless, Patrick. "Syntagmatics and Paradigmatics: Some Implications for the Analysis of Chromaticism in Tonal Music." *Music Theory Spectrum* XIII/2 (fall 1991):47–178.

Meyer, Leonard B. *Explaining Music: Essays and Explorations.* Berkeley: University of California Press, 1973.

Naldin, Charles. *Fugal Answer.* London: Oxford University Press, 1969.

Neumann, Werner. *J.S. Bach's Chorfuge.* Leipzig: F. Kistner, 1938. 2nd. edition, Leipzig: Breitkopf & Härtel, 1950.

Neumeyer, David. "Fragile Octaves and Broken Lines: On Some Limitations in Schenkerian Theory and Practice." *In Theory Only* XI/3 (July, 1989):13–30.

Niedt, Friedrich Ebhard. *The Musical Guide.* Translated by Pamela Poulin and Irmgard Taylor. Oxford: Clarendon Press, 1989.

Norden, Hugo. *Foundation Studies in Fugue.* New York: Crescendo Publishing, 1957.

Parks, Richard S. *Eighteenth Century Counterpoint and Tonal Structure*. Englewood Cliffs, New Jersey: Prentice-Hall, 1983.

Plum, Karl-Otto. *Untersuchungen zu Heinrich Schenkers Stimmfhrungs-analyse*. Regensburg: Gustav Bosse Verlag, 1979.

Prout, Ebenezer. *Fugue*. London: Augener, 1891.

Rameau, Jean Philippe. *Treatise on Harmony*. Translated by Philip Gosset. New York: Dover, 1971.

Renwick, William. "Modality, Imitation and Structural Levels: Bach's *Manualiter* "Kyries" from *Clavierbung III*." *Music Analysis* XI/1 (1992):55–74.

_____. "Structural Patterns in Fugue Subjects and Fugal Expositions." *Music Theory Spectrum* XIII/2 (1991):197-218.

_____. "Voice-leading Patterns in the Fugal Expositions of J.S. Bach's *Well-Tempered Clavier*." Ph.D. Diss., City University of New York, 1987.

Rothgeb, John. "Thematic Content: A Schenkerian View." In *Aspects of Schenkerian Analysis*, edited by David Beach. New Haven: Yale University Press, 1983, 39–60.

Rothstein, William. *Phrase Rhythm in Tonal Music*. New York: Schirmer, 1989.

Sadie, Stanley, ed. *The New Grove Dictionary of Music and Musicians*. 20 vols. London: Macmillan, 1980.

Salzer, Felix. *Structural Hearing*. 2 vols. New edition. New York: Dover, 1962.

Sancta Maria, Thomas de. *Arte de tañer Fantasia*. 2 Vols. Valladolid, 1565.

Schachter, Carl. "A Commentary on Schenker's *Free Composition*." *Journal of Music Theory* XV/1 (spring, 1981): 115–42

_____. "Analysis by Key: Another look at Modulation." *Music Analysis* VI/3 (1987):289–318.

_____. "Bach's Fugue in Bb Major, Well-Tempered Clavier, Book I, No. XXI." In *The Music Forum*, Vol. 3, edited by Willliam Mitchell and Felix Salzer. New York: Columbia University Press, 1973, 239–67.

_____. "Rhythm and Linear Analysis: A Preliminary Study." In *The Music Forum*, Vol. 4, edited by Felix Salzer and Carl Schachter. New York: Columbia University Press, 1976, 281–334.

_____. "Either/or." In *Schenker Studies*, edited by Hedi Siegel. Cambridge: Cambridge University Press, 1990, 165–79.

Schenker, Heinrich. *Counterpoint*. Translated by John Rothgeb and Jürgen Thym. 2 vols. New York: Schirmer, 1987.

_____. *Free Composition*. 2 vols. Translated and edited by Ernst Oster. 2 vols. New York: Longman, 1979.

_____. *J.S. Bach's Chromatic Fantasy and Fugue*. Translated and edited by Hedi Siegel. New York: Longman, 1984.

_____. *Das Meisterwerk in der Musik*. 3 vols. München: Drei Masken Verlag, 1925–30.

_____. *Der Tonwille*. 10 issues. Vienna: A. Gutmann, and Leipzig: F. Hofmeister, 1921–24.

Schenkmann, Walter. "The Influence of Hexachordal Thinking in the Organization of Bach's Fugue Subjects." *Bach* VII (1976):7–16.

Schmieder, Wolfgang. *Thematisch-systematisches Verzeichnis der musikalischen Werke von Johann Sebastian Bach (Bach-Werke- Verzeichnis)*. Wiesbaden: Breitkopf und Härtel, 1990.

Schulenberg, David. *The Keyboard Music of J.S. Bach*. New York, Schirmer, 1992.

Schulze, Hans-Joachim. "'Das Stück im Goldpapier' Ermittlungen zu einigen Bach-Abschriften des frühen 18. Jahrhunderts." *Bach Jahrbuch* LXIV (1978):19–42.

Siegele, Ulrich. "Bach's Theological Concept of Form and the F- major Duet." Translated by Alfred Clayton. *Music Analysis* XI/2–3 (1992): 245–78.

_____. "The Four Conceptual Stages of the Fugue in C minor, *WTC I*." *Bach Studies*, edited by Don Franklin. Cambridge: Cambridge University Press, 1989, 197–224.

Souchay, Marc-Andre. "Das Thema in der Fuge Bachs," *Bach Jahrbuch* XXIV (1927):1–102, and XXVII (1930):1–48.

Spitta, Philipp. *Johann Sebastian Bach*. 3 vols. Translated by Clara Bell and J.A. Fuller-Maitland. London: Novello, 1883–1885.

Stinson, Russel. *The Bach Manuscripts of Johann Peter Kellner and his Circle*. Durham, North Carolina: Duke University Press, 1989.

Tovey, Donald. *A Companion to 'The Art of Fugue'*. London: Oxford University Press, 1931.

_____. *Forty-eight Preludes and Fugues by J.S. Bach*. 2 vols. London: The Associated Board of the Royal Schools of Music, 1924.

Verall, John W.. *Fugue in Theory and Practice*. Palo Alto, California: Pacific Books, 1966.

Weisse, Hans. "The Music Teacher's Dilemma." *Proceedings of the Music Teachers National Association* 1935, 122–37. Reprinted in *Theory and Practice* X/1-2 (July-December, 1985):29–48.

Werckmeister, Andreas. *Harmonologia musica*. Frankfurt & Leipzig, 1702.

Williams, Peter. *The Organ Music of J.S. Bach*. 2 vols. Cambridge: Cambridge University Press, 1980.

Wintle, Christopher. "'Skin and Bones': The C Minor Prelude from J. S. Bach's *Well-Tempered Clavier*, Book 2." *Music Analysis* V/1 (March, 1986):85–96.

Wolff, Christoff, ed. *The New Grove Bach Family*. New York: Norton, 1983.

Zarlino, Gioseffo. *Institutione harmoniche*. Venice, 1558. Part III translated by Guy A. Marco and Claude V. Palisca as *The Art of Counterpoint*. New Haven: Yale University Press, 1968.

Index of Compositions

Anon.	"Veni redemptor gentium" (plainchant), 39
Bach, J.S.	Allabreve in D major BWV 589 (attr. Bach), 46

Art of Fugue BWV 1080
    Contrapunctus 1, 34, 35
    Contrapunctus 2, 35
    Contrapunctus 3, 35
    Contrapunctus 4, 35
    Contrapunctus 5, 172, 177
    Contrapunctus 6, 172
    Contrapunctus 9, 106
    Contrapunctus 10, 107

Brandenburg Concerto 2 BWV 1047, 185
Brandenburg Concerto 5 BWV 1050, 142
Canon in Einklange BWV 1072, 166
Canon triplex a 6 vocibus BWV 1076, 167
Cantata BWV 17 ("Wer Dank opfert, der preiset mich"), 37
Cantata BWV 19 ("Es erhub sich ein Streit"), 186
Cantata BWV 21 ("Ich hatte viel Bekümmernis"), 42, 58, 101
Cantata BWV 29 ("Wir danken dir, Gott, wir danken dir"), 41, 184
Cantata BWV 50 ("Nun ist das Heil und die Kraft"), 56
Cantata BWV 71 ("Gott ist mein König"), 47
Cantata BWV 105 ("Herr, gehe nicht ins Gericht"), 97
Cantata BWV 136 ("Erforsche mich, Gott, und erfahre mein Herz"), 70
Cantata BWV 172 ("Erschallet, ihr Lieder"), 68
Cantata BWV 190 ("Singet dem Herrn ein neues Lied!"), 61
Chromatic Fantasy and Fugue in D minor BWV 903, 21, 43
Concerto in D minor for two violins BWV 1043, 46
Duet 2 in F major BWV 803, 72
Fantasy in G major BWV 571 (spurious), 15
Fantasy in G major BWV 572, 15
Fantasy and Fughetta in B-flat major BWV 907 (attr. Bach), 11
Fantasy and Fughetta in D major BWV 908 (attr. Bach), 11
Fantasy and Fugue in G minor BWV 542, 74

BACH, CONT.

    Four-part chorales
        "Christ lag in Todesbanden" BWV 278, 5
        "O Mensch, bewein' dein Sünde gross" BWV 402, 5
    French Suite in D minor BWV 812, Allemande, 15
    Fugue in A major BWV 949 (attr. Bach), 133
    Fugue in A minor BWV 947 (attr. Bach), 134
    Fugue in C minor BWV 906, 79
    Fugue in C minor on a theme by Legrenzi BWV 574, 60
    Fugue in D major BWV 580 (attr. Bach), 46
    Fugue in E minor BWV 945 (attr. Bach), 73
    Fugue in F major BWV 901, 202
    Fugue in G minor BWV 578, 24, 43
    Invention 1 in C major BWV 772, 70
    Invention 7 in E minor BWV 778, 70
    Invention 8 in F major BWV 779, 167, 198
    Invention 10 in G major BWV 781, 15
    Invention 15 in B minor BWV 784, 21
    "Kyrie, Gott Vater in Ewigkeit" (manualiter) BWV 672, 74
    Langloz Manuscript (attr. Bach)
        Praeludium et fuga 52. Dis dur, 9
    Magnificat in D major BWV 243, 60
    Mass in B minor BWV 232, 184
    Mass in F major BWV 233, Kyrie, 28
    Musical Offering BWV 1079, Ricercare a 6, 188
    Orgel-Büchlein
        "Christ lag in Todesbanden" BWV 625, 5
        "O Mensch, bewein' dein Sünde gross" BWV 622, 5
    Passacaglia and Fugue in C minor BWV 582, 68
    Prelude and Fugue in A minor BWV 543, 1
    Prelude and Fugue in B minor BWV 544, 32, 93
    Prelude and Fugue in C major BWV 531, 32
    Prelude and Fugue in C major BWV 547, 62
    Prelude and Fugue in E minor BWV 548, 203
    Prelude and Fugue in E-flat major BWV 552, 48
    Prelude and Fugue in E-flat major BWV 996, 60
    Prelude and Fugue in D major BWV 532, 74
    Prelude, Fugue and Allegro in E-flat BWV 998, 46

BACH, CONT.

    Sanctus in D major BWV 241, 170
    Sinfonia 8 in F major BWV 792, 207
    Sinfonia 14 in B-flat major BWV 800, 51
    Sonata 1 in G minor for unaccompanied violin BWV 1001, 1, 31
    Sonata 3 in C major for unaccompanied violin BWV 1005, 187
    Sonata 3 in E major for Violin and Clavier BWV 1016, 65
    Sonata 5 in F minor for Violin and Clavier BWV 1018, 55
    Toccata in E major BWV 566, 45
    Toccata in F-sharp minor BWV 910, 67
    Toccata in G major BWV 916, 171
    Toccata in G minor BWV 915, 48
    Toccata and Fugue in D minor (Dorian) BWV 538, 45, 181
    Trauer-Ode BWV 198, 53
    Trio Sonata 2 (for organ) BWV 526, 182
    Trio Sonata 5 (for organ) BWV 529, 71
    Vorschriften und Grundsätze, Example 12, 6
    Rules for playing *en quatre*, No. 13, 13
    Well-tempered Clavier I
        Prelude 1 in C major, 14, 205
        Prelude 2 in C minor, vii, 14
        Prelude 5 in D major, 14
        Prelude 9 in E major, 198
        Prelude 10 in E minor, 14
        Fugue 1 in C major, 54, 136
        Fugue 2 in C minor, 19, 20, 23, 27, 79, 94
        Fugue 3 in C-sharp major, 16, 20, 125
        Fugue 4 in C-sharp minor, 20, 38, 92
        Fugue 5 in D major, 207
        Fugue 6 in D minor, 20, 70, 102, 109, 132
        Fugue 7 in E-flat major, 24, 59, 110
        Fugue 8 in D-sharp minor, 20, 42, 124, 168, 169, 204
        Fugue 9 in E major, 22
        Fugue 10 in E minor, 57, 198
        Fugue 11 in F major, 44, 53, 117, 208
        Fugue 12 in F minor, 99, 152
        Fugue 13 in F-sharp major, 17, 44, 118, 196
        Fugue 14 in F-sharp minor, 149

BACH, CONT.
    Fugue 16 in G minor, 89, 208
    Fugue 17 in A-flat major, 69
    Fugue 18 in G-sharp minor, 62, 130, 161
    Fugue 20 in A minor, 43, 202
    Fugue 21 in B-flat major, vii
    Fugue 22 in B-flat minor, 20, 120
    Fugue 24 in B minor, 11, 63, 131
  Well-tempered Clavier II
    Prelude 2 in C minor, 195
    Fugue 1 in C major, 16, 30, 116, 136, 147, 157, 158, 191–195
    Fugue 2 in C minor, 28, 87, 117, 170
    Fugue 3 in C-sharp major, 31
    Fugue 6 in D minor, 44, 121, 143, 150, 155, 180
    Fugue 9 in E major, 40, 122, 184
    Fugue 10 in E minor, 33, 91
    Fugue 11 in F major, 156, 162, 163
    Fugue 13 in F-sharp major, 21, 154
    Fugue 14 in F-sharp minor, 95
    Fugue 16 in G minor, 16, 103, 104, 105
    Fugue 17 in A-flat major, 148, 202
    Fugue 18 in G-sharp minor, 53
    Fugue 20 in A minor, 164
    Fugue 21 in B-flat major127, 159
    Fugue 22 in B-flat minor, 33, 34, 90, 119, 146, 147, 148, 158, 159, 178, 180, 199–202
    Fugue 23 in B major, 21, 49, 151, 161

Böhm, G. — Capriccio in D major, 67
Brahms J. — Variations and Fugue on a Theme of Handel, Op. 24, 103
Buxtehude, D. — Prelude in G minor BuxWV 163, 10
  Toccata in F major BuxWV 157, 52, 16
Corelli, A. — Trio Sonata, Op. 1, No. 9, 54
Fischer, J.C.F. — *Ariadne musica*
  Fuga 8 in E major, 40
  Fuga 10 in F major, 52
Frescobaldi, G. — Canzona 1, 71
  Canzona 4, 66
  Canzona 5, 71
  Ricercare 1, 39

INDEX OF COMPOSITIONS

Froberger, J.	Fantasia 12, 41, 183
Gibbons, O.	A Voluntary of Four Parts, 183
Handel, G. F.	Concerto Grosso, Op. 6, No. 6, *Allegro ma non troppo*, 21, 67
	Israel in Egypt, 41
	Lessons for Princess Anne, Fugue 4, 8
	Messiah
	"Halleluia", 184
	"Worthy is the Lamb, Amen", 50, 175
	Organ Concerto, Op. 4 No. 1, 176
	Six Grandes Fugues, Fugue 6 in C minor, 53, 60
	Solomon, 39
	Suite 2 in F major, Fuga, 1, 21, 74
	Suite 6 in F-sharp minor, Fuga, 176
	Suite 8 in F minor, Fuga, 51, 171
Haydn, F. J.	Baryton Trio 81, Finale, 50
Kirnberger, J.	Fugue in E minor, 11
Krebs, J.	Prelude and Fugue in C major BWV 553, 187
Marcello, B.	Canzone Madrigalische, Op. 4, 39
Martini, G.B.	Fugue in C major, 87
Mozart, W. A.	*Musical Joke* K 522, Presto, 24, 93
	Symphony 41 ("Jupiter"), 184
Niedt, F.	Partimento Fugue in F major (*The Musical Guide*), 7
Pachelbel, J.	Fugue in A minor, 11
	Fugue in C major, 11
Palestrina, G.	"Exultate Deo", 174
	Missa Dies sanctificatus, 112
Purcell, H.	Trio Sonata 2 in B-flat major, 183
	Trio Sonata 3 in D minor, 45
	Trio Sonata 5 in A minor, 37
	Trio Sonata 6 in C major, 181
Reger, M.	Variationen und Fuge uber ein Thema von Joh. Seb. Bach fur Klavier, Op. 81, 80
Reinken A.	Sonata VI (*Hortus Musicus*) BWV 954, 72
Roberday, F.	Fugue 9me; Caprice, 29
Walther, G.	"Nun komm, der Heiden Heiland", 39